WAKING UP
SCREAMING
from the
AMERICAN DREAM

*NPR's Roving Correspondent Reports
from the Bumpy Road to Success*

BOB
GARFIELD

SCRIBNER

SCRIBNER

1230 Avenue of the Americas
New York, NY 10020

Designed by Brooke Zimmer
Set in Apollo Monotype
Manufactured in the United States of America

1 3 5 7 9 10 8 6 4 2

Library Congress Cataloging-in-Publication Data is available.

ISBN 0-684-83218-6

Versions of these pieces first appeared on National Public Radio's *All Things Considered:* "The Numbers Man," "Jerome the Pig," "A Certain Rock in Santa Fe," "Bowling in the White House," and "As the Worm Turns." NPR and NATIONAL PUBLIC RADIO are registered service marks of National Public Radio, Inc.

The introduction is adapted from "The Pursuit of Happiness" which first appeared in *The Washington Post Magazine.* Versions of the following pieces also first appeared in *The Washington Post Magazine:* "The Serum Cure," "He Is the Egg Man," "Open for Inspection," "Press Conference," "Slam," "Wheel of Misfortune," "Spider Man," and "The Haunting of Aspen Grove."

"Concrete Benefits" first appeared in *Philadelphia.* "Jews Don't Hunt" first appeared in *Sports Illustrated.* The remaining pieces appeared in *Advertising Age.* They are reprinted courtesy of *Advertsing Age.* Copyright © 1985, 1986, 1987, 1988, 1989 by Crain Communications Inc.

For Carla

Acknowledgments

Look. I haven't exactly written a book: I've accumulated one. So maybe it will seem silly to note the outside contributions to this less-than-epic literary event. The fact is, however, that not one of these pieces would have seen the light of day without the opportunities, support, wise counsel, and occasional smack upside the head provided by a number of friends, bosses, and interested third parties who have had a crucial influence on my career.

At the top of the (basically chronological) list is Philip Klass, my teacher at Penn State, who not only steered me toward journalism, but also taught me how not to write. Ed Taggert, Eleanor Shaw, and Taylor Buckley, three of my former editors, recognized something in me which, to put it politely, not all of my former editors recognized in me, and were my sponsors and protectors in my early years as a reporter. They remain close friends.

Art Silverman, Neal Conan, and Ellen Weiss are the three *All Things Considered* executive producers who have lent me their air, their expertise, their patience, and very often their tape decks for eleven years. Steve Petranek, Linton Weeks, Bob Thompson, Liza Mundy, and Steve Coll are the most senior of the six or seven hundred editors I've worked with at *The Washington Post Magazine* during the same period, and each has been a delight to write for.

At *Advertising Age,* where I have worked since 1985, I owe great debts to the late H. L. Stevenson; to my editors Fred Danzig, the late Dennis Chase, Steve Yahn, and David Klein; and especially to editor-in-chief Rance Crain. It was he who hired me as a feature columnist in 1985, and since then he has given me the sort of freedom, editorial and otherwise, such as few journalists ever have been privileged to enjoy.

My agent, Jonathon Lazear, has been a friend, booster, and, as it turns out, very good salesman. Leigh Haber, senior editor at Scribner, and Susan Moldow, publisher, have been astonishingly encouraging and tireless in their efforts on behalf of this project, in spite of my native pessimism and bad spelling.

Finally there is my family. From my father, the late Samuel M. Garfield, I inherited my love of the offbeat. To my mother, Nancy Rowen, I credit my skeptical eye. And from them both: a sense that the unjoked-upon life is not worth living. My brothers, Josh and David, had absolutely nothing to do with this collection, but they rate a mention because, otherwise, Thanksgiving will be hell. On the other hand, my long-suffering wife, Carla, deserves some sort of trophy. Apart from her love, support, encouragement, and willingness to leave me be while I'm writing, she has been asked again and again to read my pieces hot off the word processor. She is always ready with astute commentary, a sharp eye for flaws, and her razor-sharp editorial judgment.

Then she comes to her senses and tells me, "Very good."

Contents

Introduction   11

Part I: Tilting at Windmills

Muse   27
It's Worth a Try!   29
Thank You, Thank You Very Much. Now, Please Spit.   32
Strip Joint for Jesus   34
Don't Shoot. Here's My Card.   37
Stalking History   39
Death by Footwear   41
Frankie Angel Goes Flying   44
Remembering the Day of the Cashmere Bouquet   46
The Last Zacchini   49
Campaign and Suffering   51
The Statue of Freedom   54
The Anti-Amalgamists   56
Who Killed All Those Dead People?   58
The Levee Is Dry   61
Press Conference   63
Open for Inspection   82
A Certain Rock in Santa Fe   93

Part II: The Big Score

Publish or Perish   105
Speakeasies   107
Hunger   110
Quityourbellyaching   112

Pull 115

Stung by a Bee 117

Had 'em a Minute Ago 120

Just Give Me Half a Tank 122

Miracle Whip 124

The Talking Cat 127

A Big Number 129

Freeze-Dried Fred 131

Topping the Octopus 134

The Uphill Struggle of the Kondom Kings 136

As the Worm Turns 138

Part III: Bobby Strikes Out

Wheel of Misfortune 153

The Middle-Aged Man and the Sea 174

Spider Man 183

The Haunting of Aspen Grove 198

Jews Don't Hunt 215

The Journalism Life 221

Part IV: Success, and Other Outcomes

He Is the Egg Man 227

A Whorehouse Christmas 234

Concrete Benefits 237

Shot by Cupid 245

Jerome the Pig 248

Bowling in the White House 253

The Serum Cure 262

Well, Well, Well . . . 289

The Numbers Man 291

Slam 304

Introduction

I shall never forget her beauty, slim and blonde, all blue eyes and Spandex. I shall never forget her voice, lilting and warm, patient and sweet. I shall never forget the ruddy brown suede pouch dangling from her neck, with the magically crystalline blue tourmaline nestled inside. Above all, what I shall never, ever forget about Joanna Corti is her methodology.

Her surgical methodology. Her psychic surgery methodology, as performed, for instance, on a diseased gall bladder.

"Now," she explained to me a few years back, "how that works is, I sit at the person's crown chakra, which is at the top of the head, and I go into a trance state. And at that time the different energies that I work with and the spirit doctors go through, open up the person's crown chakra, and work through and clear the spiritual bodies. Then it allows the spiritual body to heal itself."

This was in 1992, in Santa Fe, New Mexico. I had alighted there for two days as part of my decade-long search for American quirks and eccentricities. Since July 5, 1985, first for a syndicated newspaper column, then as the basis of feature stories for National Public Radio, my search has taken me to hundreds of cities, towns, and rural backwaters in forty-six states.

By the time I met Joanna, I'd been in New Mexico for barely eighteen hours and already had my aura balanced by a grocer named Ralph and sampled much of the New Age smorgasbord which increasingly Santa Fe has become. But in Ms. Corti I saw not merely a story subject, nor even my ultimate story subject. To me she was really something of a fellow traveler. The lovely young MBA financial analyst turned psychic healer had been ensconced in Santa Fe for a couple of years, but she was engaged in no less peripatetic a search than I. Indeed hers was a nearly lifelong quest, an exploration, an odyssey of astonishing scope and faith and, in a certain way, perseverance.

"I was born and raised a Catholic," Joanna continued. "In college, I studied Zen Buddhism. And I also was involved in an Eastern religion called Eckankar for many years. And during that time I learned how to meditate, and how to leave my body, and how to experience different planes of reality. I had rebirthing. I've had lots of acupuncture, acupressure. Some massage work, polarity work, chiropractic. I've done some Hakomi therapy, hypnotherapy. Lots of processing, self-motivational tapes. I listen a lot to a channel named Lazarus, and I've done a lot of his workshops. Um, sound healing, vibrational healing, music healing, crystals and pyramids. Oh, I don't want to miss anything. Oh, yes, I've done a lot of astrology, too."

Joanna Corti had yet to find precisely what she was looking for, but was of no mind to cease searching. As an American, she was doing no less than exercising her birthright of 220 years, and I don't mean only the inalienable Right to Life and Liberty. What this psychic surgeon engaged in was also independently declared, constitutionally guaranteed, and preserved by the blood and toil of her forebears. I refer, of course, to . . .

The pursuit of Happiness.

Yes, we, as a society, more or less as the founders envisioned, pursue the hell out of Happiness. We don't sit there and accept our lots and grin and bear it. This is not a fatalistic, status quo, my dad-was-a-shepherd-and-his-dad-was-a-shepherd-and-his-dad-was-a-shepherd-so-I-guess-I'll-be-a-shepherd-too kind of country. Thomas Jefferson told us we have the right to seek happiness, and by God, we're going to take him up on it—faithfully following your basic three-step program eventually articulated by Henry Wadsworth Longfellow: "Look not mournfully into the Past. It comes not back again. Wisely improve the Present. It is thine. Go forth to meet the shadowy Future, without fear, and with a manly [please allow for nineteenth-century sensibilities] heart."

•   •   •

Alphonso F. Williams Jr. certainly went forth. In this collection you'll meet the Bronx bus driver who used to lie awake plotting an escape from his mundane life on the lower rungs of the ladder to success—before investing every nickel he had in Speakesies brand disposable public-phone handset covers. You'll meet Michael Cohen, who was not thinking of his literary legacy when he socked $50,000 into the *Bathroom Journal,* the magazine especially edited for the loo. And you'll meet Cassandra Williams of New Albany, Mississippi. Imagining some sort of white-picket fence domestic bliss, she wedded Robert Green because, "We were going together for three years and it was just time"—dwelling not at all on the fact that six months earlier Robert had shot her four times in the head with a .32-caliber revolver.

This was a marriage that had no chance, as anybody could see from the outside looking in. Any outsider could have recognized instantly that the *Bathroom Journal* was a classic nonstarter, that a pay-phone condom marketplace was destined never to materialize. All of these enterprises, from the outset, were exercises in futility. They were quixotic tilts at imaginary windmills—manifestly, sometimes tragically, ridiculous. Yet I chased all over creation to document them, for do they not tell us something revealing about ourselves? Do they not suggest that sacrificing everything for an impossible dream is a peculiarly American trait? Are these doomed efforts not evidence of an American Ethic—not merely of hard work, but of hard work toward a vision of a greater, happier future—that propels and gives meaning to all that we do?

You're asking *me?*

Oh, there's an answer to that question, all right, an answer I see now, after years of reporting. Standing back to regard the patchwork sewn together from so many motley swatches of Americana, at long last I've begun to understand what the accumulation of this material might reveal. But if you'd asked at any time until very recently, I'd have looked at you like you were nuts. In fact, people have been asking me all along why I'm so intrigued with psychic surgeons, no-chance entrepreneurism, and other follies of people utterly blind to the failures destined to unfold before them—but my response never satisfied anybody else, and it certainly didn't satisfy me.

Back when I met Mr. and Mrs. Robert Green, for example, I was still writing a feature column that appeared in major dailies in Philadelphia, Minneapolis, Dallas, Sacramento, Los Angeles, and enough lesser markets that I was only about 2,500 clients away from being as widely distributed as Garfield the Cat. Among the 99.9 percent of world newspapers that did not subscribe was *The Boston Globe,* where a features editor reviewed my samples and curtly blew me off. "So man bites dog in New Albany, Mississippi," he wrote as the entire text of a rejection letter. "So what?"

So what? So *what?!* Why that smug, condescending so-and-so. I'd have given him a piece of my mind right then and there—except that I didn't know so what. If he was asking me why, apart from morbid curiosity and voyeuristic titillation, his readers would benefit from such bizarre Americana, I couldn't begin to furnish an answer. I didn't have the faintest idea what greater purpose was to be served. All I knew was, if folks were going to be out there getting shot four times in the head and letting bygones be bygones, I wanted to tag along.

In all of the thousands of conversations I've had scouting story material around the country and around the world, I never once asked for help in finding a story that somehow strikes at the core of the American psyche. What I asked after was amazing stuff. Weird stuff. Astonishing and quirky and eccentric stuff. What they used to call "human interest" material. And that was fair enough, because a guy staking his life's savings on a product nobody will ever buy is certainly of interest to his fellow humans. Story by curious story, my goal was never more lofty than what I sold my subscribers: The strange tale well-told. The trick was to scrounge around for the odd

angle and ask enough questions to elicit enough funny-sound-
ing answers to build a column or radio piece around. Thus,
without even realizing what I was accumulating, have I spent
the most fascinating dozen years of my life in hot pursuit of the
pursuit of Happiness, yielding 500 stories and a collection of
people, places, and things such as many people are not privileged to experience.

I've seen the world's largest collection of hotel-room soaps
(Camden, New Jersey), the world's largest collection of potato
chips shaped like famous faces (Fort Wayne, Indiana), and, in
Tarpon Springs, Florida, the museum/retail complex/tourist
attraction, Sponge-a-Rama.

In Las Vegas, I visited the Castillo del Sol, the home/museum
of astronomer/brain surgeon/Egyptologist Dr. Lonnie Hammar-
gren, who (as of 1986) had a scale model of a space shuttle in his
driveway, a motorcycle on a monorail in his backyard, a submarine in his swimming pool, a dinosaur skeleton in his foyer, an
Egyptian tomb in his cellar, and, as knickknacks, a dismembered
human hand in Lucite and a petrified walrus penis. I've seen, in
one action-packed day on the campus of Ohio State University
in Columbus, Ohio, the Accounting Hall of Fame, the Drainage
Hall of Fame, and the Celebrity Eyewear Collection, featuring the
spectacles of (among other luminaries) John Denver, General
Curtis LeMay, and the late Orville Redenbacher. In San Juan
Capistrano, I've interviewed a transsexual nun.

So many stories, so many characters. There was the north-
western Indiana pastor named the Reverend Win Worley, who
exorcises congregants' many demons of alcoholism, pacifism,
anger, jealousy, unemployment, acne, Catholicism, karate, and
so on by laying hands on them till they retch violently into
paper towels; the gorgeous Santa Monica, California, pet psychic who, in my presence, plumbed the consciousness of a German shepherd by telephone; the Norwegian illegal alien who
had his late grandfather and one paying customer on (dry) ice
in a Nederland, Colorado, home cryonics experiment.

To paraphrase Seuss, the places I've hiked to! The roads that I've rambled, to find the best rackets that have ever been gambled! In St. Helena, California, I visited ex-Chicago police officer Frances Herb and her working snail ranch. In New York City I met Ava Taurel, a Swedish dominatrix with a high-rent West Side dungeon and a spike-heeled staff of ten not so much catering to as controlling and humiliating a well-heeled clientele of mainly lawyers who like to be tied up, flogged, and sometimes crouched on all fours barking like dogs. I've visited the Chicago headquarters of Fun Inc., where proprietor Graham Putnam labored tirelessly to protect the domestic high-quality latex fake vomit industry from a flood of cheap, vinyl imports.

These are people with pit bull tenacity and singleness of purpose, but whose efforts in no way are eclipsed by others with singular versatility, such as Morris Fonte, New York's window-washing TV psychic, or Denise Lutz, bare-breasted Las Vegas showgirl/Fuller Brush woman. It is my opinion that you have not seen the embodiment of versatility cum rugged individualism until you've met Dr. Daniel Thomas, Indiana's only full-time practicing proctologist/coroner. You have not seen the mixture of professional satisfaction and raw desire such as you'll find in Dr. Garry Waite, the country-music performer and endodontist, who built a nice life performing root canals but sensed still greater possibilities as an artist. He sensed fame, riches, and ultimate happiness. He sensed, in short, the American Dream.

Forget that white picket fence deal. When people speak of the American Dream, here's what they're not talking about: getting a job at the big plant in town right after graduation, marrying the high school sweetheart, rearing 2.1 offspring, joining a bowling league and the PTA, Walt Disney World once, a Caribbean cruise once, and Washington, D.C., New York City, and the Grand Canyon once, borrowing heavily to get the kids

in State U., and retiring at sixty-two and a half to a nice dou-
blewide twenty miles northwest of Phoenix.

That may be the American experience, the modest and incre-
mental American Expectation of security, satisfaction, and reasonable contentment, but it isn't the Dream. When you start
talking American Dream, you're talking about the big score—
and in our relentless pursuit of happiness, there's scarcely anything that tantalizes us more. It is indelibly etched into our
culture and our consciousness, from the rags-to-riches fiction of
Horatio Alger to the real-yet-mythologized lives of Edison and
Ford, Jobs and Wozniak, Vanderbilt and Rockefeller.

"I know of no country, indeed," wrote Alexis Tocqueville
160 years ago, "where the love of money has taken stronger hold
on the affections of men."

Alas, as the Speakeasies and *Bathroom Journal* experiences
remind us, the entrepreneur's life is a penny-arcade claw
machine. Shoving coin after coin in the slot merely buys an
opportunity to manipulate that unpredictable claw as it swipes
feebly at the prize. If you are skillful, and lucky, the tenuously
gripping claws deliver you a treasure. If you are less skilled, or
less lucky, the prize slips at the last instant back into the
gravel—closer perhaps to the chute, but nonetheless on the
wrong side of the glass, hopelessly out of reach.

Jan Stuart's nose was pressed against that glass. November of
1988 found him encamped on Wall Street, in an RV, having gone
without food for twenty-two days. He had achieved phenomenal success with his Jan Stuart Skin Care, reaching $8 million in
annual sales via the counterintuitive notion of selling cosmetics
to men. But he had expanded too quickly with insufficient capital and now he was on the brink, staging a hunger strike for
capital.

"I'm willing to do everything it takes," Stuart said. "I had a
piece of the American Dream at one time, and I want it back."

The ethic of upward mobility as a path to happiness so per-
meates this society that it isn't even confined to our individual

selves. Entire cities can get caught up in the quest for the self-improvement Holy Grail, that one concept, that one gesture, that one big deal to transform them from the dreary status quo to the very realization of their civic dreams. In Portage, Michigan, a town of 38,000 just south of Kalamazoo, there was no particular feeling of community discontent—because, as some saw it, there was no real feeling of community to begin with. What was missing, they felt, was a sense of identity.

And so the city fathers undertook to build the Celery Flats Interpretive Center—the world's only celery museum.

Hamilton, Ohio, was not so fortunate as to have a (possible) former celery industry. All it had was a deteriorating manufacturing economy and the legacy of ChemDyne, a toxic waste dump that made Love Canal look like Lourdes, despoiling the Great Miami River and casting a pall over civic pride. Layoffs and environmental disaster are dispiriting for a city and a major drain on municipal self-esteem. Thus did the local muckety-mucks contrive to destigmatize, or at least reenergize, the city by swapping their comma for an exclamation point and rechristening the community Hamilton! Ohio.

For all the good that did!

Wishing doesn't make it so. In Caledonia, Wisconsin, early in 1987, the loss of manufacturing jobs had the blue-collar community on the ropes. Then, out of nowhere, came the Greatest. Muhammad Ali floated into town with a plan to build a luxury car there, a car named for himself. Nothing about the plan made sense, but the town was prepared to believe.

Yes, in 220 years, many a pursuit—perhaps America's defining pursuit—has been for a pot of gold at the end of the rainbow. But treasure means different things to different people, and often enough the big score cannot be measured in dollars. To Americans, treasure may represent something else entirely—perhaps an ideal. Or simply an idea.

"Happy the man," wrote the poet Virgil, "who could search out the causes of things." This brings to mind Dr. Simon Wikler, podiatrist and inventor of the Wikler Shoe by Buster Brown, who achieved substantial fame and fortune helping to ambulate toddlers. But when it came to his momentous theory about the genesis of disease, the medical establishment wouldn't give him the time of day. His insight: shoes cause cancer.

In Petersburg, Indiana, Lloyd Thoren was moved to open the American Atheist Museum, smack in the middle of the Bible Belt. I was there on the day in June 1987 when the Atheist Museum, God bless it, was shut down forever and ever.

In Tijuana, Mexico, in the summer of 1986, a Georgian named Allan Manny sat in Centro Medico del Prado watching an ice-blue serum drip into his vein.

"I don't think I've ever had so much pain in my life as since I've got this cancer," he said. "Everything concerned with it is pain."

Which is why he and his wife had made the agonizing decision and the agonizing journey. They knew nothing about this Mexican doctor, or the mysterious Americans who had invented this serum. They knew only that they had been promised a cure for cancer—and that unless they journeyed, unless they quested, unless they tried, there was no chance for a happy ending.

"We borrowed from parents, brothers, sisters, friends—anybody," Manny said. "I didn't take money from my people to come down and die."

This man refused to look mournfully into the Past, for he knew it comes not back again. He wished only to improve the Present, to go forth to meet the shadowy Future, without fear, and with a manly heart.

Ten weeks later, he was dead.

Man bites dust in Tijuana, Mexico. So what?

As I say, for the longest time I couldn't put my finger on it. For the longest time, apart from the utter amazement factor, I simply didn't know what drew me to these stories, these stories of dogged pursuit. Of relentless pursuit. Of utterly futile pursuit. Oh, some of them had happy endings, but most of them did not. Most of the time, what charged these variegated misadventures was the manifest destiny of failure. I knew Michael Cohen would never sell advertising in the *Bathroom Journal*. I knew Hamilton! Ohio would fare no better than Hamilton, Ohio. I knew that Allan Manny would never see his next Christmas.

Which, of course, is the answer. *That* is the so what. It took me more than a decade to figure this out, but what I finally realized fascinates me about these stories is that I almost always knew how they would end, and the subjects almost always did not. Sure, that's what drives the combination of comedy and tragedy that I've known about all along, but there's something beyond that. In the aggregate, I now firmly believe, these stories get to something poignant, something endearing, something inspiring—and maybe even ultimately something hopeful—about the American character. We refuse not to believe in ourselves. And that is not nothing. As Tocqueville wrote, "America is a land of wonders, in which everything is in constant motion and every change seems an improvement. The idea of novelty there is indissolubly connected with the idea of amelioration. No natural boundary seems to be set to the efforts of man; and in his eyes what is not yet done is only what he has not yet attempted to do."

Speakeasies-brand pay-phone protectors may not have had quite the impact of incandescent lighting, but was the effort any less heroic, the invention any less noble? I would say not. The same stubborn obliviousness that leads to flop after ignominious flop also led to the lightbulb, the telephone, and the Apple computer.

Consider Nikola Tesla. This brilliant scientist, whose experiments with radio provided the underpinnings for Marconi's invention, was the father of alternating current, one of man's revolutionary technologies. Yet Tesla spent the last forty years of his life as a piteous failure, trying to transmit electricity— like radio waves—through the air. Everyone knows Alexander Graham Bell invented the first practicable telephone and with it changed the world. But who remembers that he struggled equally on experiments at least as near to his heart: teaching sign language to dogs? So was he a genius, or a loon? The answer is: it makes no difference. And the crazy-quilt accumulation of such quixotica, I hope, speaks volumes about our national character.

The fact that most of the people I've encountered never achieved what they sought to achieve, I've finally discovered, is hardly the point. The point is that it occurred to none of them that it was hopeless or foolish or unusual to try. Quite the contrary. In America, come what may, it is second nature to try. And if at first we don't succeed, we try, try again. Ever seeking. Ever questing. Ever in pursuit of that elusive Happiness.

And this book chronicles those quests, again and again.

The first part—"Tilting at Windmills"—examines the pursuit, against all odds, of the world-changing idea. The second part—"The Big Score"—is devoted to money and the relentless pursuit thereof. The third part is titled "Bobby Strikes Out," in which I demonstrate that Big Dreams and Big Ideas are no stranger to me, either, and that I have the same capacity to heroically and pitifully crash and burn as the next guy. Finally there is Part Four, "Success, and Other Outcomes," consisting of the pieces I've done over the years that most touched me. (So, no, as you may by now have gathered, this is not exactly the humor volume you may be expecting, based on the goofy cover photo and the book's shelving in the "humor" aisle of the bookstore. Publishers have to market a book as something, and the sad fact is there is no "bizarre Americana" aisle to aim for, so this collection has been pigeonholed as humor by default. Oh, sure, there are some funny stories here, but there are some plenty unfunny ones, too. I'm not a comedian; I'm a journalist, and my journalism doesn't always lead me down a comical path.) Half the stories in this section are those which, to my mind, are the most searingly tragic—alternating with those which prove all efforts are not doomed to failure, that quixotic quests are sometimes redeemed by success.

It is the success stories, of course, that fuel the whole cycle. Some people make it. Some people beat the odds. Some people are rewarded beyond their wildest dreams. And therefore, others will always try, try again.

This brings me to a couple of young ranchers I met in 1995. Their names are John Roundtree and Eric Wentz, and when I met them at their Fallbrook, California, spread, in the shadow of Palomar Mountain, they were in the midst of some heady reckoning. *One hundred thousand head.*

They already had one of the biggest herds in southern California—probably the biggest between Temecula and Miramar—but this was just the beginning. This was just a pump primer. This was the ground floor.

"In four months, we'll have 750,000," Wentz calculated. "Once we get to 750,000, we'll sell 360,000, and then in two months the 360,000 that we have remaining will turn into another 750,000."

Never mind the funky arithmetic. With anything close to 750,000 head, anything is possible. Oh, not just the financial dividends—handsome though they may be—but the benefits for the food supply, for the environment, for the whole world. That's what earthworm ranching is all about. Yes, two young men with young families socking $15,000 into earthworms, against the chance that a process called vermicomposting would create an unprecedented worm boom.

"You have your professors and so forth sitting back and saying they don't see it happening soon," Roundtree accurately summarized. "Well . . . you have to have a ground floor. You have to have people that believe in it, and people who are willing to go out and do something about it. And the time is now.

We're alive now. We're pioneering. You know, we can't ride wagons across the desert anymore."

Well, of course, you can. But there's hardly any point to it, if you know for sure what you'll discover on the other side. Please note that the Declaration of Independence guarantees the pursuit of happiness, but says not one word about finding it. What distinguishes our society is not the succeeding, but the attempting, not the capture, but the pursuit itself.

PART
1

Tilting at Windmills

Muse

PETERSBURG, IND.—The big rooftop sign has only four letters
left: MUSE.

Precisely what Lloyd Thoren was getting at is hard to say, but
one day he got up on a ladder and pulled everything else down.
A-M-E-R-I-C-A-N A-T-H-E-I-S-T———U-M. They all came off,
leaving only one ambiguous four-letter word. It's all part of the
process as an era ends. God bless it, the American Atheist
Museum is history.

This is no temporary setback, like when Ma Bell made him
disconnect his Dial-an-Atheist phones. This is the end. The
exhibits are in disarray. The floor space is a cluttered mess, and
most of the heretical messages have long since been pulled off
the walls. The "No way, Yahweh" sign, for instance, is just sitting on a pile of magazines.

"This is the remnant," Thoren says wryly, "of what once was
the grandiose Atheist Museum."

For nine years it has been here, a shining beacon of nonbe-
lief in a vast, rural sea of faith. Here, where white-frame farm-
houses dot the corn and soybean fields, this sprawling, brown,
godless building has stood as a symbol for all that is skeptical.
Curious visitors would wander in and Thoren would launch

into his spiel: "If you were born in Spain," he'd say, "you would almost certainly speak Spanish and be a Catholic. If you were born in Israel, you would almost certainly be speaking the Hebrew language and be Jewish. People no more choose their own religion than they choose their own language."

Explaining how various versions of Absolute Truth are actually dispensed according to the luck of the draw, he'd invoke Voltaire: "Those who understand the truths of religion are those who have lost the power of reason."

But now someone else will have to do the There-Is-No-Lord's work in Indiana. Thoren, sixty-one, has sold the building, which doubles as his house, and the whole family is off to San Francisco. Today, on his last-ever tour, he is more occupied with commodity futures than with Voltaire, and he pauses to order twenty metric tons of December rapeseed before bothering to deny the existence of God.

"I see soybeans went up," he says, thumbing through *The Wall Street Journal*. "Gee, I just sold those critters."

The grandson of a Lutheran minister, Thoren was a teenager when it hit him that all of humankind was mistaken. For most of his life he was content to not worship privately, but he gradually came to see the destructiveness of religion and chose, in middle age, to fight it.

"We consider religion to be detrimental," he says. "If you are taught to be a miserable rotten sinner, you develop a low sense of self-esteem."

But evangelical atheism has its consequences, particularly when it is carried out in the middle of the Bible Belt. Thoren was perfectly willing to quit as president of the local phone company in 1978 when his areligionism became too much of a cross to bear, but when his eleven-year-old daughter gets picked on in school, "That's a horse of a different color. And it will only get worse."

Hence the move, "So that my daughter can have the delightful anonymity that you can have in a big city."

Thoren's long silver hair is swept back to his collar, his red shirt open to his breastbone, as he absently conducts his final tour. He singles out some important titles in the atheist literature, *Pagan Christs* being one of them, and shows off his giant downstairs diorama of life on Earth, from primordial slime to the ascent of man. There he grabs a handful of fossil-imprinted stones and says, "These are the pages of the planet Earth, which cannot lie. What is in the rocks *is*."

Truthfully, though, his heart doesn't seem to be in it. Maybe it's because his shrine of the unbelievers has, to be perfectly blunt, failed to disabuse the world of the Supreme Being. "We still cling to primitive religions," he says, exasperated. Yet if Thoren has lost his Unholy War, he by no means regrets having waged it.

"Even if you make a small ripple in a great big pond, it's that much," he says. "The fact that there is no God was worth everything to me."

It's Worth a Try!

HAMILTON! OHIO—National attention is nothing new to this town. We're talking about the erstwhile home of ChemDyne, a toxic-waste dump that made Love Canal look like Lourdes.

In the 1970s, anybody who was anybody in the environmental-catastrophe game knew where Hamilton was: the place just north of Cincinnati with the railroad tracks crossing the main street, so that folks in a hurry—say, to keep poisonous chemicals from seeping into the water table—frequently got stuck in massive traffic jams waiting for 112-car trains to chug by.

ChemDyne is mainly just a bad memory now. The dead fish have long since floated down the Great Miami River, and High

Street now boasts its very own underpass, but until a year ago Hamilton's identity was still pretty much grounded in the bad old days. In the last Rand McNally ratings of American cities, Hamilton ranked 202 out of 329.

Which is why the city fathers decided to act. One year ago, by official resolution, Hamilton, Ohio, was redesignated Hamilton! Ohio.

As City Manager Jack Becker had advised council the previous summer, "There is no law that says a city must have a comma after its name. An exclamation point is used to convey excitement or strong emotion, and that is the way we feel about Hamilton."

What he meant, of course, was "that is the way we feel about Hamilton!" But no matter. In every other respect he had made his point.

Clearly this was no mere stunt. This wasn't like the harebrained idea Becker's predecessor had during the worst of the ChemDyne mess—that idea to build a fountain in the middle of the river (maybe to distract attention from what was daily oozing into it). The name change would reap genuine dividends. It would generate publicity, pique the interest of potential new industries, and spontaneously boost the sagging morale of the populace. That, anyway, was the plan. One year later, the rewards have yet to cascade in.

Maybe the first bad sign came when the U.S. Board on Geographic Names refused to recognize the change, meaning the exclamation point won't ever appear on maps or road signs. "Members of the board agreed that punctuation marks are not part of geographic names," wrote board Executive Secretary Donald J. Orth. "They saw no reason to consider formally adding such a mark to the name, any more than approving a comma for use after the name, as in Hamilton, Ohio."

This was quite a blow. Subsequently, it also became clear that despite a flurry of national publicity (the mayor even got on *CBS Morning News*) millions of businesses across the country continued to not locate in Hamilton!

"We had some leads," Becker says. "We had a mom-and-pop type hotel that was interested. I think that is still pending."

Meantime, General Motors Corp. decided to close its Hamilton-Fairfield plant, which will cost Hamilton!ians 800 jobs. That development was not exactly a boon to city spirit, the revival of which also has not been quite as thorough as predicted. Of 65 respondents to a *Hamilton Journal News* poll, 45 expressed reservations about the repunctuating of Hamilton!

"What does Hamilton have besides an underpass—which every city has—high taxes, and a lot of chemical waste?" asked Robert J. Wilson. "We don't even have a nice park."

And a man named Ed Brown waxed stunningly metaphoric: "I had a friend who put a Cadillac hood ornament on his tired old Volkswagen. When he was finished, he had an old tired Volkswagen with a new, shiny hood ornament. It still stalled at every light."

Perhaps the most eloquent statement about Hamilton!'s progress can be found along its byways. A drive through town reveals all manner of signage incorporating the city's name. There is Hamilton Denture Studio, Hamilton Plaza, Hamilton Vacuum Center, Hamilton Insurance Agency, Hamilton Inn, Hamilton Church of God.

Every one is sans exclamation.

"I hadn't really given it much thought," says Robert Quick of Hamilton Insurance. "I doubt that I'd change it. I don't know that I understand why they did."

Thank You, Thank You Very Much. Now, Please Spit.

> *Nobody wants you . . .*
> *If nobody calls . . .*
> *Pretend if you want to . . .*
> *Talk to the walls.*
>
> —*from "Nobody Wants You" by* GARRY WAITE

LAS VEGAS, NEV.—This is a town of great teeth and shattered dreams. Garry Waite has seen them both.

He's seen smoky bars and vital pulpotomies, broken hearts and porcelain fused to high noble metal. He is Dr. Garry Waite, country singer/songwriter and doctor of dental surgery, a strummin' and pickin' endodontic fool.

"Music," says the forty-year-old artist, "has always been a big part of my life."

This big, dark-haired guy with silver collar tips and cowboy boots is not your run-of-the-mill singing endodontist. His "Games" is quite a song, and so is "Don't Think Twice." "Spoiled Child" is flat-out toe-tapping, and "Good Country Steel" is just that. Trouble is, the music industry is like a honky-tonk woman—and, like another Garry Waite song says, "She took my heart, put it on the floor, and stomped that sucker flat."

So now it's over. After spending twenty-two years and $100,000 trying to become a major star, Waite has hung up his guitar. His last live gig was a year ago. The recording studio is all behind him now; a lifetime of root canals lies ahead.

"I produced a real nice Christmas song for my family," he

says. " 'O Holy Night' was the name of the song. We went into a studio and for a few, you know, under $1,000, we got a very nice rendition for my aunt. That's nice to be able to have . . . But as a profession, yeah, it's probably over for me. I have a lot of albums in my garage."

The plan, of course, was to have those albums in 5 million record collections, and once it all seemed possible. Back in the mid-1960s, Waite entertained thousands of casino-hotel listeners and ambitious dreams. Then, after dental school, he defied all the odds by becoming nearly semi-significant with his first self-produced record—a disco vocal version of the *Star Wars* theme.

"We did very good on a first-time release off of that," he says. "Actually charted in Europe. And the smaller stations around the United States we were able to get a lot of play on it."

But that's a long way from being on a national label, the true measure of success. To achieve that, you must get your work into the proper hands—which is what Waite thought he'd done with his best tune ever: a song about Superman coinciding with the major motion picture. It happened that an exotic-dancer patient of his was the former secretary of a big record honcho named Danny Davis.

"She said if you'll pay my way to L.A., and cab fare, I'll take this to Dan tomorrow. And I said, 'You got a deal.' "

Not only did Davis like it, he acted instantly. He got executives from Caliope Records to sign off on a deal, had a contract-bearing secretary dispatched to Las Vegas to fetch the masters, and prepared to make Garry Waite the top singing health-care professional in the country.

"This was in October. [A Caliope executive] said, 'By December you'll have the biggest hit on your hands you'll ever have. You'll never again do as well as you do on this song.' " The following day every executive who sponsored the deal was fired.

"Management change," Waite grimly recalls. "That's a bad break."

Yet so close, as several dentistry-related contacts would be. His exotic-dancer friend was in for root canal and crowns. Later, a patient would hook him up with a board member of the Country Music Association. And then there was Tammy Wynette.

One night she was due to perform in Las Vegas but couldn't go on because of illness. Lucky Garry; he was in the audience and her problem was an abscessed tooth. Next thing you know he was treating her in her room and they've been friends ever since.

Alas, life isn't Aesop. Just because you take a thorn out of a lion's paw doesn't mean the lion can get you booked at Opryland.

"I asked," Waite says. "And she said she'd do what she could."

But it was nothing.

Strip Joint for Jesus

ST. ALBANS, W.VA.—First he looked at Satan. Then he looked at God. Then Mickey Davis, the strip-joint owner, decided to switch sides. He placed the ad July 1.

FANTASY GIRLS CLOSED
"What good would it do to gain the world
if you lose your soul?"

The answer Davis himself had come to was "none whatsoever." For months, he'd been reading the Bible—especially Revelation—and a higher truth was slapping him upside the head.

He quaked, for instance, at the prophecy of Jews returning to the promised land on wings of birds.

"The more I studied the more I realized the prophecies were coming true . . . I felt like if I shut the place down, and turned my life around, I could communicate with God and experience the Holy Ghost and stuff like that. You know the expression, 'If you ain't tried it, don't knock it'? I was forty years old and ain't never tried it."

So, amid much ballyhoo, he tried it. The Reverend David Hissom, West Virginia's foremost televangelist, dispatched a video crew, and with the cameras rolling Davis drained $500 worth of beer and liquor onto the gravel parking lot. He tore down the Fantasy Girls sign and, with red paint, scrawled the letters J-E-S-U-S on the face of the building. The grimy commercial highway between St. Albans and South Charleston was minus one sleaze merchant and richer to the tune of one house of God.

"We started having services down here once a week," he says. "I was gonna start a Christian restaurant down here." The plan was to serve meals to everybody, charging only those who could afford it. But things didn't quite work out. "My life got *worse*," he says. "The first couple of services here, man, the place was packed. Everything seemed to be going real good."

But quickly the novelty waned. People started to lose interest. Nobody wanted to subsidize the restaurant, not even the ministers who had pledged support when they urged him to close his bar. Davis pleaded with them, to no avail. Not to put too fine a point on it, this soured him somewhat to the clergy.

"They're all hypocrites. They don't worship God. They worship money. It's the almighty dollar, not the Almighty itself. Like Jim and Tammy. They're gold-plating their bathroom faucets and paying $115,000 to keep people's mouths shut. If a man's got a fancy suit, a big fancy car, he's not Christian. Can't be. If you was going to be a true Christian, like the Bible says to do, you'd end up pushing a Kroger's buggy down Main Street, because you'd be helping everybody till you couldn't help no more, then you'd be left helpless, because nobody's gonna help you.

"They said, 'I'll pray for you. I'll pray for you.' Tell that to the landlord or electric company. Seven months went by and my bank account went straight downhill. I make an honest effort to work for the other side, and I can't pay my bills. Now they's something wrong with that, ain't they? You can't eat prayer, man."

This gets to Davis's second problem in his conversion: a certain shortfall in spiritual fulfillment.

"Never once spoke in tongues. Never once was slain in the spirit. God never spoke to me, not that I could recognize. I was wantin' it so much that at times I thought it was the Holy Ghost, but I realized, that no, it was just myself."

So Mickey Davis did what he had to do. The J-E-S-U-S letters came off and a new sign went up: The Pink Pussycat. Babylon revisited. Tonight, under the strobe lights in this low-slung, brown frame building, an ample-chested young woman named Blondie is onstage doing something just on the borderline between titillating and revolting. Davis views the scene coldly, acknowledging that perhaps he never really had the requisite faith and commitment.

"The best analogy I can give you is, if you're in an airplane, and it's heading down, and you see that ground coming at you real fast, and there's a parachute in the plane, are you gonna stay seated and trust God to save you? Or are you gonna grab the parachute? I grabbed the parachute, man, but I feel like I got real close to the ground."

Don't Shoot. Here's My Card.

SALT LAKE CITY, UTAH—The first time Robert Macri met Ronnie Lee Gardner, in the records room of the courthouse, Gardner made quite an impression.

This had something to do with the gunshot that had just rung out, and with the gaping chest wound visible through the young man's overalls.

"I said, 'Is this a joke?,' " recalls Macri, a forty-five-year-old lawyer. "It was just past April Fool's Day. But another attorney, to my left, dived into a court file and said, 'This ain't no joke.' "

The other lawyer, Michael Burdell, processed the facts instantaneously: Gardner, a prisoner in the building for a hearing, had somehow gotten a gun, been shot by a guard, and stumbled into the records room with a desperate look in his eye.

Burdell recognized at a glance that this insane scenario spelled trouble, and he was absolutely correct—which was the next-to-last thing in his life he would ever be. The last thing he'd ever be was too close to Ronnie Lee Gardner.

"Ron . . . had blood pumping out of his chest," Macri says. "Then he came across and held the gun to my head. It wasn't until he moved the gun and I heard Mike say 'Oh, my God,' and I watched him blow Mike's head off that a little voice went off saying, 'Time to get out of here.' "

Macri escaped. But he and Gardner would meet again. They became reacquainted when Macri took an interest in a condemned prisoner in the Utah penitentiary—a convicted murderer Macri deemed to be a victim of society, a murderer who Macri wanted to free from incarceration. A murderer named Ronnie Lee Gardner. Yes, a year after Gardner toyed with executing him, Macri decided to be the killer's advocate, teacher, and pal.

"All of us are guilty of something," Macri shrugs, and of course he is right, although most of us aren't guilty of two homicides and dozens of felonies going back to the age of nine.

"All I can tell you," says Carrie Hill, chief of legal services for the Utah State Prison, "is it's a very unusual situation."

Bob Macri is an unusual man. Lawyer, playwright, political activist, clergyman, he has made a mark in the Salt Lake legal community by championing the rights of the downtrodden on the one hand and, as he describes the other hand, litigating "sleazy divorces."

Among his clients are the local Hari Krishna temple, Jim Hydrick—a sometime fugitive who turns electrical appliances on and off with his mind—and Summum, an organization devoted to human mummification, as taught by blue visitors from outer space.

"I have sort of a metaphysical practice," he says.

While other lawyers may leave their spiritual side home when they leave for the office, Macri totes his along. When he counsels clients such as Gardner, there's apt to be far more under discussion than writs of habeas corpus.

"I'm a Jew. I'm investigating Zen. I'm chairman of the Temple of the Rainbow Path. I'm friendly with Summum. I'm an active Unitarian. I think I'm the projection of the best in everyone."

Thus he was able to ignore that little cold-blooded killing incident and take Gardner's interests to heart. Not only did he vainly seek a commutation of the convict's death sentence, Macri found a woman in Spanish Fork willing to adopt the lad. A family unit having been established, Macri then personally took responsibility for the young man's education.

"I think the most important thing was teaching him the King Arthur myth," Macri says. "I mean, he could relate to him on a mystic level."

Recently Macri had to withdraw as Gardner's lawyer, following certain breaches of conduct by the prisoner—among them an unauthorized conjugal visit with his girlfriend, achieved by kicking through a glass partition in the visitors' room. But Macri continues to serve as friend and minister, which he says is all part of his karma. They were fated to meet, Macri was fated to be spared Gardner's violence, Burdell was fated to die, and their spiritual lives were to be entwined for the good of all men.

"Or," the lawyer says, "as my wife points out, I might be entirely wrong. He might just be a bad boy."

Stalking History

PORTAGE, MICH.—In front of City Hall here, the word PORTAGE is spelled out in begonias and dusty miller. This is only fitting for a town heavily dependent on the bedding-plant industry and which fancies itself "A City on the Grow."

"At our flower festival," says William M. Deming, parks and recreation director, "we highlighted twenty different varieties of petunias."

Not to mention marigolds and impatiens in a host of charming colors. So it was only natural, when the city was planning the new museum that will be the *pièce de rèsistance* of its park system, that it would choose, as its theme . . . celery!

The three-acre tract is being cleared now. When construction is complete in the spring, Portage will be home to the Celery Flats Interpretive Center, expected to be among the finest celery museums anywhere.

"Nobody expected it to go this far," says Michael Stampfler, city manager. "At first, the idea . . . I'd say it was roundly thought to be strange. I think even the staff at first thought it was wacky."

Silly them. While it's true that, technically speaking, there are no celery growers in Portage, there is a 100-acre celery farm in neighboring Comstock. Moreover, at one time Portage and the rest of Kalamazoo County were celery hotbeds. Nearby Hudsonville plastered "Celery Center of America" on its water tower, and Kalamazoo dubbed itself "Celery City." To this day, Kalamazoo has a celery bunch in its city seal.

"This is a known concept," says Larry Massie, Michigan historian and museum consultant, who says Portage is wise to appropriate it. After all, "In New York, they have the Big Apple."

The idea of a museum surfaced when the park system was being planned in the mid-1970s, but until recently the particular theme was as an open question. Portage has only been a city for twenty-five years and has a certain shortfall in the tradition department. The biggest export is made at the local Upjohn Co. plant, but the notion of a Kaopectate Museum garnered no support whatsoever. "People in Portage are always looking for something to hang their hats on," Deming says. "Portage really hasn't had much to grasp on to. The celery thing just kind of developed as we were looking for a historical angle."

Next thing they knew, they were deep into plans for a museum building, a small-scale working celery farm, an observation deck, and, Deming says, "a short-promotional film on 'Why celery?' " Naturally, Larry Massie was thrilled—if somewhat daunted.

"This is really an unusual project," the historian says. "Usually, when you have a museum, someone has collected information and artifacts for years and years and years."

Oddly enough, he has uncovered no celery archive of any consequence. Yet he's already amassed lots of nifty celery lore. For instance, so-called Kalamazoo celery was quite different from the California pascal celery we're familiar with. The Michigan variety was intentionally deprived of sun, producing tender white stalks. Then there's the field of celery poetry. To wit:

K-A-ka, L-A-la, M-A-mazoo
Kalamazoo, kazit, kazam
Celery city of Mich-i-gan

To some, that verse might suggest that Portage somehow has a less legitimate claim to celery tradition than its neighboring city to the north. But here again, in planning the museum, the historical options were limited.

"I guess another idea that popped up was 'portage' itself," Deming says. "At one time this was an Indian portage."

Yes, whereas the Kalamazoo city seal has the celery stalks, Portage's depicts an Indian and a fur trader carrying a canoe on their heads. "Progress, peace, prosperity," it says, with nary a word about *pium graveolens,* the parsley cousin that is celery. But Deming can only shrug.

"It isn't the Alamo or something like that, but at least it's something they can take pride in."

And Mike Stampfler agrees: "There's sort of a hunger for a sense of significance, I guess. Maybe this fulfills part of that. Or maybe people just don't care."

Death by Footwear

What Dr. Simon Wikler can't understand, what after forty years he simply cannot comprehend, is why nobody else sees what he sees.

"To me, it's so simple and obvious," he says. "I think this is the biggest story of the century. Now, everybody blows his own horn, but I really believe it."

He believes it as much as anyone can believe anything.

Research, clinical practice, and simple common sense tell the seventy-six-year-old podiatrist that civilization is literally killing itself. Not by decadence or environmental carelessness or nuclear lunacy.

He is talking about death by footwear. Wikler is certain that shoes cause cancer.

"See, we distort nearly everybody's feet," he explains from his Miami office, headquarters of Shoe Related Diseases Inc. "This is a basic element of our body that's been distorted, been inhibited. That causes stress all over the body."

Rigid, restrictive, stupidly designed shoes, he says, cause grossly distorted feet—especially in women. The feet then lose flexibility and function, putting undue pressures on the spine and entire musculature. The consequence of this, he maintains, is systemic chaos and a host of disorders. Chief among them: heart disease and breast cancer.

"When a woman has good feet, her breasts will rest on her breast cage. But when a woman has bad feet, she tends to stand round-shouldered—you know, the debutante slouch. The breasts then sort of hang limp and sort of lean a little from the armpit."

This, Wikler says, is a prescription for malignancies.

"I'm not claiming every woman, willy-nilly, is going to get cancer of the breast. I'm saying one out of ten. This is a huge contributing factor that has never been probed. Now, see, there are lots of other organs involved in the process. But I'm not going to give the whole burst. I don't want to overwhelm people."

For four decades, Wikler has been mainly underwhelming people. He has told anybody who'll listen about the historical absence of cancer and coronary disease among black Africans and Costa Rican peasants, and their subsequent lethal Westernization. He's talked about how the diseases were no menace to China and Japan, until the Chinese stopped wearing cloth slippers and the Japanese gave up their *zori* sandals.

He's shown countless diagrams of tarsal dysfunction, of atrophied foot muscles and misaligned calcanei, astragaluses, and scaphoids. As he puts it, "There's probably nobody alive who knows as much about this stuff as I do."

Certainly nobody who cares as much. Wikler first hit on the shoe-disease connection watching his own mother suffer with brain cancer. As a young immigrant, she'd ruined her feet wearing stylish but ill-fitting pumps. Wikler, who at the time was the most prosperous podiatrist in Lancaster, Pennsylvania, felt intuitively there was a cause-and-effect relationship.

"For thirty years I've been trying to get a simple statistical study of the correlation between the distorted foot and the presence of disease. But I can't get in edgewise. I'm a foot doctor, I'm not a physician, so it's hard for me to get into these clinics to make these tests."

He can't even get his own colleagues to pay attention. In 1950, having presented his hypothesis in a podiatry journal, he was to be a speaker at a conference of the Podiatric Association of Pennsylvania.

"They canceled me on the program. The same thing happened here in Florida. They said, 'Don't you dare talk about that or we'll lift your license. We're foot doctors. We remove corns. Now get lost.' "

Of late, Wikler has gotten a somewhat more sympathetic ear. He recently conducted a pilot study at the Ohio State University Comprehensive Cancer Center, and testified last month at the National Cancer Advisory Board hearings at the University of Miami (Florida).

He is the respected developer of the Wikler Shoe by Buster Brown, a spacious and flexible infant shoe that has sold in the tens of millions, so he isn't always treated like a crackpot. But for the most part, nobody wants to hear about killer footwear.

"This is something that's been totally neglected by medical science," he sighs. "It's just one of those things that people are closed to. I don't know why, but that's the way it is. In your history, surely you must remember the trouble Pasteur went through. That guy almost went nuts before he could get modern medicine to accept him. That's the way it goes. Medicine is astonishingly shortsighted."

Frankie Angel Goes Flying

PAULSBORO, N.J.—Here's what happened tonight at the Monster Academy, one of the foremost professional-wrestling training institutions in the world:

1. Talent manager Larry Zamensky, who calls himself the Bounty Hunter, agreed to represent The Atom, Thunder Mountain, and Frankie Angel on the pro wrestling circuit. Zamensky already manages a midget wrestler named Third-Degree Burns.

2. The Atom, a.k.a. Jimmie McPherson, learned he won't be billed as Fearsome McPherson as he'd planned. When Bounty Hunter signs you, you do things his way. The Atom fears his "Wrestlin' Rap with Jimmie Mac" is out the window, too.

3. Six would-be Monster Academicians looked on wide-eyed as the veteran students slammed, tumbled, bounced, thudded, and cracked through leapfrogs, wristlocks, sunset flips, step-over toeholds, and arm stretches. Then the tryouts performed a few rudimentary moves for the headmaster, a thick-browed blond gentleman named Pretty Boy Larry Sharpe.

4. Don Gates, a purchasing clerk for Atlantic City, agreed to join the Monster Academy program for the purposes of making himself an international wrestling superstar, which

will cost him $3,000, pass or fail. If he is to pass, he has a long way to go. For instance, during his audition, he employed his killer claw-grip mainly to hold up his sagging sweatpants.

5. Frankie Angel, a.k.a. "The Heavenly One," moved a bit slowly while rehearsing his preening strut around the ring. Four months of monster training have resulted in five broken ribs, multiple broken fingers, and a shoulder separation. "I came in here thinking everything was padded," he says. He was mistaken.

6. In the clutches of a clinch, Angel was overheard whispering, "leapfrog, sunset kick," to his practice opponent—inadvertently revealing the secret to pro wrestling choreography. Moments later, The Heavenly One inadvertently flew over the ropes and landed on your correspondent. Your correspondent, a wiry 165 pounds, was not injured. Angel, weighing in at 240, separated his shoulder.

In all, it's been a fairly routine night here in this converted storefront, where Sharpe has been converting pituitary cases into pro-style wrestlers since 1984. Such ring greats as King Kong Bundy, Bam Bam Bigelow, Tiny Atlas, and Kevin Von Erich learned their body slams at Pretty Boy's feet.

"Once I decide to take 'em, I keep 'em for as long as it takes," says Mr. Sharpe, a former North American Tag-Team Champion. "Then we get 8-by-10s taken, make a video, and give 'em a list of promoters. Then they're on their own."

Being on their own, of course, is not what these monsters-in-training have in mind. They haven't killed themselves spending four nights a week for five months and a tuition of three large to get a weekend club fight here and there.

"For me it's not gonna work like that. I have too much talent," says The Atom, a twenty-five-year-old father of six who quit his job as a milkman to make time for training. Early on, during a sunset flip gone awry, his nose was ripped almost entirely off his face. It took forty stitches to reattach it, but he didn't think of quitting. And why?

"He says he's gonna fight Hulk Hogan one day," explains his wife, Alicia. "He's gonna go for the belt."

Likewise, Frankie Angel, who is actually Frank Dempsky, a production supervisor at a magnetics factory. "I'm trying to live out a golden life," he says. "I know what I've wanted since I was six years old."

Thunder Mountain, a 430-pounder born David Mosier, figures he's already on his way. Bounty Hunter is negotiating a Japan tour for him that would earn Mountain $10,000 per week (40 percent of which goes to the manager) plus expenses. Mountain can already taste the sushi. "Pro wrestling!" he booms. "Every meal's a banquet, every paycheck's a fortune, every group of men's a parade."

This gets to Don Gates, the dumpy thirty-year-old tryout.

"My job is boring," he says. "Like, if we need a water pump, I call up and order a water pump . . . I wanna learn how to be a wrestler."

Can you blame him? The only nickname he ever had was "Shaggy," which wasn't exactly a chick magnet. But Don "The Outlaw" Gates—he can just see the groupies swooning.

"I got a girl to go home to, but—you know—fame and fortune. I wanna become a star. I wanna become Ricky Steamboat. Like, he's famous. Everybody knows him."

Remembering the Day of the Cashmere Bouquet

CAMDEN, N.J.—When one of the foremost scholars on international constitutional law demands you ignore his canisters, vases, and outsize brandy snifters full of matchbooks, you're apt to obey.

Here is a man who has visited eighty-seven countries and territories of the world, who has drafted the constitutions of Bangladesh, Liberia, and Zimbabwe, who has written twenty books, including *A Bibliography of the Common Law in French*. So when he instructs you to pay no heed to his matchbooks and his bowls of stone eggs and his urn full of maybe 500 pens and pencils and his heaps of baggage tags and Do Not Disturb cards—well, you just do.

"The fact that you see me here with matches is insignificant," says Professor Albert Blaustein of Rutgers University School of Law. "I'm a man with a soap collection of some scope."

Yes, yes, yes. Never mind luggage tags. The man who has influenced so many world constitutions that he's been called the Johnny Appleseed of Democracy does, indeed, have a soap collection that would blow your mind: 1,400 bars of soap, each painstakingly labeled, from 1,400 hotel stays here and abroad.

"A lot of people pick up matches," explains Blaustein, sixty-six. "These are things you just throw in a box and forget about. But this soap is something you organize and classify. You can put it in a box, date them, catalogue them, organize them, and really have a diary of your life. You really can't do that picking up ashtrays."

The collection began in 1942 when young Blaustein visited the Hotel Sherman in Chicago. In those days, years before he got into the constitution-writing racket, he was quite innocent. When he spied a soap bar personalized with the hostelry's name, "I was very impressed." So he kept it, as he has kept so many others for forty-five years ever after.

Not shampoo, mind you. Not hand lotion, or mink oil *pour le bain*. Just soap. Soap from Senegal, soap from Macao, soap from Sri Lanka, soap from Romania, soap from Lesotho, soap from Transkei, soap from Yemen, soap from Iceland. Ivory, Camay, Palmolive, Cashmere Bouquet, Lux Toilet Soap, Yardley English Lavender, French-milled coconut soap.

"See? Really nice soaps," he says, grabbing a bar from one of his ten handy carrying cases. "This is Neutrogena. The Sheraton in Scottsdale has Neutrogena."

Neutrogena or Dial, the most important thing is not the quality of the cleansing but the quality of the memory. Blaustein's 1,400 soaps constitute 1,400 life experiences. Pull out a bar at random, read him the date, and see the wistful look in his eyes as he demonstrates his soapographic memory.

"Ansley Hotel, Atlanta, early '44. Oh, you know, I think I met a girl there as a young soldier. That's undoubtedly what I was doing there at the time . . . Hotel Sofitel in Naimey, Niger. November, '84. I was down there to advise them on their constitution and charter. This is a Palmolive bar."

Should you ever get to see Blaustein and his collection in person, here's a helpful hint: When the professor is in mid-revel about any individual soap bar, *do not ask to see his pens and pencils.* Chances are he will accommodate you, but he might get in a small lather about it, possibly grabbing a pen and reading the inscription—with obvious impatience—aloud.

"Ramada Inn. East Hanover, New Jersey," he'll say, disdainfully. "How would you remember when you were in a Ramada Inn in East Hanover, New Jersey? With the soap, you would know."

Alas, as passionate as Blaustein is about his collection, the emotion is not wholly shared by the outside world. Many people regard soap merely as something to wash with, preferring to keep a diary of their lives by other means, such as a diary. Even among those with vested interest, there has been no clamor to acquire, when the time comes, the Blaustein Memorial Collection.

"I wrote to the Ivory soap people," he says. "They said they had no strict interest, but they introduced me to some people at the Smithsonian."

The Smithsonian, unfortunately, isn't exactly pestering him for it either—which puts him in a difficult position. He has but one soap collection and three children. And as Blaustein so eloquently states his dilemma, "The children don't want it."

The Last Zacchini

YONKERS, N.Y.—He must truly be a daredevil, because this is quite the fashion risk. Or what would you call a white, horsehide jumpsuit complemented by a red belt, red-leather ski mask, and red high-top sneakers?

In this getup, Hugo Zacchini looks more like a human baseball than the Human Cannonball, except that he happens to be standing on a twenty-two-foot howitzer, in preparation for being shot 160 feet through the air.

The huge silvery barrel—mounted on a freshly overhauled, nine-ton, 1940 Diamond T tanker—silently moves skyward, stopping at an angle of forty-five degrees. Hugo raises his arm above his head.

"A final wave good-bye," booms the emcee over the Westchester Fair PA system. "Good luck, Hugo Zacchini!"

Godspeed, greatest living projectile! Hugo disappears into the nineteen-inch bore as the emcee slowly counts down: 5-4-3-2-1 . . . BOOM! There he goes, slicing through the air in a graceful arc. Three seconds of wingless flight end with a bounce and a flip in the net that is his constant salvation.

"Let's see if he's okay," says the anxious announcer. "He IS!"

Of course he is. This is no garden-variety human cannonball. This is Hugo Zacchini, last and most prolific of the Zacchini Human Cannonballs. Many have styled themselves professional projectiles, but he and he alone has been shot eighty-five miles through the air, the distance between Nashville, Tennessee, and Bowling Green, Kentucky. (Hugo never actually made the flight.

He's covered the distance in the course of 4,000-some performances.)

No, he is no ordinary artillery round and tonight's is no ordinary performance. Tomorrow ends his nine-day run here, and then begins his retirement.

"I pressed my luck long enough," he says. "I do have small injuries all over my body and only one has to get worse before it's hospitalization. My bones hurt a lot. Because of injuries and age, it's time I get out."

Since 1922, when Hugo's father, Edmondo, conceived the act in Malta, Zacchinis have "jumped cannon" the world over. Edmondo himself was hampered by an old trapeze injury and never was publicly fired. But his brother Hugo (our hero's uncle) was equal to the task, as later were brothers Victor and Emmanuel. Eventually Edmondo's children got into the act, making cannon fodder out of Edmund, Duena, Victoria, and Hugo.

"I," says the last of the second generation, "have been the sole Zacchini operating the past fifteen years."

This is not to say he's been the only cannon act. The Zacchinis have *beaucoup* imitators, though the field has thinned lately after injuries to unlucky performers. Whereas it's true practically anybody is equipped to be shot out of a cannon, landing is an extremely dicey enterprise. Hugo has had the net collapse on him six times, for example.

"In 1965, at Kennywood in Pittsburgh, I hit the stage and I broke my ankle and suffered compressions in my spine. I was out for the rest of the season."

And heaven help you if the cannon—which propels its contents pneumatically—should happen to seize up at a critical moment and provide insufficient thrust.

"Then you come short," he says. "And if you come short enough, and don't make the net, it's curtains. Or wheelchair. Take your pick."

No wonder he's had enough. After all these years, it would

be a pity for the last Zacchini to become a summer squash. There are enough other things to worry about for a man of his age, which seems to be about fifty.

"I will not disclose it," he says, "simply because I'm not a twenty- or thirty-year-old man, and that's what people want to see in the air. People want to see a daring young man in the air, and it's ridiculous to show the daring *aging* man in the air."

That's logical . . . but wait. If he's retiring, what difference does it make how old he is? And, for that matter, if this is his last run, why did he bother to overhaul the truck? Here's why: Tomorrow's performance is his last ever *unless somebody wants him to do more.* Aches or no aches, if the money is right the Zacchini tradition will live on.

"The demand will call me back, I'm sure," he says. "It will call the act back."

Campaign and Suffering

JUPITER, FLA.—In 1948, Richard Kay was an Ohio organizer for the Harold Stassen presidential campaign. The experience must have left an impression.

Stassen, of course, raked in 157 delegates toward the Republican nomination that year, or just 70 percent short of those needed to carry the day. He also lost in 1952, '64, '68, '72, '76 and '80—becoming, in the process, the archetype of American political futility.

That is Stassen's legacy to Richard Kay. The sixty-nine-year-old semiretired lawyer is a candidate for the presidency of the United States.

"I just felt I have to have some input in national dialogue," Kay says as he prepares for a petition-filing trip to Louisiana.

"It's limited, I agree. But I'll tell you this: You don't know unless you try."

Actually, the impact of his candidacy is far less than limited—on everyone but Kay, who is spending about $10,000 of his own money on his campaign for the Democratic nomination. And he knows precisely how he will fare, because he's been through the exercise before. Carrying on the Stassen tradition, he ran in both 1984 and 1980, and didn't become president either time.

In '80 he was on the ballot in six states. In '84, two. This year: only Missouri, Louisiana, Kentucky, and Kansas. His own home state of Florida has refused him on the grounds of obscurity. No matter, he says:

"Ideas are more important than Richard Kay."

Today the idea is to get to Baton Rouge and file for a ballot position. He dresses in a gray pinstripe suit, one he hopes is photogenic for the TV cameras—not that there will be any. Then he takes his lone "Richard Kay for President" button from the lapel of his brown suit and sticks it onto the gray. He does so swiftly; it's a procedure he's mastered over the years.

In the 1950s, back in Cleveland, Kay came within sixteen votes of unseating a key Republican councilman. But he lost. And soon thereafter he was twenty-one votes shy of a nomination for the Ohio legislature. But he lost.

"I couldn't get beyond a primary," he sighs. In 1952, after working on Dwight Eisenhower's presidential campaign, "I was supposedly in line for an appointment in Washington as an assistant secretary of the Navy." But he lost that, too—this time through the devices of political foes, of whom he had many.

"I always used to be somewhat of a maverick," he says.

That never exactly changed. He got out of politics for a while, but then jumped right back in after representing Lieutenant William Calley Jr. in the My Lai court-martial. That time an Army court voted, and Calley lost.

The early 1970s found Kay in the thick of George Wallace's

American Party, for which he sought a U.S. Senate seat from Ohio. About 94 percent of the state's voters thought it was a bad idea. Still, he enjoyed debating Howard Metzenbaum and Robert Taft Jr., and was stimulated by the whole experience.

"That's when I began to realize that I had as much of a grasp on international and national problems as they did," he says. So he ran again in 1976, for the Democratic senatorial nomination, and lost. "Then I started gravitating toward races for more national offices. Some people felt this was foolhardy."

His performance in the last two presidential races did nothing to silence them, but Kay has long since stopped worrying about it. What concerns him is issues. So consumed is he by the quest for public service, he says, that he never took the time to marry and raise a family. "Politics," he says, "is my family."

Kay gulps a fistful of vitamins in the kitchen of his big, nicely appointed apartment. Here and there around his flat are artifacts of his public career: a photo of him with George Wallace, a plaque of recognition from the Greater Cleveland Young Republicans. He speaks wistfully of his fact-finding trip to South Africa and his hour-long audience with King Faisal of Saudi Arabia.

"I've been fairly successful," he says, "for a nonentity."

He speaks passionately about a balanced-budget amendment, global literacy, and invocation of the Monroe Doctrine in Nicaragua. Only when his guard is down does he show how pained he is that nobody's listening.

"I've had people say, 'We're not interested in having you on the ballot unless you're a serious candidate.' What the hell do they mean?" he asks. "Do they think I'm having a good time?"

The Statue of Freedom

SPRING VALLEY, CALIF.—The difference between ordinary mortals and real idea men can amount to something as simple as listening, really listening to Miss South Dakota.

Had Herb Ketell not been a seasoned philosopher, the significance of what he was viewing probably would have been lost on him, as no doubt it was lost on the millions of others who got all the way to the margarine commercial without realizing what they'd seen and heard.

"I watched a TV show one night and it was the Miss America contest," says Ketell. "The fifteen finalists were put in a booth and brought out one at a time and all asked the same question: 'What do you like best about America?' And more than fifty percent of them said, 'Freedom.' I thought, that's a good idea. Why not immortalize the word 'freedom'?"

Why not, indeed? Yet as obvious as the next step was, Ketell was the only man in America to discern the essence of the telecast and get busy. He alone has conceived, designed, and sponsored a 300-feet-tall monument overlooking San Diego Harbor of a muscular man, arms outstretched, clad only in a jockstrap—2,400 cubic yards of concrete molded into a physique as classic as the concept it represents.

Ketell calls it the Statue of Freedom.

"This will be a lot better than the Statue of Liberty," he says. "You need a strong man to represent freedom, because it takes strength to stay free. You don't want a weakling representing America."

Don't get him wrong. Ketell is as fond of Miss Liberty as the next guy, but having come up with a superior concept, he's not about to let sentimentality get in the way. He's charging ahead with all the energy that got him elected Mr. Spring Valley by the Spring Valley Chamber of Commerce.

At eighty-two, Ketell is the very picture of vigor. Today he's wearing a Hawaiian shirt in striking Day-Glo colors and a pair of handsome white slacks. Never mind the chain-smoking; he's tall and muscular and blessed with a good head of hair. In short, for his age, he looks incredible—but he says it isn't incredible at all, "if you know the laws of nature and the divine."

And that gets to the soul of the matter. Ketell is a walking advertisement for *Keys to a Good Life,* which is a book of philosophy he penned at the age of eighty.

"This book," begins the introduction, "is dedicated to help Human Beings to rise above the frustrations of the brutal physical world and to have the Joys of the Good Life." What follows are 356 fact-filled pages, a synopsis of Ketell's eighty-two years of accumulated knowledge. Such chapters as "Many people are unhappy," and "How to brush your teeth," and "Homosexuals are not greatly different from heterosexuals" get right to the nitty-gritty of what makes the world go round. "If you want to lead a peaceful, happy life," he says, "listen to me."

Just for one example, whereas many scientists are wasting time looking for a cure for cancer, Ketell's book demonstrates at least two cures that you can find right in your own refrigerator: garlic and asparagus. Simplicity is his watchword. In chapter 64, he distills Plato's life and work to one and a half typewritten pages. Is there any doubt that this is the man to spearhead a project so vast as the Statue of Freedom?

Not that there aren't obstacles. "Two or three people objected to my little jockstrap, so I'm putting a pair of tennis shorts on him," Ketell says.

And there's the matter of air rights at Point Loma, the federal land jutting into the harbor where Ketell envisions the statue being built. Point Loma happens to border both the San Diego Naval Air Station and the San Diego Airport. Asked whether there is a possibility of a 300-ft. monument being built there, port director Don Nay responds with a hearty "No."

But Ketell is undeterred. He harkens back to his days in Portland, Oregon, when, through his efforts, citizens overcame political intransigence to build a city zoo.

"There's always someone against you, whatever you do," he says, noting that before his chairmanship of the zoo committee the proposal was voted down twice.

"I imported an elephant," Ketell says. "We had a parade."

The Anti-Amalgamists

ORLANDO, FLA.—Nancy McEwan has her mouth open and Michael Ziff has his hand inside.

This is not entirely unusual, Ziff being a dentist and McEwan having teeth. What makes the scene somewhat extraordinary is that Ziff is not introducing a filling but removing one. He is removing it because, as he's explained to Mrs. McEwan, it is lethal. He is removing it because, he says, it will slowly erode her health and maybe eventually kill her. He is removing it because, like every filling in your mouth and mine, it is made of silver-mercury amalgam.

"Make sure you breathe through your nose," he warns his patient, "and make sure you have your eyes closed until I tell you I have the whole filling out."

These are the words of a true-blue anti-amalgamist, a fearless, fearsome dental renegade. Ziff is at the forefront of an incipient movement of impassioned dentists with a disturbing message: your mouth is hazardous to your health. Mercury vapor seeping from your fillings can damage your brain, they say. Also your heart, lungs, thyroid gland, pituitary gland, adrenal glands, blood cells, enzymes, hormones, and immune system—which is alarming because many of these things are useful on a daily basis.

Where the American Dental Association sees as a harmless and useful tool they see an environmental threat that makes the asbestos hazard, in Ziff's words, "look like a picnic." They aim to stamp it out.

"Amalgam is dead," he says. "It's just a question of when."

Answer: Not terribly soon.

The American Dental Association doesn't believe amalgam is a sinister killer. What the ADA does think is that removing patients' fillings to protect their enzymes is unnecessary, unduly expensive, unethical, and grounds for losing your license. Even the most sympathetic establishment researchers are skeptical.

"I'm not saying they're talking nonsense," says Cyril O. Enwonwuo, who concluded in his report for the National Institute of Dental Research that new studies on mercury toxicity are called for. "I'm just saying they're stretching things."

Ziff is unswayed. He is Chicken Dental saying the sky is falling, and his father says so, too. Sam Ziff, erstwhile Air Force officer and physiology hobbyist, has spent six years and $30,000 gathering data on the mercury issue, which he circumspectly describes as "the greatest health controversy of our time." His home office is crammed with six filing cabinets and three bookshelves, all overflowing with medical literature on mercury toxicity—1,800 scientific references in all. Though the literature doesn't necessarily prove the dangers of dental amalgam, he says, it is full of enough indicting evidence to make your teeth rattle. This evidence he presented in his book, *The Toxic Time Bomb*.

"Can it be possible," the book asks, "that mercury may be the single factor responsible for so many unexplainable health problems experienced by man?" Emphysema, multiple sclerosis, shyness—you name it and he figures your fillings could be causing it.

"The studies that have been done everybody is pooh-poohing as insignificant," he says. "The thing nobody has ever done is look at chronic low doses over a long period."

Nor is there anybody rushing to do so, which demoralizes the Ziffs to no end.

"I don't need to work as hard as I've worked and spend my own goddamned money to do something that would fall on deaf ears," Sam says.

"Frustrating," Michael agrees. "Having to deal with people who are close-minded and won't deal with the research."

But they press on. While Sam labors to find support in the medical community, Michael yanks out fillings and replaces them with polymer composites. It is a molar crusade, and one not undertaken lightly. With every amalgam filling he removes, Michael risks his license and livelihood—which is to say, he's putting his money where your mouth is.

"I fully realize the position of jeopardy I'm in," he says. "But I've come to realize that I have to do what I have to do."

Who Killed All Those Dead People?

Between the homicide that was a suicide and the suicide that was a homicide—to say nothing of the homicide that was either homicide, suicide, or neither—Dr. Daniel Thomas has had a turbulent year.

So now, on top of everything, the beleaguered coroner of Lake County, Indiana, has been publicly humiliated. Indiana's only full-time coroner/proctologist has been summarily dumped from the Lake County Law Enforcement Council, on the grounds that he's annoying.

"It's a real soap opera," Thomas says. "I could write a book."

When last we checked in on Doc Thomas about fifteen months ago, he was mainly preoccupied with the Cooley case. Probably you recall that James Cooley, a fifty-two-year-old Hobart man, was found dead in his basement darkroom with thirty-two claw-hammer blows to the head—not all that bizarre a circumstance until you factor in the police ruling of "self-inflicted."

Thomas, an admittedly stubborn fellow, got it in his head that the deceased actually had been murdered. "Something smells from fish," he remarked, and sure enough the Hobart police ultimately changed their minds—but not before a flurry of Thomas's public statements portraying the investigators in a less than flattering light.

Then came the Fisher case. This was a fairly straightforward situation wherein Mr. Fisher discovered an armed robber in his garage and tussled with him, during which struggle the robber bit him. The minor twists were that 1) the intruder, Mr. Scott, actually was Mrs. Fisher's lover, 2) Mr. Scott has AIDS and tuberculosis, and 3) a day later Mrs. Fisher died of heart failure.

Informed that the Hobart police contemplated charging Mr. Scott with murder in Mrs. Fisher's death, Dr. Thomas again favored reporters with his autopsy findings. To wit: Mrs. Fisher died not of a heart attack, but of congestive heart failure brought on by an overdose of tranquilizers.

Here again, certain parties did not appreciate the ensuing press coverage.

"I feel there are times when there are differences of opinion regarding an ongoing investigation that we sit down and discuss it privately," says Chief Lawrence Juzwicki of the Hobart police.

The final blow came with the Agee case. Mrs. Agee, fifty-three, was charged with shooting Mr. Agee, sixty-six. The prosecution said it was an execution-style murder, meticulously planned and perpetrated while Mr. Agee slept. Mrs. Agee first claimed she shot in self-defense, while being sexually brutalized and threatened with her death and the death of their two children.

Then, based on the autopsy, Dr. Thomas weighed in with his ruling.

"You can't ignore the physical evidence of the autopsy," he said. "This was a suicide."

This was what you call "a new development." Shortly thereafter, Mrs. Agee remembered that, oh yes, it was definitely a suicide. What with the sodomy and everything, it had slipped her mind. But she was still convicted. "One never knows what motivates a jury," sighs Roger Moore, her lawyer.

One can speculate jurors were influenced by the testimony of multiple Agee relatives, who said Mrs. Agee has been threatening to kill her husband for years. But whatever the circumstance, Thomas stuck by his suicide analysis. After the verdict. Publicly. In the newspapers.

That's when the Lake County Law Enforcement Council, an unofficial professional organization headed by a certain Chief Lawrence Juzwicki, blackballed Indiana's crime-bustin' proctologist.

"He's in hot water," says County Prosecutor Jack Crawford. "I think the Agee case was the straw that broke the camel's back."

Not that they question Thomas's competence, the prosecutor says. It's just that "police feel he should confine his expertise to the medical area. They don't like him telling them how to do their jobs."

Thomas, of course, says he does no such thing.

"Actually, what's occurring is I'm standing up for what I think is right, and it's agitating," he says. "I'll never miss them, but just the idea of what they did is wrong."

For starters, the hubbub has people thinking he's been removed from office. Who needs that kind of publicity? Says Thomas, "They're driving me ape."

The Levee Is Dry

And it shall come to pass, when many evils and troubles are befalling them, that this song will testify against them as a witness.
—DEUTERONOMY 31:21

PALMER, TEX.—Don McLean's song "American Pie" had been out for seven years when it first started working at Roy Taylor. But it tantalized him. It frightened him. It consumed him, and it changed his life.

"When somebody mentioned to me that it was a prophecy— I don't remember who it was—and I started just thinking about it," says the forty-four-year-old freelance electronics technician. "I just kind of pieced it all together."

The process began in 1979. For nine years since, Taylor has devoted himself to analyzing the song, interpreting it, and spreading the word about the cataclysm he says it foretells.

"It's singing about the Battle of Armageddon. Everybody knows that the Bible says there will be a war between the forces of good and the forces of evil in the last days. And that's exactly what 'American Pie' is singing about, musically speaking."

The revelation didn't come immediately. For two years, Palmer sat in the dining room of his double-wide mobile home and worked out the details on thirteen cassette tapes in line-by-line annotation.

"I had prayed to God and asked him to give me time to do this song, so two weeks later I was fired from my job. I really had no control over it. I was actually driven—out of some power that I couldn't understand myself. And it went together like you wouldn't believe."

Taylor ran an ad in *Spotlight,* a far-right-wing newspaper, and sat back waiting for the response. He was disappointed to get but seven requests for his tapes, but it turned out they were widely circulated in certain circles of the religious right. Amid the blank cassettes and recording equipment in Taylor's dining area are stacks of letters from fascinated correspondents around the world.

Perhaps they'd never given any thought to the McLean lyric, "Helter-skelter in the summer swelter / The birds flew off the fallout shelter." But Taylor made it all clear: "Helter-skelter" referred to nuclear terrorism to be committed here by Soviet infiltrators equipped with A-bomb backpacks. This will lead to calls for disarmament, which will make America vulnerable to overthrow.

"Now we all know that there's a secret organization or secret power in this world that makes wars and brings down nations," but it wasn't until he happened upon a *Soldier of Fortune* article about the Soviet terrorists that it all made sense. That article cited a secret government report about the grave nuclear threat and an ominous "H-hour."

"And what gets me, if you use the words 'Helter-skelter,' it starts with *H.* And also nuclear holocaust starts with *H.* Holocaust. Helter-skelter. And what's amazing about this government report: it uses a time when they set off these bombs as H-hour. Why didn't they use zero hour as most military people do? But they said H-hour, which I couldn't believe."

He also can't believe, after all this time, that there are still skeptics. His own wife resented all the time he devoted to one silly song.

"You know, a wife, if she don't have a job, she can always revert back to a housewife. But if a man, if he don't have a job, he's just a bum. I believe it almost cost me my marriage, but I would have done it anyway."

The other skeptical party in all of this is Don McLean himself. Dave Burgess, McLean's manager, threatened to sue if he sees his client's name even mentioned in connection with Taylor. That surprises Taylor not at all. A few years back, when the singer played in Dallas, Taylor managed at length to get McLean on the phone and discovered a prophet ignorant of his own prophecy.

"I said, 'Mr. McLean, do you realize the song you're singing, the symbols that you're singing, are directly out of the Bible? And what you're saying is foretold in the Bible 2,500 years ago?' And he said he didn't realize that . . . He didn't understand the song himself."

Verily, the Lord works in strange ways.

"Like I said," Taylor shrugs, "if this song doesn't come to pass, I apologize to the whole world. If it's not true it won't happen, but it is true and I know it's true and I knew it was true and I knew it would happen and it's happening."

Press Conference

Charles W. Wixom freezes.

It may be the Chicago-in-February weather, approximately 17 million degrees below zero at the south end of the LaSalle Street drawbridge, where Wixom steps out of the Institute of Food Technologies into the teeth of a paralyzing wind. Or it may be the ghost of Clarence Birdseye (yes, there was a Birdseye), the granddaddy of food technology, doing to the IFT executive's nose and ears exactly what he did to fish fillets in 1924 to alter the course of food-storage history.

But, in all fairness, Wixom's reaction probably has very little to do with the subfreezing temperatures (the guy's a Chicagoan and an inveterate skier), nor with any supernatural Halibut

Chiller from Beyond. What does it is the mention of the Balkan Muslim Association press conference.

Wixom freezes partly because tens of thousands of innocent Muslims are being uprooted, raped, and slaughtered in mounting ethnic genocide so horrific that the Balkan Muslim Association on November 24 summoned the entire Washington press corps to the National Press Club and demanded that the world intercede.

He freezes partly because, in spite of the manifest urgency and historical significance of the routing of Bosnia, NBC did not show up for the press conference. And because CBS didn't either. Or ABC. Or CNN. Or *The New York Times.* Or *The Washington Post.* Or *The Wall Street Journal.* Or *USA Today,* the Associated Press, UPI, National Public Radio, *The Christian Science Monitor, Time, Newsweek, U.S. News and World Report, Grit, Weekly Reader,* or any other news organization you've ever heard of. Mainly, however, Chuck Wixom freezes because, in his capacity as public affairs director at IFT, he is himself in the process of planning a Washington press conference, scheduled for March 9 at the press club, and unlike the Balkan Muslims' warning of apocalypse now, which drew virtually nobody, his topic is "Research Needs into the 21st Century. A Report of the Research Committee of the Institute of Food Technologists."

Which is to say, in terms of marquee value, a little on the esoteric side. As a practical matter, Wixom harbors no illusions about attracting the major networks. IFT's goals are far more modest: ten to twelve reporters, including the trade press. But he's arranged for the IFT's press club meeting room to be set up for forty, and upon learning that the Balkan Muslims had arranged for exactly the same thing, what stops him cold, finally, is the phrase "thirty-seven empty chairs." It is then, for a chilling, pregnant moment, that Chuck Wixom freezes.

Just never you mind what you've seen in the movies. Never mind those televised presidential news conferences. Especially never mind the daily press briefings you saw during Operation

Desert Storm. Millions of Americans were aghast at the ugly spectacle of stupid questions being asked and badgering questions not being answered, yet never bothered to read the news stories that resulted, and thus, taking sausage-making for sausage, grew ever more to loathe the media. *Especially* never mind those briefings, because they are to the typical press conference what the Branch Davidians are to a church group, what *Jurassic Park* is to a petting zoo, what *The McLaughlin Group* is to political discourse—i.e., a grotesque exaggeration of mundane reality.

There are probably 2,500 press conferences in Washington each year, and in 2,495 of them, no reporter must shout above the din to be recognized. No photographer has to elbow into good camera position. No Sam Donaldson type needs to put a choke hold on a Helen Thomas to land one, final, withering, interrogative blow ("Mr. President, if two trains leave Washington headed in opposite directions, and one is traveling sixty miles per hour while the other is traveling fifteen, how many of the passengers will be former clients of the Secretary of Commerce?").

Most press conferences are far more prosaic affairs, typically small gatherings in the radio-TV press galleries of the Capitol or the thirteenth-floor meeting rooms of the National Press Club, where more than 1,400 were held last year. On a recent weekday, the press club's various meeting rooms held events sponsored by the Committee for a Responsible Federal Budget, the Coalition to Preserve Health Benefits, the American Medical Association, and Greenpeace. Somehow, ABC, CBS, and NBC managed to get their evening news broadcasts on the air without covering a single one of them.

That's not to say the Coalition to Preserve Health Benefits, for instance, had nothing of value to report; health insurance is a big issue. It's just that press conferences aren't necessarily called with the expectation of enticing the media elite.

Chuck Wixom, for one, knows better.

"We're not trying to get on the evening news," he says. "We're not trying to get on the front pages of the major dailies."

This is February 25 in Chicago, exactly twelve days and 612 air miles from the IFT's session at the National Press Club. Wixom's tentative invitation list covers forty-four news organizations, but he'd be perfectly pleased with the inside pages of the big papers, a squib on the wires, and a good ride in the trades: *AgriPulse, Kiplinger Agriculture Letter, Food Business, Science News,* and so forth.

Food technology research, he well understands, is not one of those hot-button issues that makes assignment editors foam at the mouth. While there may be some general interest in such developments as aseptic packaging, aspartame, fat substitutes, low-cholesterol egg products, and, yes, Birdseye-process flash freezing, it all seems quaintly low-tech next to space stations, Super Colliders, information superhighways, virtual reality, ultra-fast computer chips, and high-definition TV. On the other hand, Wixom knows that the IFT research committee's 129-page report—a year in the making—yields important insights with wide-ranging implications for the nation's economy, health, and food supply.

"I'm a great believer in not holding news conferences or issuing a news release unless you have something to say," he explains, but if news equals "the economy, stupid," this certainly qualifies. The IFT's news hook? By vastly increasing the amount of federal dollars applied to food-technology research (versus, say, agriculture research concentrating on greater crop yields), the nation would be rewarded with jobs, food safety, and environmental benefits with economic value far exceeding the research investment.

Aha! "Jobs. Investment. Environment." Buzzwords! As he surveys the economic and political landscape, Wixom sees plenty of reasons to be hopeful for greater-than-usual media interest. Food technology, per se, may not be the sexiest of subjects, but in the context of the Clinton revolution, it seems to fit right in with the Washington *Zeitgeist*.

"A lot of stuff," he says, "is blowing our way." First President Clinton pledged to transform government spending into investment. Then three children died from *E. coli*-tainted Jack in the Box hamburgers, a food-borne bacteria issue addressed in the food safety section of the IFT report. Then the president weighed in again with the notion of shifting military research funding to industrial technology. Wixom's deputy, Ellen Brooks, brandishes a *New York Times* clipping about the possible funding shift as evidence of IFT being in the right place at the right time.

"Everywhere you turn," Brooks declares, "somebody's saying something that's setting us up beautifully."

Still, she and her boss are leaving nothing to chance. The marketing plan for release of the report was drafted well before any of the six IFT research teams had written word one. In a multipronged effort aimed at IFT members, food processors, scientists, economists, government regulators, the administration, and Congress, the press conference is planned from the outset to be the focal point, and thus are Wixom and Brooks gradually completing an elaborate checklist of preparations.

"Feb. 15–19: Draft press releases. Draft themes to play up. Draft tough question list. Set up press list. Notify daybooks. Plan advances, call, write. Feb. 22–26: Develop contact lists. Obtain advance copies. Write op-ed pieces. Refine themes, questions. Send themes, questions, schedules (IFT officials). March 1–5: Confirm National Press Club. Call advances. Daybook update. Washington news bureau notices. Notify key list of government, scientific societies, trade associations. Set up appointments. Set up one-on-one interviews. Dummy press conference. Run (on duplicating machines) reports and releases."

And so on, endlessly, inexorably toward March 9. Today, Wixom is bogged down with one crucial errand: finding a single, hard-hitting statistic to put an unwieldy 129-page report in crystalline perspective.

"The data, as so often is the case, are not as sharp and convincing as they should be to make the case," he says. "We need to have something you can get in a quote, a sound bite."

What, specifically, he'd like to say is the following: "For every dollar invested in food technology research, there is a tenfold return to the economy." Ten to one. A simple, powerful multiplier that everyone can grasp, even reporters. The problem is, he's not sure of the number, and neither, apparently, is anyone else.

"I talked to both [IFT ad hoc research team chairman Arnold E.] Denton and [IFT President David R.] Lineback about it. Denton's reaction was, 'I thought it was 7 to 1.' And Lineback said, 'Gee, in the agriculture schools they say 22 to 1.' "

So, in the nondescript offices of IFT, where the dull hum of the heating system battles the Chicago winter, and his old brown desk chair fights the new teal carpeting, Chuck Wixom goes dialing for dollars. Chewing, as is his wont, on an unlit cigar, he calls his pal Mike Phillips of the congressional Office of Technology Assessment, but gets no multiplier he can use. He tries to phone a newsletter called *Food Industry Report,* but discovers it no longer maintains an economic database. Learning that Brooks has drawn similar blanks with the Bureau of Labor Statistics and the U.S. Department of Agriculture, he finally calls John Connor, a Purdue University agricultural economist and author of the most thoroughgoing food economics statistical abstract.

"John," he says, "it's Chuck Wixom at IFT. How are you? It's been a long time."

He explains what he's after, "something that's direct, but with a number we can support as rigorously as we can," and he scribbles notes from the conversation. But when he hangs up, he just shakes his head. Connor can provide no magic multiplier.

"When you're looking for the right fact, number, whatever,"

he sighs, "it always turns out to be something nobody has ever published."

At which point, a visitor once again brings up the Balkan Muslims, who had civilian annihilation sound bites to offer and still couldn't draw a crowd. But this time Wixom doesn't freeze. He's a PR veteran, and he doesn't need an outsider to remind him how terribly things can go awry.

"You want a horror story? I worked at OTA [Office of Technology Assessment] in the seventies. When OTA was just getting started, we were just scrambling for media attention."

And therefore, he says, when in 1977 the office came up with a major report, about nuclear proliferation or some such subject, he and his colleagues notified eighty news organizations, from the networks on down. And when the moment arrived, "it happened to be the day George Allen was fired from the Washington Redskins.

"The bottom fell out, for no reason that we could control. I have thought of that occasionally over the past couple of weeks."

Here, Wixom gently places his gnarled and slimy Macanudo on his desk, above which, one suddenly notices, is a bulletin board where Chuck Wixom, the skiing enthusiast, has pinned a small cloth patch. It reads:

"Think snow."

David M. Petrou, of Eisner, Petrou & Associates Inc., once forgot to think snow. It was December 1984, and his client, the owner of a big new gym called the Center Club in Alexandria, wanted a huge press turnout for his grand opening. So Petrou hired the centers (get it?) of the Redskins, Bullets, and Capitals, ordered prime rib and gulf shrimp for one hundred, spent $10,000 in catering and appearance fees, and prepared an outdoor extravaganza.

"And wouldn't you know it?" he says. "The first snow of the

season. Talk about 'what if somebody gave a party and nobody came'!"

Mind you, this was no blizzard. It was more like a dusting, but in Washington, D.C., a half-inch snowfall has the effect of curare in the water supply; the region's central nervous system goes into complete shutdown. Schools in six counties were closed upon the sighting of a flake just west of Warrenton. Child-care arrangements were thrown into disarray. And radios blared with admonitions for all nonessential employees to stay off roads—whereupon, the ego line having been drawn in snow, everybody within ninety miles of the District rushed to his car and headed for work. Except snowplow operators.

All in all, a bad day for an outdoor media event.

Oh, the athletes showed up. And so did the help, in their big puffy chef's hats, at the roast-beef carving stations. But not one reporter.

"The client was a bit disappointed," Petrou recalls. "Like, 'What the [expletive] happened?' He went berserk."

So, in that sense, Chuck Wixom is exactly right. Notwithstanding the terrifying implications of the Balkan Muslims' debacle, there is no reason for him to obsess about the malignant indifference of the press when any number of other random external events can blow him out of the water just as well. Many of them fall into the category of "timing."

In addition to bad weather, for example, there is also the nightmarish truth that news usurps news. To wit: the George Allen situation, in which one news event is trumped by another. As Donovan McClure of the Kamber Group says: "It remains the most awful thing you'd ever want to contemplate."

The most awful, but not the most unfamiliar. In 1971, when he was a principal in the now-defunct firm of McClure, Schultz & Hoyt, he had a client who wanted to announce the development of an international airport in Utah catering specifically to Asian business people. At length, the agency notified every Asian news bureau in the city, a list numbering in the dozens, and arranged for a big 11 A.M. news conference at the press club.

"The morning of our press conference," McClure remembers, "the White House scheduled an 11 A.M. press conference where Nixon announced he was going to China."

In the face of bona fide History, an airport story was rendered insignificant, and McClure's clients sat forlornly at the press club with an untold story that even a day earlier would have been fairly big news.

"The pastries were good," he says. "We had them all to ourselves."

Occasionally, when the stars are aligned just right, an organization can actually achieve the confluence of multiple plagues. Last winter, for example, Mel Schettler knew from the outset that his press event might be regarded by some media cynics as somehow slightly trivial. Yet, in mid-January, he nonetheless forged ahead with plans for a press conference celebrating the largest tree root excavated from a sewer by any Roto-Rooter franchisee in 1992: 57 feet 9 inches, bagged by Jerry and Joe Bristol's Roto-Rooter Sewer Services of Contra Costa County, California.

On January 17, public relations specialist Tara McGuire from Roto-Rooter's Des Moines headquarters was phoning major media outlets looking for takers on the story. At 1:30 P.M., National Public Radio producer Art Silverman happened to take her call, but was not instantaneously moved by the surpassing human interest. At the precise moment of their conversation, he was distracted by the first confirmation of American warplanes bombing Iraq in a tense, preinaugural Desert Storm redux.

NPR took a pass on the big root story.

"It just happens that way," said the exasperated McGuire. "What are you gonna do?"

Though the response was similar from the rest of the national media, what Roto-Rooter did was press on with its news conference, which happened to be scheduled for the next morning at the Bristol brothers' business in Concord, California. Schettler, vice president of franchise services, flew out from Des Moines. The San Francisco press was invited. A continental breakfast was on hand.

And so was the biggest rainstorm and flood in Northern California in five years.

In terms of reporters and photographers, said Joe Bristol later that afternoon, "we never had none physically walk in," but it's just as well. The Bristols had themselves pretty much lost interest, because sewers were backing up all over the county. Seven hours after Schettler presented him a plaque with no outsiders present, Bristol said, "I got eighteen service trucks out in the road, and I had 'em out all day and I still got 118 jobs on the board." By which time the big cheese was on his way back to Iowa, shrugging at the contrivances of fate:

"It rained," Schettler said. "Someone in Washington decided it would be a good time for a mini-war. We were somewhat the victim of circumstances."

It is March 5, and Joe Gibbs has just shocked the city by announcing his retirement from the Washington Redskins.

"Thank God," Chuck Wixom says.

Not that he has any strict interest in Gibbs's health or state of mind or even the fate of the Redskins: he's just having a terrifying flashback about the George Allen episode. Had Gibbs waited four more days to announce his decision, Wixom would have been head-coached out of media coverage for the second time.

This is Friday, his last working day in Chicago before heading east, and he and Ellen Brooks are busy tying up loose ends. He's been on the phone most of the past two days, arranging meetings with the staffs of key senators (Richard G. Lugar, Bob Dole, Patrick J. Leahy, Thomas A. Daschle) and representatives

(E. "Kika" de la Garza, Robert H. Michel, Dan Rostenkowski, Henry J. Hyde) to brief them on the IFT's findings.

"It's important to make them aware that this is coming," he says, "before they read it in the public press. It's a matter of courtesy and good common sense."

Among the other chores: packaging 250 press kits for the conference itself and general distribution in the agencies and on the Hill. This errand is complicated by some last-minute document duplication, after his staff inadvertently ran off 500 copies of the IFT president's statement without correcting a late revision.

That is no mere detail. IFT's leaders are determined not to jeopardize their case with incautious wording. For example, where President David Lineback initially was to have said, "We do call for an allocation of research funding to food science," he now will say, "We do seek a reallocation of research funding to food science areas . . ."

By the same token, Lineback will not risk provoking Agriculture Secretary Mike Espy or congressional leaders by demanding a certain dollar figure in increased funding—a decision Wixom understands, but one that inhibits his ability to pique the interest of editors. It is axiomatic that big numbers make news. Still, even though he is already handicapped by not having the economic multiplier he was hoping for, he agrees with Lineback's decision.

Waving around big figures, he muses, makes for a "good story, bad politics."

Brooks, meanwhile, is facing the reverse side of the problem. She has been making phone calls to every news organization on her press list, and finding that the very mention of money gets her transferred to the financial desk. This is akin to dialing 911 and being transferred to the community relations officer. At most newspapers the financial departments are in varying degrees limited in news space, readership and clout. At TV networks, they are categorically an afflicted child nobody ever sees or talks about. Brooks happened to be trying to spark interest at science desks, themselves a backwater, but "I think reporters have trouble finding the appropriate hook. I'm sitting here thinking what button to push, but once you brought in the concept of money, you couldn't backtrack. They didn't want to talk about it any further."

Brooks is somewhat encouraged that in virtually every case her final contact seemed enthusiastic in requesting a press kit, upon which everybody said he'd base his ultimate coverage decision. But she also understands that this is what all reporters tell all PR people just to get them off the phone. It is all a part of the dance, and the dance is a consequence of what all participants understand about what so many press conferences have become.

They originated as a tool of convenience, enabling an individual organization—from astronauts to reactionary Wisconsin senators to self-absorbed quarterbacks—to get a message out to all interested parties in one, compact forum. Of course, as with so many Washington institutions, its rational essence has mutated. What began as principally a labor-saving device has taken on other forms. In the vast majority of instances, a press conference is not a means for catering to media interest; it is a method for generating press interest—with all the degrees of substance and cynicism that implies.

Yes, a press conference can be where America gets a terrifying tutorial on nuclear meltdown, or where Magic Johnson confirms he is infected with HIV. But it can also be theater of the overblown, attempting to lend gravity or drama to thin, manufactured "news." It can be a cheap PR trick, a mere pretext for the press release to the home front ("In a Capitol Hill press conference Friday . . ."). At its worst, it can be a sort of recreational drug for the powerful and would-be powerful, for whom the sight of the TV crew is the most vivid high and the ultimate aphrodisiac. There are several members of Congress so conditioned to reacting to bright lights and wires, they're apt to speak extemporaneously for twenty minutes into a floor lamp.

"The news conference, in my opinion, is a contrived event," says Bob Franken, Capitol Hill correspondent for CNN. "It's a less than desirable way to get information."

As a consequence, invitations such as Brooks's, and the daily wire-service "daybooks," where press conferences are briefly summarized and announced, constitute the world's longest-running example of "The Boy Who Cried Wolf." Congressmen and CEOs and policy analysts and trade groups shout, "News! News!" and the media come running up the hill, and when they arrive there is no news after all, and each successive time the media hear shouts, fewer and fewer bother to run up the hill. Outsiders are still bewitched by the pomp and glamour of it all, and every day clients approach major public relations firms about arranging a news conference. But every day the PR shops counsel, in the sage words of Manning, Selvage & Lee's Joseph Gleason: "Don't bother."

Why? Ask the Balkan Muslim Association. It knows only too well that sometimes, even when wolves are really eating the flock, the townspeople are disbelievers. Or, if you prefer, think of press conferences as a sort of Field of Broken Dreams.

If you hold it, they might not come.

CNN called.

Brooks didn't call CNN. The network called her, and on March 8 she's allowing herself to imagine the best. Even if Wolf Blitzer doesn't camp on her doorstep, the call is "another real indication of people noticing" IFT's story.

The press conference is tomorrow morning, and a check of the AP wire reveals that, sure enough, the daybook notice is right there:

"9:30 A.M. FOOD—Institute of Food Technologists holds news conference concerning food science research.

"Location: National Press Club.

"Contact: Charles W. Wixom, 312-783-8424."

Wixom, who is not in Chicago to be contacted, stands inside the National Press Building and frowns. The AP has edited out the substance of his release.

"It doesn't have any of that good stuff in there," he says.

Brooks notices too: "They gave everybody else three lines and they gave us two lines."

On the other hand, they're heartened not to see Michael Jordan and Julia Roberts testifying before the House Commerce Committee, or J. D. Salinger doing a ribbon cutting, or a notice such as:

"9:30 A.M. REUNION—musicians Paul McCartney, George Harrison, and Ringo Starr announce plans to reunite the Beatles."

There was, of course, no way for Wixom to know, months ago when he booked the room, what competing news events would be on the daybooks for the morning of March 9. As it turns out, there are eighteen congressional hearings and about a dozen press conferences and briefings throughout the city, but none with catastrophic news-usurping potential. The biggest event: the first day of Janet Reno's attorney-general confirmation hearing before the Senate Judiciary Committee.

In any case, Wixom says he's ceased to be worried about it. He's done everything he can do. The media have been alerted and re-alerted. All the preparations have been made. Two dozen IFT members have converged on the Loews L'Enfant Plaza Hotel. As of 5 P.M., the forecast mentioned not one word about snow. The universe will do what it will do; he'll live with the result.

"I'm not hyped at all," he says. "It's on automatic pilot."

Outside, it is raining lightly. Temperatures are beginning to dip.

• • •

"FOOD RESEARSH NEEDS IFT."

At last the day has arrived. It's Tuesday at 9:15 A.M. The press conference, a year in the planning, is finally about to begin, and a sign at the press club advertising the event is misspelled, unpunctuated. Food researsh needs "IFT." Pray, how much "IFT" does food "researsh" need?

Hoping this is not some kind of horrible foreshadowing, IFT Executive Director Dan Weber removes the second *s* in "researsh."

Otherwise, though, things look pretty good. First and foremost, the weather is fine. Sunny and mild all the way. Moreover, the room will categorically not be empty. The press conference isn't due to start for fifteen minutes, but already the Edward R. Murrow Room and the foyer outside are crowded. Not with reporters; they aren't here yet. But the area is teeming with people from IFT, including almost the entire research committee and all of the six team leaders responsible for the various sections of the report. Among them, Jack L. Cooper, of the AAC Consulting Group Inc., who led the environmental team. Cooper is admittedly nervous.

"This is really my first media event," he says. "I don't know what the reporters are going to ask."

Not an idle concern.

The one thing more horrifying than nobody showing up for a press conference is reporters being there, armed with questions you are not willing or able to answer. In the early 1960s, no less a personage than the prize-winning economist John Kenneth Galbraith was stunned, embarrassed, and infuriated by the utter impertinence of a question put to him at an American Association for the Advancement of Science gathering in New York. The question itself, from science writer Earl Ubell, then of the New York *Herald Tribune,* now of WCBS-TV, is lost to history. But Galbraith's answer was one for the annals: "You, sir, have no soul."

As Ubell recalls: "I clutched. He didn't answer the question;

he attacked the reporter and he won the round." Others in similar situations have been less fortunate.

For an unanticipated-question nightmare, it would be hard to top the experience of Paula Hawkins. The former U.S. senator from Florida was lucky enough to attract the major networks to her first media event, a luncheon in the Capitol's Mike Mansfield Room to announce her first legislative initiative. Thereupon everything unraveled.

The center of the fanfare was Hawkins's proposal mandating jail terms for food-stamp cheats, precisely the sort of populist issue that had propelled the conservative gadfly into high office. But then several reporters—notably Robert Ryan, then of the Knight-Ridder News Service, and Phil Jones, of CBS News—began to notice the incongruity of the issue and venue. What was Hawkins doing fussing about petty food-stamp fraud while serving up New York strip steak and fresh strawberries to one hundred well-heeled lobbyists and agriculture industry figures, and by the way, who was picking up the tab?

"She dissembled," recalls Ryan, now deputy managing editor of the *San Jose Mercury News*. "I said, 'You're using tax dollars for this.' And she said, 'Absolutely not.' So I pointed out that the caterer had just told me the opposite."

Hawkins finally pledged to pay for the luncheon out of her own pocket, but before the commotion was over, she also wound up acknowledging that her initiative would cut only about two-hundredths of one percent from the federal food-stamp budget. And she wound up on the CBS and NBC evening news, fleeing her own press conference under a barrage of reporters' shouts.

"Senator, why are you leaving?" hollered NBC's Tom Pettit. "Why are you leaving? You called us here to cover this thing, and now you won't answer our questions."

Nobody at the Institute of Food Technologists is expecting hostility from the press, of course, but nobody wants to be embarrassed either. Thus, last evening, IFT's officers and the research team leaders convened for a dry run. Chuck Wixom peppered them with questions, and they did their best to respond.

Respond they did. To a fare-thee-well. To a numbing extreme. The first hour of the dry run, everybody agrees, was pretty brutal.

"It was long-winded, and examples were not specific," Wixom says. "They were general. Answers were in scientific terms, not consumer terms. At one point, someone said, 'If you were a real reporter, you wouldn't be asking questions like this.' I said, 'If I were a real reporter, you'd be mincemeat.' "

By the end of the rehearsal, though, all eight participants had gotten the hang of giving brief, pointed, coherent answers. Wixom is delighted at how they came around, and he's satisfied his people can address all the issues of substance clearly and concisely in about an hour. Yet as the clock hits 9:25, he is visibly anxious.

"Palms sweating," he volunteers. "Perspiration on the brow. Quivering in the knees."

This may have something to do with the sign-in list, which, at T minus five minutes and counting, has only three news organizations represented.

"The reporters coming?" he asks Brooks. "Huh?"

At this moment a man walks in carrying a TV camera. Brooks's eyes light up. Could CNN have turned up after all? Is IFT going to get a spot on *Moneyline,* or, better yet, on *Dollars & Sense,* every half-hour all day, on *Headline News?* Brooks clambers from behind the sign-in table and follows the camera guy into the room. A moment later she is back. "King Broadcasting," she says. They own four TV stations in the Pacific Northwest, site of the Jack in the Box contaminations. They're not interested in research; they're interested in *E. coli* and food irradiation. Oh, well.

By 9:30, of the forty seats in the Edward R. Murrow Room, twenty-seven are filled. This would be extraordinary, except that they are occupied mainly by IFT people. In the entire room, there are five reporters. One is from King. The others are from the Agriculture Radio Network, *Food & Drink Daily, Science News,* and *Food Chemical News.* Not a single daily newspaper or consumer publication is represented.

So be it. At 9:36, Wixom introduces Lineback, a blond, broad-faced *doppelgänger* of a ten-year-younger Boris Yeltsin. The press conference, at long last, begins.

"Good morning. Thank you for coming," Lineback begins, with not a hint of irony. "We want to tell you today about investments to increase knowledge in food science and technology, and what the results from this would mean to the food supply, consumer health, and the nation's economy . . ."

He reads his remarks in a matter of three minutes, then yields to Denton, who takes four minutes to read his introductory statement. Then, finally, to the heart of the matter: The men will entertain questions from the floor. Without hesitation, the reporter from *Food Chemical News* addresses Lineback.

"You say you don't want to increase funds [of overall federal research dollars] for this research. What areas would you take funds from?"

The preparation, the anticipation, the rehearsals pay off. Lineback has the answer at his fingertips. "It would be presumptuous," he says, for him to tell the government what other funding might be reduced to increase food technology's share of the research pie. He'll leave that to the policy makers. The response is perhaps a bit disingenuous—everybody knows IFT thinks preharvest research is overendowed—but diplomatic. Just as they had agreed.

Next question, from *Science News:* "About those [*E. coli*] outbreaks on the West Coast. How much of that can be prevented with more inspection and public education? . . . Is 'not enough science' really the problem?"

Lineback's response: You bet. As detailed in the section on food safety and health, only research will produce the technology that can detect microbiotic contamination.

Next question? Next question?

"Any other questions?" Wixom asks, rising from his seat in the corner. "The team leaders are up here in front to fill in any specific info on particular areas you may wish to have."

Lineback introduces all six team leaders, and Wixom once again scans the room for more questions. There are none.

"Thank you very much," he says. "That concludes our press conference."

It is 9:46. The event has lasted exactly ten minutes.

Lineback, looking more Yeltsin-like than ever, seems dazed. Jack Cooper, who had been unnerved about facing the press corps, expresses mild disappointment.

"Well," he says, "I was ready."

And Chuck Wixom, who always knew it might turn out this way, is utterly expressionless. His eyes are focused on some indeterminate point in space. Not for the first time, he is frozen in thought. Then, dispiritedly, he speaks of the practical reality behind a non-triumph, which is potentially less un-triumphant than meets the eye.

"The point of it is, we got the message launched," he says. "Now we're going to fan out and carry the message around town." (And, sure enough, the message will get out. *Food Chemical News* will do a nine-page takeout on the IFT report, coverage that will lead to a dozen calls from other trade press within two weeks of the press conference.)

Meanwhile, at 9:52 A.M. on March 9, the reporter from King Broadcasting walks up to the sign-in table and speaks to Ellen Brooks.

"Do you have a press packet?" she asks.

Brooks glances at the corrugated carton perched nearby, overflowing with handsome IFT folders, laboriously stuffed in Chicago a week ago with background material, transcripts, and seven separate press releases, each painstakingly crafted and re-crafted to state the institute's case in the most precise, politic way.

Reaching toward the carton, she casts a look back at the reporter.

"How many," she asks, "do you need?"

Open for Inspection

ALEXANDRIA. $136,900. COZY NEST. 2 master suite TH.2
ba, washer/dryer on BR lev. Great fenced patio. Immac.
Plenty of prkg. Close to Van Dorn Metro. Easy commute to
the Hill! 5552 First Statesman.

It's 11:45 on a crisp and cloudless Sunday morning. Marta
Tanenhaus sits in the immaculate kitchen of her cozy nest,
relaxing with her coffee and newspaper.

Okay, fine, not relaxing exactly. More like concentrating.
More like bristling with intensity. More like sunspots of flar-
ing neurons dancing invisibly but wildly all about her, like
arcs of current around a Tesla coil. *Bzzzzz. Bzzzzz. Bzzzzz.*
Bzzzzzzzzzzzzzzz.

Like mllns of Amricns from brdr to brdr and cst to cst at the
vry same mmnt in this wndrfl cntry of ours, Marta is careering
over the real estate section. She just happens to be a bit more
focused than some as she scans Mount Vernon–Weichert Realtors' full-page "open for inspection" ad. Like twin lasers, her
eyes lock on the Alexandria TH with the great fenced patio at
$136,900. *Bzzz. Bzzzzzzz.* Oh, no. Oh, no! No, no, it can't be . . .
Oh, *NO!!! BZZZZZZZZZZZZZZZZZZZ.*

"DAMN IT!" she yells. "Every time. Every single time. 'Two
baths'! It's two and a HALF! Every SINGLE TIME!"

Marta is intimately aware of the ad's .5-bathroom deficiency
because the particular .5 bathroom happens to be situated eight
feet away. With her husband, Marc Schwartz, Marta is the
proud owner of 5552 First Statesman Lane. Alas, the couple
have been endeavoring since last May to become the proud *former* owners of the condominium town house—which, while a

handsomely decorated Hill-commuter's dream convenient to the Van Dorn Metro, is increasingly a cozy albatross around their necks. They'd like to move to a bigger, detached house in Montgomery County, but first they must unload one immaculate TH in a small subdivision where, at any given time, ten other immaculate THs are for sale in a still-depressed market.

"As time goes on," she says, "we're sort of getting *shpilkes,* if you know what I mean." What she means is a case of nerves. The jitters. Apprehension. Frustration. Worry. In Yiddish or any language, it is the anxious feeling you get when you begin to think your cozy nest with the great fenced patio is your prison forever.

"And we're not trying to make a killing," says Marc, who bought the house in 1986 when he was still single. "It's like, 'Give us an offer'. Somebody."

Which is why, in ninety minutes, for the third time in eight months, 5552 First Statesman is open for inspection. With luck, young first-time home buyers from D.C. and Virginia will pick up the same real estate section, breeze past CHAMPAGNE & CAVIAR, ignore both DOLLHOUSE and A REAL DOLLHOUSE, dismiss WANT TO BE ENVIED?, forsake FAIRY TALE SETTING, disregard DIRTY BUT STURDY, and home right in on COZY NEST, apparent .5-bathroom deficiency notwithstanding.

Yet one more time, the place has been painstakingly prepared. The coffee is brewed. The signs are erected, blazing a trail to the property. The Realtor is in the dining room, setting out brochures, each with a glossy color photo of the house glued to the cover. All that remains is for the buyer to walk through the door.

Lose the avocado.

If, Mr. and Mrs. Homeowner, you have any wish of selling your house, get rid of the avocado at once. I know. I *know.* Major appliances are expensive, but if they are avocado-colored—or anything in the entire pale-green family—they will frighten away prospective purchasers, because, let's face it, objectively speaking, they are nauseating. This goes double for coppertone.

Harvest gold? You might as well hang dead cats from the chandelier. In terms of merchandising your home, harvest gold has exactly the buyer appeal of satanic messages scrawled in blood.

On the other hand, it's better than flocked wallpaper. Or shag carpeting.

"Gawd, you'd never believe the shag carpeting that's still out there," says Rosie Harsch, a Prudential Preferred Properties super agent who bills herself as "a real estate legend."

"And people are proud of it. Oh, Lordy! And it's orange!"

And, along with the avocado dishwasher and the kitty-cat decals on the kitchen cabinets and the mural of Venice in the hallway, it has to go. What must replace it is a hardwood floor or a cut-pile carpet in light gray or beige. The walls must be white or off-white, or, if some other color, muted in the extreme. Large pieces of furniture must be removed to reduce clutter. Those dramatic original clown paintings you lovingly selected at a weekend designer art show in a Rockville hotel conference room must be taken off the walls, along with your limited-edition collector plates of Hank Williams Sr.

In other words, to every degree possible, your house must be radically cleansed of all the personal little touches that make a home not just a habitat but an extension of your identity.

You may at first balk at the idea of systematically denaturing your home. You may resent the Orwellian process of single-family historical revisionism. You may take umbrage at what seems like a personal attack on your tastes, treasures, and family values, but you've got to stifle emotional response and accede to your agent's passionless professional judgment.

Or the place will never sell.

Don't think of the agent's advice as an intrusion. Think in the terms of a marketer trying to give a product the broadest possible appeal. What to you may seem like a condemnation of your very self is to real estate experts nothing more than routine "staging."

"You try to take away as many negatives as possible," says Millie Sydnor, manager of Mount Vernon–Weichert's Fairfax office.

Fixing sidewalk cracks, trimming shrubbery, painting the front door, opening drapes, putting in higher-wattage lightbulbs—it's all part of the staging process, and that's not the half of it. From their entry into the real estate business, agents are repeatedly tutored on the finer points of merchandising properties. At one such session for new Prudential agents in Tysons Corner, training executive Valerie Huffman dispensed one bit of critical advice after another.

"Secure pets away from the property," she advised eleven home-sales novices.

"Put music on [classical for high-end homes, light country or light rock for low-end].

"Look and act professional.

"Escort every single solitary purchaser through that property. People actually open drawers, open closets. You'd be surprised by what people do in other people's houses.

"*Always* carry air freshener. Keep it in your car. I would use Airwick solid. I'd have two of them."

The reason, of course, is that some people's houses—as they say in the elusive technical parlance of the real estate industry—stink. The home truly is an extension of the person, and in the same way a person can't usually tell that he has bad breath or body odor, he often isn't aware that his premises truly reek big-time.

Obviously, an open house is no place for odors—only aromas, as per page 57 of the Prudential training manual: "Freshen the air by opening windows, spraying with air freshener, and creating a mouthwatering 'baking aroma.' This can be done by

warming a spoonful of vanilla in the oven, or by actually baking rolls."

Boiling cinnamon sticks or potpourri on the stove does the
trick too. But, here again, delicacy is called for. Realtors are
trained to be firm but tactful in working with homeowners to
stage a house, using phrases like "making the property invit-
ing" as opposed to "Let's kill that awful stench." Agents are forever struggling with the challenge of promoting the seller's best
interest without cutting him to the quick.

"One of our agents," Huffman recalled for her pupils,
"arrived at an open house and found unmade beds and dirty
dishes. So he made the beds and did the dishes—and then after-
ward dirtied them back up, so as not to offend the owners."

The other school of thought *is* to offend the owners, to jolt
them into reality, to shame them into preparing their property
for maximum appeal. Then, when the open house commences,
and the first couple appear at the door, Mr. and Mrs. Home-
buyer might be instantaneously infatuated. Seduced.

Blown away.

"Wow!"

Now there's an opening line, just the naked declaration of
blownawayness listing agents love to hear. It means emotional-
ism has arrested reason, allowing the seller, even in a glutted
market, to deal from a position of strength.

Not that anybody has necessarily uttered this upon entering
5552 First Statesman, which is a cozy nest by virtue of being
maintained, tastefully decorated, and approximately the same
size, in cubic feet, as Oprah. No, "WOW!" is merely what the
sign says a block away—sign number three in a series of four,
each with a pair of balloons tethered to it and each enticing
motorists toward the property, itself marked by a looming,
gaudy, veritable free-for-all of signage.

Dangling from the familiar white right-angle post is the basic

"For Sale" sign, on which is plastered an "Open Sunday" sign, over which is affixed a "Bring all offers!" sign, atop which is a sign advertising "Warranty." Then there's the metal box, attached to the vertical post, holding "Free Brochures," and the twin yellow balloons, and, of course, hanging just below the "For Sale" plate are the name and phone number of the listing agent: Dick Yates.

"Some Realtors would say, 'That's tacky,' " says Yates, examining his extravagant creation. "But I'm not afraid to do something different. And, yes, balloons are illegal in Fairfax County on real estate signs. Theoretically, I could be arrested and pay a $50 fine, but it hasn't happened yet."

Why not take the risk? As his office manager, Millie Sydnor, likes to say, "Whatever you can do. It's got to be made to look like there's a party going on. Not just an open house, an *event*."

It's all about getting noticed, establishing a mood, just as in composing the ad. Why "Cozy Nest" instead of, say, "Super Value" or "No Annoying Basement" or some such?

"I just reached up and . . ." Yates says, making a grasping motion with his right hand. "You're just looking for anything that will grab somebody's attention."

So far, so good. At 12:15 P.M., forty-five minutes before the open house is set to begin, a man knocks on the door. He hasn't actually come in response to the ad (and thus can't be considered a more serious shopper). He's a cabdriver who saw the signs and got curious. With the homeowners sitting a few feet away, Yates briefly shows the man around—a tour that is 100 percent WOW-free. The guy is interested in three levels, not two, and three bedrooms, not two, all for less than the $136,900 Marc and Marta are asking. If he is impressed with the half-bath on the ground floor, he doesn't say. Yates gets the man to fill out a visitors form and sees him out.

Still, not a bad start for an event that hasn't officially begun. Already the yellow balloons have attracted more interest than the ads Marta persuaded Yates to place in *Roll Call,* the *Hill Rag,*

Legal Times, and the *Arkansas Democrat,* all playing up Hill-commute convenience and timed to coincide with the Clinton transition.

"I've pushed for some strategies Realtors weren't particularly open to," she says. "I just feel they're not doing enough."

Coldwell Banker certainly didn't suit her. When their second listing period expired in December, Marc and Marta declined to renew. Instead they found Yates, a "million-dollar club" Weichert agent, who had impressed them when he quickly sold a neighboring two-bedroom town house.

"We're looking for drive, enthusiasm, creativity," Marc says. "He came up with some good strategies that were effective . . . well, I don't know how effective. Bottom line is, the place hasn't sold."

Bottom line is, they haven't had so much as a decent offer. They haven't even had an *insulting* offer, which is why—as it nears 1 P.M.—they are once again preparing to clear out of their own home so that, once again total strangers can tromp through their LR, DR, great fenced patio, two *and a half* baths, master bedroom, spare bedroom, and no basement. The staging of the cozy nest wasn't particularly traumatic, because this isn't an orange-shag, clown-painting kind of couple. Yates recommended removing two leaves from the dining room table, uncluttering the living room to the tune of two potted plants, changing the wattage of a few lightbulbs, and not much else. The couple chose to leave hanging in its upstairs display case their prize collection of condoms from around the world, factory-sealed in their colorful packaging.

Marta was up till 3 in the morning working on a legal brief, and Marc was up getting the house shipshape, but by 1 P.M. they are on their way. Sellers generally aren't welcome at their own open houses, so out they go, simultaneously demoralized and hopeful. And to where? Why, to search for the detached house of their dreams, of course—the one that calls to them, beckons them, blows *them* away.

The one they're not sure they'll ever be unchained to buy.

Or will this be their day of liberation? Marc and Marta are long gone when, at 1:20 P.M., arrives a couple with "Cozy Nest" written all over them. Young, childless, a perfect fit. It's uncanny; they look like they belong in this neighborhood already—and, in fact, as Yates greets them, it becomes clear that they do.

"Hi. Dick Yates. Come on in."

"Hi. We just live down the street."

Ugh. Nosy neighbors, here for no other reason than to snoop around in an exact twin of their own home. Still, Yates is attentive.

"How long have you lived down the street?" he asks.

"A year and a half."

"You folks thinking about changing your situation down the street?"

"Oh, no. Not really. It depends. Maybe in two or three years."

He gets them to sign a visitor's card, stuffs a brochure in their hands, offers to answer any questions they might have, and prepares to usher them around when, at the door, another young couple appears.

"Hi, Dick Yates. Please come in." And they do, looking somewhat sheepish.

"We," the wife says, "live down the street."

Neighbors eyeball neighbors and everybody pretends to be delighted to see everybody else, although it's perfectly clear nobody knows anybody's name. ("Hi-iiiii! How ya doin'?") What follows is four-part ogling of the Schwartz-Tanenhaus dry bar, a combined storage area and room divider between the living room and the dining room. Excepting the fenced-in, ground-level deck and the condom collection, it is the only feature of the Cozy Nest they couldn't have enjoyed by simply staying home.

Still, traffic is traffic, and early traffic is reasonably brisk. At

1:36 P.M. comes a couple in their late thirties or early forties, renters so unaccustomed to the mechanics of home buying that their first question is, "What's the availability date of this one?" (Answer: Whenever you find it personally convenient to surrender $136,900.) But 5552 First Statesman is tailor-made for first-time buyers, and Yates gives them the tour. They do not say "Wow!" They do not ask questions about financing. They do not even marvel at the dry bar. They simply express regret about the lack of a third bedroom and leave. Still, though Yates isn't certain they are truly in the market, he vows to follow up.

"You never know," he says. "You just never know."

It's 4:30 P.M. The open house was called from 1 to 4, and nobody has darkened the doorway for three hours. Grand total of parties coming through: four, neighbors included. "Looks like it's dead now," says Yates, an observation made with no trace of disappointment. Resignation, perhaps, but not disappointment, because he devoted his Sunday to this open house with no expectation whatsoever of selling the Cozy Nest. None. Zero. He staged the home, placed the ad, hammered the signs, duplicated brochures, glued on color photos, blew up balloons, brewed coffee, and chatted up nosy neighbors all the while knowing there would be no contract offered.

"I tell all sellers up front that it is uncommon for someone to walk into an open house and say, 'I'll buy it.' "

Uncommon? In the sixty or so open houses he's handled over the five and a half years since he left U.S. Army intelligence with the rank of colonel to become a full-bird Realtor, he's had that happen exactly once. And his record is about average, and every real estate agent in America knows it.

They learn the odds at the same time they're learning about boiled potpourri.

Valerie Huffman, to her Prudential trainees: "Why do we hold a home open?"

Trainee: "To sell the house."

Huffman (smiling): "That should be the least of your concerns."

The *least* of an agent's concerns! Did you actually think they were baking cookies and putting furniture in storage and stockpiling Airwicks to complete a transaction at an open house? How naive can you get?

"Your number one reason for holding an open house," Huffman explains, "is to meet prospects."

Not prospective buyers for the house they've just staged the living bejesus out of. Prospects for the agents. Potential listings. Potential buyers for *other* properties. People of no interest at all to the optimistic sellers whom Realtors have dispatched to seek the homes of their dreams, or to the mall, so that they won't be underfoot while the Realtors create enticing aromas in immaculate kitchens to drum up business for themselves.

Luckily, homeowners usually insist on open houses, because they foolishly believe they will attract buyers. So, yes, Huffman instructs, there is a side benefit, "and that is to appease the seller, but mostly it's a vehicle for marketing yourself."

That's why Dick Yates isn't inconsolable. At Marc and Marta's open house, he met one pair of renters who don't yet have an agent, a cabdriver looking for a three-bedroom town house who doesn't seem to have an agent, and two sets of neighbors who, inevitably, will be trying to escape their cozy nests. Now they know just how aggressive Yates is with balloons and signage. They know how professional he is with prospects. They know how handsomely he packages brochures, with a glossy color photo of the property glued right to the front. And they all have his card. In two days, they also will have follow-up notes.

"You never know," he says, "where something's gonna lead you."

(It will turn out that the renters will promise him an appointment to look at Multiple Listing Service listings, the cabdriver will blow him off, and one pair of neighbors will list their own house through another Realtor—within a week. Yates will thus kick himself for not closing in for the listing when he had the chance, and he'll bemoan "yet another two-bedroom for sale" for Marc and Marta to compete with. The other couple won't commit to anything, but will stay on the phone with him for ten or fifteen minutes, which Yates regards as "sort of an investment in the future.")

For their part, Marc and Marta came home having indeed found the home of their dreams, and having come not one step closer to actually being able to buy it. So does that mean their open house, from their point of view, was a cruel and pointless charade?

Not exactly.

Cruel? Yes. A charade? Absolutely. But pointless, not at all, because an open house does not occur in a vacuum. It happens in a larger, real estate ecosystem. While Marc and Marta let strangers tromp through their bedroom on Sunday, somewhere across town someone else was tromping through somebody else's bedroom—maybe just a nosy couple of young neighbors who may, through the miracle of Realtor self-interest, be persuaded to make an appointment with an agent, whereupon they may look at properties he pulls up from the multi-list, one of which may be a cozy nest at 5552 First Statesman, which may take them, utterly unprompted by signs, balloons, or Airwick, three weeks from now to behold a great fenced patio, custom dry bar, and one-of-a-kind global condom collection, and exclaim, with naked enthusiasm, "WOW!" In the overall scheme of things, a lot of three-hour Sunday charades in a lot of aromatic homes stimulate activity that eventually will mean the sale of a certain Alexandria TH at or near $136,900.

And that will be money in Marc and Marta's pocket. Whether Mount Vernon–Weichert and Dick Yates will get their 6 percent commission, however, is uncertain. The listing is due to expire shortly, and—*Bzzz, Bzzzz, BZZZZZZZZZZZZZZZZ*— shock of all shocks, they're looking for a new agent.

A Certain Rock in Santa Fe

In 1992, I went to Santa Fe for two days on a speaking engage-
ment, and—as always—took my tape recorder along just in case
I ran into something. Oh, did I ever run into something.

This is a radio story, and is printed here in basic transcript
form, with some few parenthetical descriptions of sounds heard
by the listener. The italic type is the text of my direct narration.
All voices heard in the piece, including mine when I am inter-
viewing subjects, are printed in roman type. This format will be
used for all of the radio pieces in this collection.

*So I walk into the hotel gift shop to buy newspapers—you know,
foraging for local oddities, as roving reporters are sometimes
reduced to doing. And as I'm frantically ripping from page to page,
the cashier wants to know what I'm up to.* "Looking for weird
stuff," I say. "That's what I do. Do you know of any weird stuff in
Santa Fe?"

"That depends on what you mean by weird," she says.

I say, "Well, I was just in California chasing after a lady who
balances people's auras by cutting their hair. Unfortunately, I
never tracked her down."

"Aura balancing," the cashier says. "What would be weird
about that?"

*This is my first clue that there is another dimension to Santa Fe,
apart from the chic, excruciatingly hip turquoise and adobe temple
to southwestness that tourists know. It turns out that part of the
city's 14 percent-population growth in the past decade is attributable to people who don't think aura balancing is strange at all. It
turns out this lady has a friend who balances auras, a guy named
Ralph down at the health food store.*

FOOD MARKET CASHIER: That's $3.93, please.

The store is called The Marketplace, a grocery on the fringes of downtown. Frankly, lots of cities have a health food supermarket like this, where you can get all the dried kelp and tofu enchiladas you need, fast, no questions asked. But as the manager leads me to Ralph, she takes me past clue number two about the other Santa Fe. This isn't just any organic food outlet in just any town. We're in the vitamin aisle and where I'm expecting to find Flintstone Kids, I'm seeing an array of bottles with little labels and big promises.

STORE EMPLOYEE: Luminous Spirit, Positive Attitude, Women's Courage, Emotional Rescue, Clearing Hate, Clearing Greed, Humiliation, Children of Divorce. . . .

Herbal remedies. One for every complaint, all made in Santa Fe. Unfortunately, there's nothing here for bad timing. It's noon at this point, and Ralph can't see me until quitting work in the evening, so I decide to hit the Central Plaza and grab a bite to eat. Now, I'm not an eavesdropper by nature, but having been in town for an hour and already having discovered an aura balancer and herbs for emotional rescue, I can't help being struck by a conversation between two other people at the fajita stand—people who realize they know each other from the drum-making workshop they took last year. Their names are Margie and Miguel.

MIGUEL: The intent of the workshop was to go simply beyond how to stretch skin over wood, but . . . but to use the drum-making process as . . . as a . . . as a route to access some inner . . . inner stuff. Inner feelings and thoughts.

The tom-tom as a route to the greater truth. This, I was rapidly coming to understand, is quintessential Santa Fe. The Marketplace organic grocery turns out not to be an oddity so much as a metaphor for a city that itself is a supermarket of the supernatural—a hall of mirrors for the inner self. And as Margie says, people are drawn here for precisely that reason.

MARGIE: I think people are looking to get closer to the earth. They come here because the sky is so blue and the sunsets are so, you know, rich, and the land somehow speaks to their soul, and it's a . . . it's a journey related to that. That's why I came here.

I look in the calendar section of the daily New Mexican, *and the magnitude of Santa Fe's preoccupation reveals itself. There's a full page of opportunities to minister to the troubled soul: Jhoo-Rhee healings, Sufism, homeopathy, and spiritual development, A World In Need of Therapy workshop at the Sipaupu Center, Spiritual Emergence Support Clinic, plus thirty-eight other twelve-step programs, support groups, and other roads to holistic health. And that's just on Thursdays, in this mecca of psychic tourism, where the very bedrock is said to pulsate with healing energy.*

JOANNA CORTI: In Santa Fe and around Santa Fe there are many vortexes of energy, and these vortexes connect the Earth's energy with other dimensions, and that's why I came here. I came to find a vortex.

Joanna Corti is a thirty-eight-year-old transplanted Easterner who advertises in the Sun, *an alternative newspaper specializing in the healing arts.*

CORTI: A wonderful way to experience what's happening here is to go outside the city limits and take your shoes off, and just stand on the ground and feel Mother Earth, and just be silent for a moment, and then you'll know what I'm talking about.

Originally from Syracuse, New York, Joanna ventured here to take advantage of the unique obsidian rock bed and the vibrational emanations therefrom. Moving to Santa Fe, she says, was the natural evolution of a lifelong quest for personal growth.

CORTI: I was born and raised a Catholic, and when I was in college, I studied Zen Buddhism, and I also was involved with an Eastern religion called Eckankar for many years, and that . . . during that time, I learned how to meditate and how to leave my body, and how to experience different planes of reality. I had rebirthing. I've had lots of acupuncture, lots of acupressure, some jinshin-jitsu, massage work, polarity work, lot of chiropractic. I've done some Hakomi therapy, some hypnotherapy, lots of processing, self-motivation tapes. I listen a lot to a channel named Lazarus, and I've done a lot of his workshops. Sound healing, vibrational healing, music healing, crystals and pyramids. Oh, I don't want to miss anything. Oh yes, I've done a lot of astrology, too.

Also pendulums and tarot, color healing, and the I Ching. Oh also, balance sheets. We forgot to mention the balance sheets, which she used to do in France as an MBA financial analyst for Burroughs Corporation. But numbers crunching is a thing of the past now. Ensconced in Santa Fe, a leather pouch dangling from her neck with blue tourmalines inside, she is practicing spiritual medicine. Joanna Corti is a psychic surgeon, performing ten to twenty spiritual procedures a week at $75 a pop.

CORTI: Now how that works is I sit at the person's crown chakra, which is at the top of the head, and I go into a trance state. And at that time, the different energies that wo . . . that I work with and the spirit doctors go through, open up the person's crown chakra and work through and clear the spiritual bodies. Then it allows the physical body to heal itself.
BOB: [interviewing] Does Blue Cross and Blue Shield cover this?
CORTI: No, it doesn't.

But, it's not such a ludicrous idea, says James Tamarelli, editor and publisher of the Sun, *where Joanna and scores of others advertise their metaphysical services. To him, the distinction between Joanna's psychic surgery and internal medicine is nothing more than a difference in belief systems. And if spiritual assistance is strange, he wants to know, "What about Christianity? What about prayer?"*

JAMES TAMARELLI: If they have power in them, you know, like sensitivity and energy and a connection with something higher that they call praying to God, she has power in her and a connection with something higher that she calls working on the psychic level. They are the same thing, and people get help that way.

BOB: [interviewing] What percentage of this stuff should I be expected to take seriously?

TAMARELLI: Well, I would take it all seriously because they're all serious.

[An eerie, high-pitched sound changes the scene]: *This is the Temple of Light Healing Center and Bed and Breakfast where Jean Gosse, the proprietor, is circling the rims of seven crystal bowls with the rubber-tipped edge of a doorstop to create the proper sound environment for her work. She's another advertiser in the* Sun, *and her suburban Santa Fe rambler is one-stop shopping for healing and transformation. It just depends on which of her diplomas you want to exploit. Jean is a certified biomagnetic healer, certified energetics practitioner, second-degree Reiki healer, certified aromatherapist, licensed massage therapist, and a certified medium.*

The bedrooms of her home are filled with electromagnetic gizmos and crystals, but her pride and joy is in the backyard. It is the ascension chamber, built according to the sacred geometry for nothing less than a spiritual voyage to the stars.

JEAN GOSSE: [outside] It's made up of fifteen equilateral trian-
gles. If you step over the little ethereal wall here, this was
channeled in so that I can keep the energy spinning as
they're meant to in the main part of the chamber. And in the
main part of the chamber here, one sits under a copper pyramid. This copper pyramid is built with the same specifica-
tions, only smaller, of course, as the Giza pyramid in Egypt.
A cassette player if one chooses. There's also a synchro-ener-
gizer with light-sound machines. There's also a crystal ball
out here.

*She doesn't actually do anything to you out here. She just sticks you
in a fleece-covered BarcaLounger, tilts you back to astronautic
angles, and frees you to privately commune with the pantheon of
Gods, mystics, and prophets whose pictures she's laid out against
the wall.*

GOSSE: Satchidananda, our Lord Jesus, Buddha, Kwan Yin, Mas-
ter Katumi, Sai Baba, Commander Ashtar, Commander of the
Ship of Jerusalem . . .
BOB: [interviewing] Ship of Jerusalem?
GOSSE: It's a . . . one of the spaceships.

*That's spaceships from another planet, but never mind that. I
have an appointment with Ralph, the aura balancer.*

RALPH FIRE EAGLE: [performing an incantation] I ask through this
light that any karmic action that can be released up into the
light take place today for Bob and for myself, that that light
fill, protect, and surround us . . .

*Ralph Fire Eagle works days at The Marketplace, but on his off
hours, he's a biomagnetic healer, adjusting people's body auras to
get their seven chakras of body energy in proper balance. Right
now, his subject is . . . me. I'm supine on a massage table and he*

is painstakingly guiding his hands around my aura, which evidently, is way out of tune. Rainbows dance on the ceiling, courtesy of prisms suspended in front of the windows, and Ralph slowly molds my auric field like so much modeling clay.

FIRE EAGLE: Each of us has an individual center on certain parts of the physical body so what I'm doing is checking to see . . . they're all little individual spinning wheels of energy, which spin in a positive clockwise form. So what I'm doing now is checking to see if they're in balance. Do you have a family?

BOB: [interviewing]: Wife and two kids.

FIRE EAGLE: I'm asking you these questions because when I came to this part of your field here, I received like a little picture, and I saw your family. OK. I can see that you have kids. So you carry the people who you are really close to with you in your field.

BOB: [interviewing] Did you happen to see if my wife picked up the shirts at the dry cleaners? [Laughter]

The treatment takes twenty minutes, but when it is complete, I don't feel particularly balanced. What I feel mainly is puzzlement, puzzlement about how a kind and sincere man like Ralph can believe in this hocus-pocus. Or maybe it isn't hocus-pocus. Maybe if I'd only stand barefoot outside the city as the psychic surgeon has recommended, I'd feel the energy resonating from the obsidian rock bed, but clearly, all these healing therapies can't be for real. So you'd have to do a lot of balancing, a lot of questing, a lot of check writing to separate the therapeutic wheat from the chaff. Where does it all end for the true seekers and spiritual hypochondriacs searching endlessly for the external meaning they're destined never to find?

This is precisely the question I posed to Alexandra Windsor-Betts, who sells overpriced artwork to tourists in her own downtown gallery. I've stopped here looking for a souvenir, but naturally I discovered that Windsor-Betts herself has sampled the psychic smorgasbord. Eventually, though, she got weary at the process, which she likened to kids wandering around at recess.

ALEXANDRA WINDSOR-BETTS: And we're sort of waiting for the bell to ring, and then for someone to tell us what to do next, but we're all out there kind of waiting for someone to give us instructions, and there really aren't any. We have to make our own.

A mecca for healing, or a magnet for neurosis? More feckless Californians and Coloradans and Easterners put roots down here each day, and the city is thriving, but at what cost? What will all this spiritual self-absorption do to Santa Fe? [Excerpt of traditional music heard in background] *On the Central Plaza, Native American buskers commuting from their pueblo play street music, and jugglers toss around Indian clubs. One of them is Roque Marquez, who resents what's become of his town.*

ROQUE MARQUEZ: I think it's for the worst. I think we're losing a lot of what we have.

BOB: [interviewing] How so?

MARQUEZ: Well, the people . . . the original people, the people that . . . that have been here developing all these arts, people whose grandparents were curanderas and herb . . . herbalists and healers of all sorts can't even afford to live here because they can't afford thousand-dollar-a-month rents. It's impossible. They can't stay. There's a big resentment because we have to leave. People have to leave. Natives have to leave. People who have been here ten years . . . you know, people that have been here before Santa Fe got hard to live in have to leave.

BOB: [interviewing] Is Santa Fe the most healed place in America, or is it something else entirely?

MARQUEZ: I think there's a lot of sickness coming here.

BOB: [interviewing] To get healed?

MARQUEZ: To get healed, but it's been just a whole lot of sickness.

BOB: [Beside a highway, with cars speeding by] I'm on the road outside of Santa Fe heading towards Albuquerque, standing in the desert, taking off my shoes, and I'm now going to try to connect with the positive energy of this place. [Pause] I definitely feel something. [Pause] Yep, it's . . . it's a rock.

And it wasn't obsidian. It wasn't tourmaline. It was just a rock, and it was stuck in my foot, and—in spite of the ancient spirit doctors—it hurt.

PART
2

The Big Score

Publish or Perish

NEW YORK—It's a good thing coffee cures cotton mouth. A few minutes ago, Michael Cohen was so nervous his every tentative utterance came with background noise approximating a dry squeegee on dirty glass. He had a cough, too—the kind you get when you find yourself trying to win somebody over, and that somebody is looking at you like you've just beamed down from the Planet Moron. But the meeting is over now, and Cohen can reflect yet again whether his new publishing venture has merit or whether—as some skeptics have suggested—it is the Stupidest Proposition Anyone Ever Thought Of.

"At first I thought it was a stupid idea, too," says the twenty-six-year-old Cleveland entrepreneur, "and I'm the one who thought of it."

The enterprise at issue is *Bathroom Journal,* the magazine "for people who value their time." If Cohen's grand vision materializes, it will be a monthly digest filling a notorious publishing void: reading matter designed exclusively for consumption on the hopper.

"It's more than a magazine, really," he explains. "It's a decorative item. We offer a wall rack to keep it on display. I guess you could say it adds personality to the bathroom, a room that needs that in a lot of homes."

The idea had long percolated in Cohen's mind, but only when he read a survey finally confirming the bathroom as America's prime magazine-reading venue did he courageously take the plunge. He quit his job in public relations, sank a fortune into a pilot issue, and ventured into that perilous Ty-D-Bol that is magazine publishing.

You may have heard of the *Bathroom Journal,* because Cohen's unveiling of the concept last summer led to a gush of publicity, a valuable promotional commodity upon which his plans for regular publication hinge. But at the just-adjourned meeting in the offices of Rosenfeld, Sirowitz & Humphrey—the first advertising agency to hear him out—it became starkly apparent that Cohen's brainchild is severely underdeveloped at birth.

David Madoian and Marie Wolpert, media planners at the agency, sat stunned as Cohen stumbled through his presentation. They were polite but nonplused as this smiling, curly-headed young man insisted, "It's a good magazine to read if you have the time, and you do have the time."

It didn't help that the pilot issue's editorial format has been scrapped for one not yet fully devised. It didn't help that Cohen coughed, fidgeted, and basically phoomfed through his spiel. And it certainly didn't help when he volunteered—with what in mind there's no telling—"Newsstand magazines usually have a benefit; this has no benefits. You could call it a dual-interest service magazine. Or you could call it a lifestyle book . . . not even a lifestyle book."

But none of that really mattered, because Madoian was pretty much hung up on another basic point: the portability of magazines in general. It occurred to him that a person who set his mind to doing so could transport, say, *Sports Illustrated* into the bathroom with him.

"Is there a need for something like this thing?" Madoian asked. "Don't people leave magazines in their bathroom already? I know I do."

Cohen had a ready response. "I get this question all the time," he said. "You've got to [cough] factor in the [cough] editorial and the wall rack."

In the end, no advertising pages were purchased. Both ad people assured Cohen they'd monitor his magazine's progress and consider it for their clients' 1988 media schedules, but the parting was reminiscent of a good-night handshake after a disastrous blind date. Thus Cohen sits in the coffee shop across the street, lubricating his palate and wondering all over again what he's gotten himself into. He and his investors have plowed $50,000 into this project already, with the promise of many thousands more in expenses ahead. Yes, people picked up on the novelty of this thing, but, as he notes, "The publicity will stop one day, and we'll have to make it on our own."

"It's an emotional roller coaster," he says. "I really sometimes have to convince myself that it's a good idea. But any new idea sounds stupid until people accept it. I'm trying to think of an example. . . .

"Airplanes."

Speakeasies

Enterprise, Alphonso F. Williams Jr. knows, is the cornerstone of success.

Henry Ford took a simple notion—the assembly line—and built an immense fortune. Jobs and Wozniak tinkered their way to Apple Computer riches. Debbi Fields built a better cookie, and the world beat a path to her door.

What they all had in common was an idea, and the conviction to pursue it, damn the obstacles and deaf to the naysayers. So too Al Williams. Two years ago, he and his wife resolved to build their own business and they have risked everything to make it happen.

"We were just thinking," says Williams, a thirty-six-year-old Bronx school-bus driver. "We were trying to think of something to help the public that didn't exist yet. There's a saying, 'A great idea is always there. What is missing is a great mind to grasp it.' So I tried to be a great mind and come up with something different. That began the long road."

That began the brainstorming, the conception, the patent search, the product development, the incorporation, the quest for a manufacturer, the formulation of a business plan. That began Patal Inc. and the gestation of a product just now entering the world. That began Speakeasies, disposable public-phone handset covers in two decorator colors.

"Think," advises Williams's brochure. "Hundreds of people have used the public phone daily, and so do billions of germs. Germs don't discriminate. Germs can lower our resistance and/or immunity to disease. *Diseases can kill!* You can speak at ease with Speakeasies, our disposable public phone covers."

The product itself, made of spun-woven paper and elastic, looks like the surgical slippers doctors and nurses wear in the operating room. Speakeasies slip over the phone handset, providing a protective layer of fabric between the user and unseen bacteria—with no audio distortion. "Save on unnecessary medical expenses," the brochure says, and, "YES, NEVER WIPE OFF A PUBLIC PHONE AGAIN!!!" Only $4.98 for a package of ten.

"I tried to make it shamelessly seductive, with impeccable class and readability," Williams says. "Hopefully, they'll read that and have to have it."

The key word there is "hopefully." Williams is only too aware that, in the pantheon of public-health menaces, telephone bacteria isn't exactly top of mind. Yet his intuition tells him he's onto something. He's betting that once people get to thinking about it, their lifetimes of pay-phone recklessness will flash before their eyes.

"Who knows?" he says. "It's a shot in the dark. Time will tell."

Williams drives a school bus to support his wife and three kids, but he has the soul of an entrepreneur. He isn't content to play it safe and ride the status quo, and he isn't afraid to delve into the unknown.

"I've done other things," he says.

For instance, he once came up with an idea he thought Procter & Gamble could use in its Scope commercials—an adaptation of Wilson Pickett's song "Don't let the green grass fool ya." The Scope version would go like this: "Don't let the good taste fool ya / Don't let it change your mind / Although it is sweeter than the other kind / don't let it change your mind."

Another time, he noticed an old lady feeding pigeons on the same street day after day. Though he'd never done anything like it before, he took pictures and wrote a story for a newspaper photo essay, and got it printed in the New York *Daily News*.

"That," he says, "gave me confidence to try this thing to the utmost."

This thing, this Speakeasies thing, is the ultimate dabble. He couldn't get a business loan, ("Believe me, I tried. But I got turned around. 'Startup, startup, startup.' ") and has socked everything into it but the rent money. He basically blew his last $475 to buy 10,000 subscriber names from *Prevention* magazine.

"As a matter of fact," he says, "I'm down to zilch."

So, as he distributes free samples, trying to spread the word around Manhattan, Williams is understandably nervous. And as if the launch of a new product with no marketing budget weren't worrisome enough, he harbors a lingering fear that he's given the thing the wrong name. He thinks maybe he should have gone with his first instinct.

"At first I called it Phone Condoms. I had a slogan, 'Phone Condoms work!' I liked that, but a number of people told me I at once grabbed their attention and turned them off. I had a cousin who said she couldn't see going into a store and asking for Phone Condoms.

"My friends still tease me about that. They'll say, 'Hey, Al. Phone Condoms work!' "

Hunger

NEW YORK—If you want to distinguish Jan Stuart from the other hungry capitalists on Wall Street, you'd be well advised to ignore the dark suit and $200 Brooks Brothers shoes. Focus on the Winnebago.

The clothes are strictly *de rigueur,* but Stuart's recreational vehicle is among the finest parked in front of the New York Stock Exchange these days. All right, it's the only RV of any kind within the vicinity of the stock exchange. Then again, Stuart—chief executive officer of the Jan Stuart Skin Care Co.—is the only CEO actually living on Wall Street.

"I've got running water," he says, giving an impromptu tour. "Refrigerator, freezer, microwave. The microwave doesn't come in too handy."

It doesn't come in handy because, at this writing, Stuart hasn't eaten in twenty-two days. Oh, that's the other thing. He's living in a RV *and* staging a hunger strike.

"My heart, my soul, my religion—everything is tied into this," says the desperate entrepreneur, who has lost control of his financial future and about seventeen pounds. "I'm willing to do everything it takes."

Stuart is fasting because it's a good attention-getting protest, expressing his disappointment with Wall Street, which he thinks is hostile to small businessmen, a condition he thinks was amply demonstrated when nobody jumped to give him several million dollars, which he had been polite enough to ask for nicely, when he took an unusual full-page ad in *The New York Times,* which was headlined "PLEASE HELP ME SAVE MY COMPANY!"

In less than ten years, Jan Stuart Skin Care had grown from a standing start to $8 million in sales. The expansion strained Stuart's meager capital base, and when two attempts to go public failed, the company was critically short of cash. This led to unpaid bills, lawsuits, layoffs, and lost shelf space for his moisturizers, masques, and body sprays.

Friends and advisers suggested shutting down and starting from scratch, but, "To me bankruptcy is a bad negative. That's when I knew we had to do something dramatic. I had a piece of the American Dream at one time, and I wanted it back."

Hence the *Times* ad last August—an ad that led to plenty of response and zero cash offers. Now the company is on the brink and Stuart is in his Winnebago, smack in the middle of perhaps the world's first-ever hunger strike for skin care. He is undercapitalized, undernourished, and—to his way of thinking—underappreciated.

"It's been very lonely," he says, sipping purified water from one of fifteen gallon jugs. "The response from the people on the street has been very positive. But the type of people I need to attract, as you know, don't walk the streets of New York. They are driven through the streets of New York."

His most hopeful sign to date was a brief visit from billionaire industrialist Donald Trump, who praised Stuart's resolve. Trump didn't get out his check book, but he did suggest that fruit juice might be an acceptable dietary adjunct that wouldn't compromise the integrity of the protest.

Shortly after Dr. Trump departed, the papaya juice and local news coverage flowed.

At this stage, Stuart acknowledges, everything is riding on publicity. Luckily, apart from the sloughing off of dead skin cells, this is his greatest area of expertise. His scrapbook is thick with clippings from publications large and small, all seemingly stunned by the notion of under-eye cream for men. As Stuart says, "It was a concept—men's skin care."

And so is a Wall Street hunger strike, but not exactly the same kind of concept. Whereas speaking out publicly about facial cleanser is widely regarded as an appropriate way to promote facial cleanser, there are those who will question the Miracle No Foodstuffs Diet as a means to lure corporate investors.

Gandhi fasted for independence. Mitch Snyder fasted for the homeless. Jan Stuart is fasting for the rights of all men to have clean pores and healthy, resilient skin.

"The biggest risk was that people wouldn't take this serious enough," he acknowledges. "But I needed to speak out. I'm gonna go on as long as it takes to be heard."

Quityourbellyaching

ALEXANDRIA, VA.—A credit card that earns you money. It just can't miss.

Erik Schrader has finally hit the big one, and you can tell from his taped phone message that he's excited about it: "Wouldn't it be nice to walk into your favorite new-car dealership and say, 'Hey, I'll take that car'? And the best part is, you pay no interest and no monthly payments out of your own pocket!

"No wonder it's being called the 'credit card of the future.'"

And it's also no wonder people are clogging Schrader's rented conference room four times a week to learn more. They come to hear about C.I. Systems, Schrader's consulting organization, and about the Omni Card, which he says will bring them $300 to $1,000 a month within three to six months, doubling every six to nine months until eventually they're in a $9 million-a-month situation. All anybody has to do is go out and recruit two new card subscribers, who each in turn recruit two more and so on forever more. And no selling. It's just a matter of stuffing flyers in doorjambs and under windshield wipers—flyers that look like $500 bills inscribed with this message:

QUITYOURBELLYACHINGANDCALL 369-6094.

Schrader takes care of the rest with his taped messages and meetings—so it's an expert who explains the ingenious multilevel marketing method guaranteed to make you rich.

"Over six hundred millionaires said, yes, this is how they became rich and successful," Schrader tells me and two dozen other candidates at a Thursday night meeting. "So would you do it? Would you try a method that took no work, is very simple, doesn't cost you any money, takes very, very little time? Would you do it for six months?" Two dozen heads nod yes.

But there's more. Once you pay your $60 membership fee and your $25 monthly dues, you're eligible to join three other companies: GEMS International, The Silver Letter, and Success Synergistics. "I'm telling you," he says, "any one of those companies will make you more money, faster, than the Omni Card."

Claudia, a fiftyish-looking woman with a purple-and-white print blouse, purple vest, bouffant hairdo, and "I love Herbalife" button, is psyched. "I want to go for it!" she volunteers. Sharon, a nurse, tells everybody, "I can see the light at the end of the tunnel."

Sitting next to me is Earl Reynolds, president of Earl's Advertising Specialities Printing & Gift Shop. Earl isn't very emotional about all of this. He's more of an analytical guy, and he quietly explains to me the potential of what is being described: "This thing is just starting, and I can get in on the ground floor. If you get in on the ground floor and get a hot dog underneath you, you can make it go.

"I'm in it to make money," Earl whispers. "That's my second plan. My first plan is to serve God."

Schrader doesn't much care who Earl serves, as long as he forks over the first $85 and distributes about 10,000 flyers. After sixteen years in the multilevel marketing business, this bald, fifty-four-year-old, former U.S. Navy Band tuba player figures he's earned his first big score. He's done Shaklee. He's done Coscot. He's done Sir Erik's Lodge (his own company). He's done Cambridge Diet. Genesis. Herbalife. Universe Foods. Morning Sun Cosmetics. Stamp investing. Newsletters.

He's tried them all. Yet, somehow, the riches have eluded him. Every time his organization gets hot, pow! The supplier company goes out of business.

Or he gets arrested. Three times he's been busted, and even though he's been found guilty only once—he's awaiting sentencing on a November conviction in Maryland—the law always seems to turn things sour.

"There's something about this type of organization," he observes during a phone conversation. "Once you get arrested, the people get scared off."

People are funny that way. And so are the legal authorities, like the New Mexico justice department, which has booted Omni Card International out of the state under threat of criminal penalty. It turns out that attorneys general regard this sort of multilevel marketing as an illegal pyramid scheme. Pyramiding is what Schrader was found guilty of in Maryland, though he says it's a bad conviction that will be reversed on appeal. The real problem, he contends, is "circumstances of laws and Goody Two-Shoes that complain."

Don't even suggest that the authorities simply hate seeing Claudia and Earl blow good money on no-chance rackets. And don't rub Schrader's nose in the fact that, after sixteen years, he has nothing to show for his efforts but a well-polished sales pitch and a closet full of flyers.

"Don't ever say that," he says, hurt. "Don't ever say somebody doesn't have a shot at it. Sooner or later, something good's going to happen."

Pull

NEW YORK—It is 12:30 P.M. on Wednesday, Feb. 4. Liberace is in grave condition 2,800 miles away.

In point of fact, the famed entertainer has four and a half hours of life left within him, but here in the offices of MSG Advertising his current nonexpiration is an inconvenient technicality and temporary obstacle. The assumption is that he will succumb presently. Preparations have been under way for days.

MSG is a direct-response ad agency/merchandiser that has given us, among many other tempting TV offers, the Liberace fortieth-anniversary record album. This exclusive collection was modestly popular two years ago. Now, unlike the artist himself, the record is destined to live again. Immediately upon hearing the grim medical news last Monday, the ad-agency masterminds began scrambling to prepare the Liberace memorial TV record offer.

"It's a tribute to him," says Diane Handler, MSG president. "Liberace was an amazing man."

Was, is—we're dealing in semantics. The fact is, Liberace's passing could be the stuff of which TV-offer legends are made. The record's potential to attact orders—called "pull" in the argot of the trade—is bound to grow exponentially with the eventual tragic news. One thinks of what happened following the drowning death of the Beach Boys' popular drummer.

"We had the Beach Boys when Dennis Wilson went into the drink," recalls June Keane, MSG media director. Next thing you know, she says, they had a gold record on their hands. "Before that nobody would touch the Beach Boys.

"We did Ricky Nelson. He was no good when he was alive. He went [in a fiery air crash] on a Sunday. We had [a posthumous record offer] on stations Tuesday or Wednesday. Pulled like crazy."

Keane's only regret is that reports Nelson triggered the explosion while freebasing cocaine may have slowed sales. "It would have been better if the plane had just gone down," she says.

Cynical? Maybe to you. But to the sensitive marketers at MSG, it's just a question of opportunity. When it knocks in this business, even if you're in mourning, you've got to be ready to open the door.

"I knew Ricky Nelson," Handler says. "He was a nice guy. However, it was 7 P.M. on New Year's Eve when I heard the news. I came to the office on New Year's Day to get his tapes out."

That's not to say there are any guarantees, and MSG has not exactly batted 1.000. Handler lost small fortunes on her home pizza pan, her ladies' tool kit, her Walkmate mini-speaker (it attached to Walkman stereos for music you could share), and her Roll-a-Round, a novelty toy she was convinced was the next hula hoop.

And, of course, there was the Christian dating service. "The guy was so Christian," she says, "he screwed me out of $20,000."

Because record albums don't have to be pressed until the orders are already in, they are somewhat less speculative, but the risk can still be substantial—even when you're dealing with a famous, not-quite-dead showman like Liberace. Other noted celebrity passings have been strictly mediocre, pull-wise.

"You never know what's gonna work," she says. "Bing Crosby didn't do that well. Jimmy Durante didn't do that well. The first big death was Elvis. Elvis was humongous."

It all boils down to instinct. Handler turned down Dream-Away, the pill you took at bedtime to shed weight while sleeping. She turned down Dan from the Holy Land, who was peddling water from the River Jordan. She turned down Gary Waite, the country-singing endodontist from Las Vegas.

Yet she ignored Keane's warnings and went with a jewelry offer—seventeen pieces for $17, pieces so obviously worthless, Keane says, "It really insulted the intelligence." Pulled like gangbusters.

Strange business. One minute you're selling hermit crabs with little pompons tied around them, the next minute you're negotiating the rights to offer a treasury of concert pianist Vladimir Horowitz's greatest hits.

Sadly, Horowitz is eighty-two years old. I point out to the agency principals that we can't expect to enjoy his genius much longer.

Handler nods confidently. "We know that."

Stung by a Bee

CALEDONIA, WISC.—If this were a dream, you'd wake up in a sweat.

Here's a town clawing at the dirt for sustenance, so wracked has it been by unemployment. It's a milky white place with no love lost for neighboring Racine, whose black population is suspiciously regarded as the competition in the labor pool and worse. It's a hard-luck crossroads that has been disintegrating, in economy and spirit, for years.

Then out of nowhere comes The Greatest.

Muhammad Ali floated into Caledonia with a vacant smile, a retinue of protector/partners and the damnedest idea you've ever heard: an expensive luxury sports car called the Ali 3.WC, which his associates propose to assemble locally and sell overseas. Sell to whom? To ludicrously rich Arabs and other gulls unduly impressed by Ali's legendary name.

Three months ago Ali arrived, short-circuited nervous system and all. He floated in not so much like a butterfly as a stray hot dog wrapper—but there he stood nonetheless, bigger than life. "I made boxing better than it ever was," The Greatest told the local press "I promoted it and I'm going to promote this car."

Since then there's been a lot of ugly publicity about the Ali Motors Inc. principals, nasty stuff about bankruptcies and illegal securities sales and a troublesome paucity of capital. But even before word spread of the backers' dicey financial histories, folks here pondered fitfully over what this all really means. Could it really be? Three hundred and twenty new jobs? A black man more famous than Martin Luther King rescuing Caledonia from economic ruin?

"The numbers are right," says Bruce Nielsen, whose firm would be general contractor on the $10 million Ali plant. "They're gonna make big money."

Yet for three months the partners have been mum on how they'll finance the project—not a small detail in an automotive venture, for which capital is typically measured in the billions. And nobody has seen so much as a drawing of the car. It's all so fuzzy and insubstantial, so attractive yet so elusive. In a word, surreal.

"There's two groups of people," says Patrick Motley, chairman of the Caledonia Town Council. "There's people who don't think it will ever take place. They're just biding their time and waiting. And there's other people who are hopeful, who are unemployed, who have spoken to me and asked me about the odds of getting a job."

Motley may be correct, but there seem to be more Caledonians betwixt and between. There are guys like Jim Dean, a self-employed contractor whose land adjoins the proposed site. On the one hand, he'd love to see it all fly.

"I've talked to twenty young guys who have been to every place they could go to and always get the same story," Dean says. "If they employ half what they say it'll be good." But he still worries about carpetbaggers trying to rape Caledonia of what little self-respect it still has. "If this thing don't pan out," he says, "they just pick up their satchel and the heck with it."

Over at the Corner Connection bar, Roger Houle's regulars have already figured out how the plans could materialize and still be bad news: if Ali Motors management, mainly black, gives hiring preference to black workers. "It's niggers gonna be movin' in," Houle says of the bar talk. "That's the big scandal."

Clayton Nielsen just about chokes at reports like that. Bruce Nielsen's father and partner at Nielsen Building Systems doesn't want anything—least of all percolating racism—to jeopardize the sweetest deal going. Not only would his outfit design and build the plant, they own the land upon which it would rest. Thus he trumpets the Ali Motors concept ("Some of these oil sheiks got so much money they don't know what to do with it") and dismisses the negative publicity surrounding Nelson Boon Jr., Ali Motors managing partner.

"He's very, very open. He's very, very likable. I personally think he's a great guy," says the elder Nielsen. "Everybody has a dark spot in their past."

No gloom and doom from these fellows. They have seen the profit and its name is Muhammad.

"Did you know he's a magician?" Bruce asks. "We were walking out of the hotel room, fifteen of us, and he turns around [Bruce spins around himself, mimicking The Greatest]. And we look. His feet were off the ground about that much." Bruce spreads his hands twelve inches apart.

Says Clayton: "You figure it out."

Had 'em a Minute Ago

The third of five surprises in one hour came when the fellow walked in wearing nothing but red jockey shorts. This was just before Christmas at the White Pines Lounge in New Athens, Illinois, and the other patrons were pretty sure the guy wasn't Santa Claus.

But nobody could get too worked up over a mainly naked stranger, because they were still reeling over two other big surprises—the first of which was the robbery. At 6:15 P.M. on a quiet Thursday night, in the quiet bar at a quiet rural intersection, some disquieting menace had barged in with a sawed-off shotgun.

"We thought it was just a joke—a Halloween joke—'cause he had the ski-mask on," recalls Harry Reynolds, the seventy-seven-year-old owner of the White Pines. "He said, 'This is a stickup.' We said, 'You must be kidding.' "

No such luck. The bandit had no sense of humor whatsoever. Not only did he steal hundreds of dollars from patrons and employees, he also forced one man to tie everybody up, including Reynolds's three young great-grandchildren, who cowered terrified on the floor.

That's when the second big surprise of the evening arrived. In the midst of the holdup, the door swung open and in walked a regular customer. Paying no heed to what was transpiring around him, he walked up to the bar and ordered a beer. Reynolds is still shaking his head about it:

"He says, 'You're not gonna believe this, Harry. All I got is a $50 bill.' The robber says, 'I'll just take that.' " And the robber did.

Naturally, before fleeing, the gunman threatened to blast

anybody who dared to move. To demonstrate how serious he was, he grabbed the poor soul he'd enlisted to bind the victims and brained him with the butt end of the shotgun. Out the door the intruder then fled.

At this stage, you should be aware that robbers at the White Pines historically have had mixed success. Last time, about two years ago, a bandit shot Reynolds in the shoulder, which made him very angry. So the proprietor plunked his adversary with a heavy bar ashtray, stunning him. The ashtray fell to the floor and shattered, allowing Reynolds to pick up a shard and slice the bandit's face to ribbons.

Alas, Reynolds sighs, "I'm getting too old to fight anymore," and he let this new crook escape unmolested. A minute or so after the getaway, one hostage managed to wriggle out of his bindings, lock the door of the bar, and phone police. In just another minute, squad-car sirens could be heard heading to the scene.

That's when someone started pounding on the door from outside. It was the man in the red underwear.

"We opened up the door," Reynolds says. "He come in and said, 'Did you people just get robbed? I just got robbed in the parking lot.' "

That explained the wardrobe, so one of Reynolds' employees took the shivering stranger back to the kitchen where there was a shirt and a pair of pants. At about the same time the police arrived, whereupon came Surprise No. 4. The barmaid had solved the crime. The culprit, she announced, was Underwear-man. With a shotgun. In the kitchen—right now.

"It was one of the damnedest things I ever seen," Reynolds says. "The girl says, 'That's the guy! I recognize his voice.' "

And, according to the St. Clair County Sheriff's office, she was correct: Thomas L. Winfrey, twenty-six, of St. Louis, was both the man in the ski mask and the man in the red drawers. He had reentered the bar reluctantly after realizing that his get-away plans were, to say the least, foiled.

"Outside the building we found this guy's car," says Detective Rick Siekmann. "Inside the car was a shotgun laying on the front passenger floorboard. There was a bunch of money inside. The bottom line on the story was the guy lost his car keys."

The bandit had fled the bar, dumped the loot in his car, and patted his every pocket in a panic, the detective says. No keys anywhere. By then police sirens were blaring. It was time to act fast. His own flannel shirt and jeans would have been instantly recognized, so he did the only thing he could think of. He stripped to his underwear. A disguise in reverse.

"He's got a record of robberies in the past, but he obviously isn't very good at it," Siekmann says. "He has a habit of getting caught."

As for where the keys were, that's Surprise No. 5. He'd left them in the ignition.

Just Give Me Half a Tank

ARLINGTON, VA.—It began as a more or less ordinary Tuesday afternoon for Fahed Subartani. The pump islands were busy at his Columbia Texacare service station, and he was occupied tuning up an African diplomat's Volkswagen. Then the explosion came.

"I hear it," Subartani recalls. "I raise my head from the hood where I am working. I see fire at the pump."

He saw sixty-foot-high flames and thick black smoke. In that first instant, he did not see that his pump jockey was hurt, nor could he see the two injured customers. He definitely didn't notice two other customers hightailing off in a pickup truck. He was too busy shutting off the valve to the underground 10,000-gallon tanks and cutting the electric. (Otherwise, in a few seconds, there would have been a crater where Texacare had once stood.) Then he and a bystander knocked down the fire with a garden hose.

In general, Subartani acted cooly and decisively, especially considering it was the first time his gas pumps ever were blown up by a 30mm antitank shell. But now—now that Robert Dilger and Joseph Donahue face charges relating to the immoderate use of artillery weapons in a major suburb—Subartani is just puzzled.

"Who believe a customer gonna having cannon in his car and shoot pumps?" he asks. "But it's happen."

He has reason to be incredulous. In point of fact, in this part of Northern Virginia, tanks are a rarity. As far as enemy tanks are concerned, there are virtually none. And, by the same token, as far as anyone knows, cannon attacks on gasoline pumps are more or less unheard of. As Subartani observes, "I don't think anybody would [knowingly] put shell on gas pump and hurt the public."

So the theory now is "accidental." When all is said and done, it's likely Robert Dilger will be found to have lacked hostile intentions in this unprovoked assault on the self-serve island.

Dilger is a freelance defense contractor, who, hoping to plug a grievous hole in the Army's infantry capability, made a big gun that goes boom. On this Tuesday, his intention evidently was to make it go boom at a rural Virginia firing range. It appears he was merely transporting his homemade 30 mm antitank gun from point A to point B, stopped for a fill-up, went to the back of the pickup to inspect his weapon, inadvertently let the barrel slip out of his hand, and then watched in horror as the gun discharged. You could say it went boom prematurely, because, yes:

He didn't know it was loaded.

"It's different when it happens with a .22," notes Chuck Myers, president of Aerocounsel, a small defense-industry think tank, rolling his eyes at the triteness of the explanation. A man more than casually familiar with both Dilger and his devastating gas-pump immobilizer, however, Myers was equally unimpressed with the damage done. It turns out this shell was merely a practice round. A combat shell with a spent-uranium penetrating rod "will go in one side of the Pentagon and out the other. That gun that went off in the gas station will take out any tank in the world from the side or rear."

"Dilger was doing all right," Myers says, "until he screwed it all up."

The screwup being, of course, more than just the accidental firing. If, as Myers insists, Dilger's gun is the only infantry weapon ever developed that is truly capable of killing a tank (he says the bazooka is worthless), and if it is true that Dilger, a former Air Force procurement officer, was gradually penetrating the Defense Department bureaucracy and generating interest in his development, it might actually have been to his advantage to take out a gas pump or two. The news coverage was your basic publicity bonanza. Every general and armed-services committee member in town now knows about the gun.

The real screwup is that Dilger, a patriotic guy just trying to help his country, turned tail and ran—thus making his clout, like a combat antitank shell, go in one side of the Pentagon and out the other. The public may be willing to forgive an innocent accidental gas-station shelling, but it will not abide a shelling-and-run.

As things stand, public relationswise, Myers says, "that didn't help him at all."

Miracle Whip

NEW YORK—To get an appointment with Ava Taurel, first you have to listen to her recorded message, which runs five minutes.

Then you have to call her secretary, who will set you up with a preliminary appointment.

But before you meet—maybe in Central Park, maybe in a coffee shop—Taurel will have you walk to a certain spot outside Carnegie Hall. You'll stand there for sixty seconds, long enough for her to scan you with binoculars.

Only if you look lean and presentable will she actually show up for the interview, which costs $30.

Then, if she's sure her brand of therapy is right for you, she will accept another $150 and lead you to her building. At the elevator, she will blindfold you. Inside the car she will frisk you for weapons. The blindfold will not come off until you are safely inside her studio.

Then and only then will she tie you up with leather thongs and whip you and tickle you with a feather and otherwise dominate you into therapeutic submission.

"Men need to switch roles completely," says the forty-one-year-old Swede who, for this particular interview, has foregone the leather lingerie in favor of a conservative blouse and skirt. "Sometimes it involves pain. Sometimes it results in restriction or bondage. Sometimes it involves cross-dressing."

Around the studio are the various tools of Taurel's trade. You have your whips, your ice picks, your spiked wristbands, your waffle turner, your mechanical meat tenderizer. You have your spike-heel boots, your nurse and policewoman and governess costumes, your Q-Tips, your rubbing alcohol, your latex examining gloves.

But don't be jumping to conclusions. Taurel is no kinky prostitute. She is, as her advertisements say, a Scandinavian woman psychodramatist. In her recorded messages and in person she makes emphatically clear that she will not be used sexually (though she will, in some instances, permit limited foot worship). Her job is to let men restore balance to their lives by playing out submissive roles they have been forced to internalize in our male-dominated culture.

"I've played someone's mother. I've played someone's wife. You play the role of somebody who's important in someone's life. You make that person live through a situation that he might have been in in childhood."

Taurel is tall and attractive, though hardly ravishing, with deep-set eyes, short blondish hair, and a soothing Swedish lilt to her voice. Her background includes acting, psychology, and occupational therapy—all of which stand her in good stead in the burgeoning discipline of psychodrama.

"I had a rather interesting experience the other day which is kind of unusual. A man came to me to be dog trained. I had him bark out the window. I had him walk around the floor and kind of lift his leg up. . . . He had to eat dog food. He had to bring me a can of dog food. And the moment I pushed his face into the dog food, he realized his whole past!

"His father—being a veterinarian—never gave the love and attention to his son that he needed. He gave it to the dogs, and the child desperately wanted to be in the place of the dogs."

This gentleman, like all her clients, found Taurel through her ads in *New York* magazine and *The Village Voice*. (The cable TV commercials are on the drawing board.) Among her 300 submittees are lawyers, bankers, brokers, and advertising men—precisely the upscale, intellectual clientele she prefers.

Having pursued domination as a hobbyist for several years, Taurel went professional a year ago, knowing full well her craft might attract a certain weirdo element. The last thing she needs is to find herself dressed as a chambermaid, walking her leashed client around the studio on all fours, only to discover—too late—that the guy's some sort of kook. Hence the meticulous screening. So far, apart from a few phone calls threatening her with mutilation, everything has gone smoothly. But what bothers her is that some people think she is a little strange.

"Society doesn't accept it yet," she laments, "They don't see the beauty of it or the spiritual side of it. People who have no knowledge of culture, no knowledge of art—how could they understand? That's the sad thing about America."

The Talking Cat

DETROIT, MICH.—Accordionists, naturally. Also cloggers, contortionists, dulcimer players, and leprechauns. Then there's the pizza gourmet with piano, the pipe-smoking dog, and the one-and-only Helmut Kokey, eastern Michigan's foremost lederhosen-clad yodeler.

When it comes to entertainment in and around Motor City, the Marce Haney Agency has booked them all. "We cover from *A* to *Z* in showbiz," says Haney, a twenty-seven-year veteran of the booking wars. "Whatever you want, we can get it."

Someone wanted a trained rabbit. Haney found one. Fire eaters? No problem. Of course when the chiropractic clinic needed entertainment for its grand opening, Haney had just the thing: Tommy Dee and Gail. He plays accordion. She's a puppeteer. And their motorized calliope converts into a buckboard and a chariot. "They're quite unique," she says.

Yet with all the amazing talent she's encountered over the years, Haney has never, ever seen anything like Rose Lokey and Katrina, the talking cat.

"This animal does talk," the agent says. "She does not meow. She has a guttural sound. I've yet to hear that cat meow. Everything comes out in syllables, one syllable at a time."

Okay, strictly speaking, the cat doesn't talk. What she does, with Lokey manipulating the furry underbelly just so, is mimic human speech—Lokey's speech, to be precise. But talking cats of any sort are darn rare nowadays. They're so rare, in fact, that Haney and Miss Lokey herself feel they can transform Katrina from a local feline novelty into a national media star, provided they can drum up a clientele, which, thus far, incredible as it may seem, they have not.

"We haven't booked her in a big commercial yet," Haney

says. "We've been working on it and working on it for a year. Maybe more."

It's a puzzlement. Not only is a talking cat a serious conversation piece, Rose Lokey is a dynamic personality in her own right. She is an ample woman of middle age, with not one but two cable-access TV talk shows of her own, a collection of immense wigs, a pair of false eyelashes larger than twin Madagascar hissing cockroaches, and the capacity to speak extemporaneously on most any subject—especially the subject of talking cats.

"I want to be on a commercial with Katrina, a cat food commercial," says Lokey in the crowded, pink, Louis XIV 'n' lace bedchamber. "That's my main goal. I see all the other people on the cat food commercials and they're talking to their cats, you know. Why shouldn't I be on there talking to my cat?

"She could say, 'I love you' or 'Buy this cat food. You'll love it!' You know, and people would run out and buy that cat food because they see a cat on there talking, and they'd say, 'Well, maybe that cat food might make my cat talk.' "

Lokey has been imagining such a thing for four and a half years, ever since she adopted the stray Katrina and discovered her pet's facility for language. This occurred, she recalls, when the cat began calling her Mama.

" 'Mama, Mama.' She never says, meow, you know, like cats usually. She says, *bbddbdbr,* and I wondered about that. So I said, 'Katrina, if you can say Mama, you can say something else.' So I started teaching her words. She can count. She can spell. She's a little mimic and whatever I tell her to say, she'll say it. Now, she doesn't say everything perfect, because she's a cat."

And Katrina can't get on a cat food commercial, it turns out, because:

a) she doesn't work alone.

b) cat-food advertisers like their commercials to focus on cats.

c) Lokey isn't a cat.

"This is where our problem comes in," Haney explains.

"They would love this cat if it could stand all by itself and say something about the product. But the cat will only repeat what the mistress says," with the mistress gripping the cat's belly and yelling shrill commands in the cat's ear—a collaborative effort which for some reason conflicts with cat-food makers' sense of advertising impact.

"They don't know what they're missing," Lokey says, and she's absolutely right. Hugging Katrina, she shouts into the cat's ear: "Say, 'Bob.' " Katrina opens her tiny little mouth. "*Meow,*" she says.

A Big Number

NEW YORK—Attention art collectors: the Morris Katz collection is available.

The fastest, most prolific painter in history will release, to a suitable buyer, his portrait gallery of thirty-nine American presidents, his religious series, and certain other master-works—105 paintings in all.

Act now. This one-of-a-kind collection, according to the artist, has been appraised at $3.5 million, but he is offering a rare opportunity:

"I accept any offer under $1 million within reason," Katz says. "I'm looking for financial independence."

Morris Katz, fifty-four, whose accomplishments have been certified by the *Guinness Book of World Records,* already is independent in a number of other respects. For instance, he has long since eschewed the paint brush in favor of a palette knife and wads of toilet paper. Contrary to another sacred principle of the medium, he routinely custom-colors paintings to suit the decor of the customer. And, most significantly, he flouts artistic convention by completing his average canvas in five minutes or less—usually in public.

Rembrandt shmembrandt; to Katz there's a bona fide thrill creating a ninety-second woodland scene for shoppers at the Iselin, New Jersey, Shop Rite.

"It's the highest form of art," he says. "They sway with me. They follow me in space. I call it imagination in motion. My mind flies into the painting as I paint it, and they fly with me."

His problem at the moment is that artistic air traffic is on the decline. The man who has painted a snowscape in forty-five seconds to gain the world's oil-painting speed record now finds himself squeezed by the rent on his decrepit Greenwich Village studio, which is situated in a garlic and turpentine fog above a bagel bakery on Sixth Avenue. He doesn't want to give up his collection, but he needs to hit something big.

"I'm trying to get a connection with the Home Shopping Network," he explains. "Johnny Jones calls up from Hickstown, you know, and says 'I want a painting.' It could be a whole new thing, a different type of entertainment. Very exceptional. What, twenty-five dollars you're not going to pay? All I need is a meeting with the executives. Twenty minutes. All I need is a chance."

Meanwhile he scrapes by, turning out 5,000 or so paintings a year. Grand total, at this writing: 162,270. His most lucrative commissions come en masse at Catskill Mountain resorts and trade shows, where his art becomes a novel entertainment. Knifing though forty paintings in a seven-hour sitting, he finds himself surrounded by curious passersby. His next gig will be gracing the Ultra-Seal booth at the National Automobile Dealers Association convention in Las Vegas.

"I do also weddings," he adds. "March 1 I have a wedding in San Diego, California. That's for a very big number."

There were times that Morris Katz was riding high. He'd carved out a nice niche for himself in the mass-produced wholesale original art business, but lost a fortune in the commodities market in 1969. Then, diligently working the resorts and pumping local publicity, he gradually become a New York demi-celebrity. This culminated in 1979, when he was named the male "Real Person of the Year" by the *Real People* TV show.

"I'm more famous than Johnny Carson will ever be from the people direct," he says. "These people interlock with me."

So now it's just a question of locking into the right gimmick. He'd like to paint on an airplane, or a cruise liner. An off-Broadway show would be nice.

"Call me a one-man art circus. A one-man art revolt. I make fresh paintings. They are as fresh as the bagels in the bakery. As a matter of fact, I'd like to have a contest with the guy who makes pizza in the pizzeria. He makes a pizza, I make a painting, and we see who finishes first. This could generate tremendous publicity. I constantly need publicity. It is like blood in my veins."

The down side of the exposure, of course, is that his high profile is actually impeding the sale of his private collection, some of which masterworks he labored over for up to an hour.

"People do not know I am the super artist," Katz laments. "They think I'm the toilet paper painter."

Freeze-Dried Fred

LARGO, FLA.—The furniture store fired him after three days. The waterbed-sales job lasted three hours. His tenure at the convenience store wasn't much longer, and the opportunity to market satellite dishes turned out to be a pressure-sales nightmare.

"That was another failure," says Jeffrey Weber, a thirty-four-year-old transplanted Indianan. "I just had a tough time adjusting to Florida."

Then he saw the newspaper story about the Minnesota equipment manufacturer, and just like that his future was determined. Weber decided to spend the rest of his life freeze-drying dead animals.

"It just intrigued me, especially with as many elderly people as there are in this state that have pets," Weber says. "I just thought it would be a fantastic opportunity to make good money."

Shortly after reading the article about the novel technology, Weber bought a $30,000 freeze-drying machine and opened shop as Preservation Specialties Inc. When your pet dies and you don't feel you can part with it, just send it off to Weber and have it placed in his 105-cubic-foot machine, at minus 5 degrees F in a near vacuum, and gradually sapped of its precious bodily fluids. Just like with instant coffee, but more so—and with fur.

"When the animal is completely dry," he says, "they weigh about 70 percent less than they do going in. There's no hair loss, no odor, and it'll last virtually forever. A small cat under ten pounds would take about twelve weeks. A Doberman will take six to eight months. Your average cat or dog, you're looking at two to three months. It's a slow process, but the animal has no place to go."

With Weber, at least, King or Fluffy will have company; the drum is one crowded menagerie. Today it holds three dead flying squirrels, five dead cats, one dead shark, one dead Doberman, two dead coral snakes, one dead garter snake, one dead Yorkshire terrier, one dead cockatiel, and a flounder (dead).

"The white cat here is just about finished. The Doberman has about four weeks to go or so. He's down to about fifty-one pounds. He was about ninety when he started. Pretty incredible. And every time we've returned a pet, the owner has cried."

Could it be over the bill? This process is not inexpensive. The average house cat in the lying position costs $350 to freeze-dry. A Doberman in an attack position runs about $1,800. Small birds start at $150. But when someone loves a pet, expense isn't always an issue.

Take John Scheuren. When his cat got nose cancer, the St. Petersburg businessman was loathe to simply put the animal to sleep. So after the euthanasia he freeze-dried Fred, and is glad that he did.

"It looked like a good alternative," Scheuren says. "A lot of people look at him and start petting him and don't realize he's freeze-dried . . . Sometimes we keep him on top of the TV, other days on top of the stereo, sometimes down behind the plant on the floor—just depending on what kind of mood we're in."

Cheryl Masciotra, a veterinarian's assistant, was less satisfied with the drying of her husband's pet lizard, Monte. She says Monte was freezer-burned, due to Preservation Specialities' inexperience with lizards. Yet, she says, she still believes in the process and would be pleased to try again.

Others are just as eager. Bait marketers are excited about the technology. Shrimp brokers are excited about the technology. And, of course, funeral homes are excited about the technology.

"They are very interested in the process," Weber says. "The biggest drawback seems to be the length of time it would take to freeze-dry a body.

"One funeral home in Miami said they would charge anywhere from $25,000 to $35,000 . . . Legally there are no laws against it, but ethically and morally there are questions I'm sure that are going to be raised. But the market is probably there. We envision the day of glass-top coffins and perpetual viewing chapels, 'cause once freeze-dried, the body will not deteriorate."

Like the drying itself, he says, "It's just a matter of time."

Topping the Octopus

WASHINGTON, D.C.—There's something very poignant about Ken Hakuta's office. Could it be the slime?

Yes, maybe it's the slime, the slime-in-a-can he has stowed amid the paperwork clutter on his desk. Or maybe it's the mechanical cat leg in the back room. Or the Celebrity Dirt. Or possibly, in the display case, the PocketSneeze-brand latex mucus.

Who's to say? In the end, maybe it is all these novelty items in the *aggregate* that bathe Hakuta and his business habitat in the smoky light of pathos.

For, after all, what is more pathetic than a man who has sold 150 million Wacky Wall Walkers and still hasn't had enough? What is more tragic than a sophisticated businessman (Hakuta is a fellow so connected that he can purchase his Silly Putty directly from the manufacturer by the pound) spanning the globe foraging for the nifty, sifting relentlessly through good ideas and bad in a vain quest for the next big fad.

"All I need is one item," he says.

He believes it, too. He believes to quench his desire he needs but one more toy phenomenon on the scale of the Wacky Wall Walker—the unctuous, bite-size thermoplastic octopus that sticks to smooth vertical surfaces and slowly crawls down. Thus Hakuta travels far and wide. Thus he haunts the toy fairs. Thus he pays $3,000 a month to monitor more than 100 calls a day on 1-800-USA FADS, his fad hotline. He has even devised for himself a heroic alter ego, Dr. Fad, the High Priest of Fads.

Ken Hakuta's whole sense of self depends on tasting it again: the power and the exhilaration of inciting mass hysteria.

"Not that I'm going to die if I don't," he says. "But if I can't come up with one . . . I'll be disappointed quite a lot."

Of course, should he manage to be struck by lightning a second time, Dr. Fad wouldn't be sated. The quest would only begin again. Ken Hakuta is not like the others, the others like Gary Dahl, who created the Pet Rock, basked in the spotlight, then slipped irrevocably back into obscurity.

"They are like their products," Hakuta says. "They are one-shot deals."

Is the compulsion not understandable? To have made millions producing glow-in-the-dark, wall-crawling octopods—to know that, had it been a different place and time, it might not have been a Wacky Wall Walker. It might have been a mood ring. It might have been a Slinky.

Oh, what Ken Hakuta knows. He has a factory, so he knows how to make toys. He has a battery of lawyers, so he knows how to secure patents and licenses. He has a research-and-development operation, so he knows how to turn an idea into a tangible prototype. He has a contact at every major media outlet, so he knows how to get publicity. He has a Harvard MBA, so he knows how to run a business.

And he has common sense, so he knows—in his heart of hearts—the odds of him producing the next big fad are infinitesimal. The problem, as he well understands, is that fads, by their very nature, are not made. They are phenomena. They just happen.

But that didn't stop Hakuta from trying to make a go out of the bird-shaped bird whistle you half fill with water and warble through. That hasn't deterred him from researching a superior bounceable modeling clay. That didn't keep him from promoting rainbow-vision novelty eyeglasses for all they were worth.

In some respects, Hakuta is like the author of a brilliant first novel, striving futilely to match his seminal inspiration. But he is not just a myth maker. In the world of Stupid Little Items, he is part of the myth. He is Wacky Wallwalking Hamlet, an Octopus Oedipus, a tragic hero for the ages.

"I could be. It's been four years since I did the Wall Walker.

If you'd asked me in January or February '83 am I going to come up with the next fad by the end of '86, I'd have said, 'Of *course* '86.' "

Of *course* he didn't make it. Of *course* he never will. Because he is searching the world for the answer found only within.

There is no peace in a butane Godzilla. The octopus has given you riches, Dr. Fad. Now, physician, heal thyself.

The Uphill Struggle of
the Kondom Kings

PRINCETON, N.J.—The world headquarters of The Logistix Group Inc., the international marketing concern, is Dennis Meseroll's bedroom.

Here, between the bed and the closet, next to the ironing board, just across from the Telex machine and beneath the portrait of Jesus, is the carton of merchandise: about 144 keychains with latex condoms encased in the fobs.

The box hasn't been disturbed in a while. The keychains are the sole item in The Logistix Group's "Imaginotions" line, and business is on the quiet side right now.

"Condoms just aren't moving at the moment," says Meseroll, a twenty-four-year-old graduate student and entrepreneur. He and his pal, marketing maven Mark Petravic, have joined forces to cash in on an unprecedented societal trend—a trend so momentous that Meseroll instantly retracts his initial characterization of the marketplace.

"Actually," he corrects, "the condom market is real hot. It's the condom keychain market that's sluggish."

Truth be known, it's really too early to tell. It was only last

April that Meseroll returned from his studies in Thailand, carrying with him what he regarded as a can't-miss novelty item. He'd never before seen a keychain whose clear plastic fob contained a removable prophylactic.

"We showed it around to a number of people," says Petravic, who has some previous experience in importing. "Everybody loved it. So, now that the thorough marketing research was done, we proceeded to get letterheads and business cards."

And spared no exaggeration doing it. The letterhead lists Meseroll and Petravic as specialists in marketing, public relations, and "social awareness programs"—all of which is true in the sense that it's only mostly false.

In any case, having reckoned that AIDS' effect on the overall condom market would make condom keychains an ideal by-the-cash register item at places like Spencer's Gifts, they set out to make their fortune.

They reasoned that our society is unquestionably highly sensitized to disease transmission—and a spate of other new products proved it their point. But unlike, say, the Speakeasy, a disposable pay phone–mouthpiece cover, and Le Funelle, a flushable paper device enabling women to urinate in public restrooms while standing up, the keychain would have both disease-prevention and entertainment value.

"We thought it was a great idea," Petravic says, "so we set out to put one in everybody's pocket and, I guess, become the Kondom Kings."

Thus their surprise at resistance from retailers and distributors.

"We haven't sold fifty-thousand or anything like that," Petravic says.

Twenty-five thousand?

"No."

Ten thousand?

"Just put: 'He was reluctant to disclose sales figures.' "

It wouldn't have taken him long. The only substantial order

so far, for one gross, came from an outfit that makes a body-flavoring product called Heaven Scent.

"They make things to squirt on your girlfriend in various flavors," Meseroll says. "They got a gross of them. We're still awaiting their check."

And while they're waiting, they're also wondering if maybe they didn't in some way miscalculate the demand for contraceptive conversation pieces.

Meseroll: "Spencer's said it just wasn't interested. A lot of people are really conservative about the legality of selling basically a pharmaceutical item. They don't want to get a phone call: 'The rabbit died. The stick turned blue.' It's not like a Pet Rock or whatever, where it's completely frivolous. It has a serious side some people don't want to be reminded of."

By no means are Meseroll and Petravic ready to surrender, however. These are uncommonly canny young men with a lot of instinct about business and not too many illusions.

The one thing they don't have going for them is genetic credentials. Meseroll's father was a government engineer and his mother a secretary. Petravic's parents are Ph.D. fusion researchers at Princeton's plasma physics lab—that is, not a single family member in the birth-control-novelty industry. But Petravic isn't worried. All he needs, he says, is patience.

"Also, a few large orders beyond our wildest dreams would be nice."

As the Worm Turns

While visiting California in February 1994, I happened to find myself scanning the classified section of the *Los Angeles Times*. There I spied a provocative two-line ad. In five brief words, the ad described an urgent need for growers, growers of a commodity you wouldn't think there would ever be an urgent need for. I was curious, so I dialed the advertised phone number, beginning what would be a strange odyssey of hopes and dreams and extravagant claims of both fabulous wealth and environmental salvation.

The ad was in the Business Opportunities section of the classifieds. It said, "Earthworm growers wanted. Huge profits. $ $ $." Then a phone number. So I dialed it and reached an outfit called Hy Hunter Industries, where a fellow named Bill Block told me an astounding story. The great Hy Hunter, the worm king, six decades in the earthworm business, was coming out of retirement not just to help folks make huge profits growing earthworms, but also to preserve the environment, to double the world food supply, to do nothing less than save mankind. It was an enticing idea.

I was in L.A. with some time to kill, so that very day I ventured out to Hunter's home and headquarters in suburban Grenada Hills. There, I strolled down a path dotted with giant statuary, beside the lobster pond and into his sprawling ranch home, over the creek running through his kitchen and up a winding steel staircase to worm central, a cluttered office with brown patches of mastic on the Sheetrock where the L.A. earthquake had rattled wall-to-wall mirrors into shards. Bill Block was busy working the phones, but he took a moment to explain how a small investment in what he called "the intestines of the world" could not help but rapidly multiply.

BILL BLOCK, HY HUNTER INDUSTRIES: Well, earthworms double every two months. You've got 500 earthworms one month. You got 1,000 in two months. You got 2,000 in four months. You buy the breeders, and you hold them for six, seven months. Let's see, if you've got 10,000, you go to 20,000. You got 40,000, you got 80,000. You got 160,000, you got

320,000. You got . . . you got a half million worms in less than a year.

BOB: [interviewing] And to sell them to who?

BLOCK: You sell them for the landfill people. You sell them . . . the people right now, the landfill people right now are needing billions of earthworms.

What he referred to was California Assembly Bill 939 mandating a 50 percent reduction in solid waste to the state's landfills by the year 2000. Among the ways to reduce organic wastes before they ever reach the landfills, it turns out, is to feed them to worms. Yes, to simply let nature take its course, not only taking these organics out of the waste stream, but yielding worm excrement, called castings, a rich, natural fertilizer. So to hear Bill Block tell it, there is a sudden demand for billions of earthworms, and, therefore, for thousands of enterprising earthworm growers. The phone calls responding to the same ad I saw rang through regularly.

BLOCK [on telephone, speaking to caller]: Okay, earthworm growers, huh? Okay, your name, please. Okay. Every day the phone rings with people like yourself. We have a six-acre ranch up here in Grenada Hills. Everything is organic up here. We grow tomatoes as big as grapefruit, and they *taste* like tomatoes, man. Where are you from anyway? What part of the . . . okay. What kind of work do you do? A machinist? Okay. Do you have a backyard? Do you own your own home? Okay. You qualify.

Block is voluble and very enthusiastic. Hy Hunter is world famous, he tells people. A real-estate tycoon, he says. On the board of lots of major corporations. In Block's estimation, Hy Hunter is just short of being a Christ figure, an environmental messiah, performing the solid waste equivalent of turning water into wine. So I was naturally keen on meeting the man—which, soon enough, I did, in the greenhouse out behind the garage.

Blinded with diabetes, Hunter is an unhealthy seventy-year-old who looks like a healthy fifty-year-old, with thick white hair and a pink baby face. Inside the greenhouse, he dug his hand into a container of what looked like potting soil.

HY HUNTER, HY HUNTER INDUSTRIES: This . . . it was all garbage, and if you look you can see that it looks like dirt. That . . .
EMPLOYEE: There's an earthworm right there.
HY HUNTER: Okay, there's . . . this is earthworm castings, and it's . . . people think it's black dirt. It's the finest fertilizer in the world. I can grow vegetables twice as fast as a farmer twenty-four hours a day.

That's why he's excited. That's why he suddenly revived a business that had been all but shut down, selling growerships like he hasn't done since the early 1970s. He is a man with a vision of environmental revolution, a sort of annelid alchemy, not water into wine so much as garbage into gold. He imagines turning landfills into theme parks, a sort of Six Flags over Refuse. And he wants you to join him.

HY HUNTER: I'm the most knowledgeable person in the world today in earthworms, or we call it vermiculture. And if people will listen to me, we can change the world.

[Over the sound of a large grinding machine]: *Garbage into the world's finest soil? Is this a fairy tale? The answer is: not necessarily. This is Canyon Recycling in La Jolla, California, just north of San Diego. Here each day, 100 tons of yard waste and scrap lumber are ground up, separated, cured, and spread out in eighteen vemiconversion wind rows. Trucks water them daily, but other than that nothing is done to the mounds but the addition of thousands upon thousands of earthworms. John Bierman, manager of Canyon Recycling, does what vermiculturalists love to do. He grabs me a big handful of crud.*

JOHN BIERMAN, CANYON RECYCLING: This is a combination of green waste and manure, and we slurry it into about . . . a solution about 70 percent moisture. The worms like it moist. And then we feed it on the beds with the side-discharge truck here. There's our workers. I just picked up a handful of manure and green waste in my hand, and I'm going to let Bob smell it here, and you can . . . you can tell me what it smells like.

BOB: [interviewing] It smells like nothing.

BIERMAN: That's right. The beauty of earthworms is when they get into the waste medium, the microbial populations that work in concert with them, they go right for the worst-smelling material and they mitigate it real effectively very quickly, within twenty-four to forty-eight hours.

Then after thirty to forty-five days, it's just a question of running the material through a worm separator, bagging the castings, and selling them as Vermi-Grow brand organic fertilizer at up to $120 per ton. Money to accept the green waste, money per bag to sell the byproduct, and all the while the workers are multiplying like crazy. No wonder entrepreneurs have pricked up their ears.

[The scene changes, to the sound of a baby cooing and a mother speaking baby talk]

This is the home of Eric and Debbie Wendt in Fallbrook, California. Eric's friend and longtime employee, John Roundtree, is visiting with his wife and baby, and it's a homey scene: two lovely families with small children and big dreams, distinguished from other middle-class Californians only by having 100,000 earthworms out in the backyard. Eric, thirty-six, and John, thirty-five, all of a sudden are ranchers in a big way all because, as John recalls it, he saw a newspaper lying in the street.

JOHN ROUNDTREE: I picked it up, looked down, and started looking through the classifieds, happened to see that there, called them up, and here I am growing earthworms.

ERIC WENDT: Yeah, he hit me with this, and it was, like, wow. You know, "What are you talking about? Earthworms?!" I knew nothing about it, absolutely nothing. And so we just got into it as far as the numbers that you need to make a profit. What we did was we bought a distributorship, which gives us an area in which basically we control, and within that area we are the only ones who can sell this worm.

They paid Hy Hunter Industries $15,000 for an exclusive distributorship and a 100,000 head of worm, now grazing out back in a greenhouse. But in eight or nine months, they expect to have 750,000 head and a quick return on their investment, even though Hunter does not guarantee he'll buy any worms back.

ERIC WENDT: No, there is no guarantee, and the reason for that is that he's got to get into a whole new set of contracts to be able to guarantee something like that. It has to do with . . . it has to do with a lot of things, and I'm not really sure. That did not bother me, getting into this business, because on my own I did some research just talking around, and I'm totally confident I can get rid of all of them myself.

BOB [interviewing]: What did your wife say when you said, "Hey, guess what?"

ERIC WENDT: That was an interesting evening.

DEBBIE WENDT: We said, "What?! You're going to invest *what* into *what?!*" But, you know, after they explained it to us, it seemed to be a pretty good idea. And so we stand behind them. We think it'll be fun. It'll be a good adventure.

ROUNDTREE: And the time is now. I mean, we're alive now. We're pioneering now. You know, we can't ride wagons across the Old West anymore, so we have to take what we have and make it better and make is usable, make it feasible.

There's only one problem. It may not be feasible. Experts in vermicomposting seem to agree that for now in the foreseeable future there is no burgeoning market for earthworms, in landfills or any-where else. Canyon Recycling, for instance, is running unprofitably at half capacity despite experienced, well-capitalized management with understanding of receiving, production, finance, mainte-nance, permitting, and marketing. It isn't making huge profits because, according to state officials, there are no huge profits to make.

WESLEY CHESBRO, CALIFORNIA INTEGRATED WASTE MANAGEMENT BOARD: Well, there seems to be an underlying assumption that earthworms are the single key to California's solid waste problems, and that's not the case.

Wesley Chesbro is chair of the California Integrated Waste Man-agement Board, which is actively encouraging individuals to throw their kitchen waste in small garage worm boxes, but in no way envisioning large-scale, statewide vermicomposting. At best, he says, worm ranching will be one of many methods used to reduce a fractional part of the state's waste stream.

CHESBRO: I don't see it as emerging as the . . . even for organics, as the . . . in the near future, as the central solution for organ-ics.

CLIVE EDWARDS, OHIO STATE UNIVERSITY: Well, it sounds a little bit dubious to me, to say the least.

Clive Edwards is professor of entomology at Ohio State University and probably the world's foremost academic authority on com-mercial vermicomposting. He's generally bullish on various pilot projects around the world, but he says that right now there is no industry to speak of and certainly no pent-up earthworm demand. To him, claims to the contrary are eerily reminiscent of the mid-1970s, when a vermiculturalist named Ronald Gaddie ran a com-bined pyramid and Ponzi scheme with earthworm profits as the bait. The network grew to more than 10,000 mainly West Coast investor/growers. Then in 1978, a can of legal worms opened and the annelid pyramid collapsed.

EDWARDS: It's not the first time that this sort of operation has been marketed, and it's not turned out very well in the past in my experience. In fact, it's turned out very badly once or twice. So I would have some certain reservations about that market being there.

Ominous warnings or no, Hy Hunter's salespeople are having little difficulty selling growerships and distributorships to eager entrepreneurs. In May, three months after my first visit, I returned to Hunter Industries, and I hadn't even gotten out of my car when I saw a growership deal on the verge of being closed right in the driveway. The salesperson was Hy's niece, Holly Hunter. The prospect's name was Vicki Shafner.

BOB: [interviewing] So how close are you to getting involved in the worm industry?
VICKI SHAFNER: Well, as close as you can get without doing it.
BOB: [interviewing] Are you impressed with what you see?
SHAFNER: Yeah, I really am. Holly seems like a very nice person, and I agree with organic fertilizers and our problem of landfills. I've always liked worms.

And she seems to like worm ranching, at least more than previous investments in gold mines, oil wells, even an ostrich farm that never quite fulfilled its promise.

SHAFNER: Yeah, I'm a risk taker. There's an awful lot of people that are afraid to do anything that sounds the least bit offbeat, and I always investigate everything. Why not? One of these times something's going to work. I like the worms. They seem like actually the best. At least the initial . . . the initial investment is not huge, and that's nice. That sounds real good to me.

HOLLY HUNTER, HY HUNTER INDUSTRIES: To buy into a business that's going to be good for the environment as well as for your pocketbook, per se, this is probably the least amount of money I've ever seen to get involved in a business to double your original investment after ten months and the second year make $20,000 to $30,000, if not more, depending on how aggressive you want to be.

[Over the sound of a heavy object banging down on a truck bed]: *A few minutes later, I ran into Brian Lehman, whose brand new worm bin was being loaded into his pickup truck.*

BRIAN LEHMAN: It's not a lot. It's not a big investment, actually. I just forked over $5,000, but I'm sure that I should be seeing that back very quickly, being a distributor, just to do what I just did, set people up and to start them into the growing of this business. Everybody thinks it's a great idea, and now it's just a matter of convincing them to go ahead and take a little bit of risk and get in where the market is.

LUTHER HUNTER, HY HUNTER INDUSTRIES: [the scene shifts to Hy Hunter's living room] Do you want to finance it through Beneficial?

PROSPECT: Well, we don't know if we want to spend that much money yet.

LUTHER HUNTER: Well, if you want to be a distributor . . .

Even as Lehman drove off with his worm bin, Hy Hunter's brother, Luther, was pouring it on to sign another couple to a distributorship deal, and it was a scene to behold.

PROSPECT: Well, I have to crawl first, though.

LUTHER HUNTER: Well, if you want to crawl . . .

HY HUNTER: I always suggest that.

LUTHER HUNTER: . . . at the $2,000 level. All right, that's 10,000 worms. I would suggest, if you're going to do it, to do it at the 2,000 level because you're going to be . . .

PROSPECT: That's our average goal.

LUTHER HUNTER: You're going to have 300,000 . . .

As it happens, two weeks ago Luther Hunter left his brother's company in pursuit of another opportunity, and promoter Bill Block last week followed him out the door, leaving others to assume the mantle of salesmanship and exaggeration. For instance, Hy Hunter isn't, as Block told me, a real estate magnate. He freely admits losing a fortune speculating in real estate. And he isn't on the board of lots of major corporations. He's on the board of zero major corporations. And if he's world famous, it somehow slipped past the attention of Who's Who. *But he did make a big killing in worms back in the late 1960s and early 1970s when pyramider Ron Gaddie built his great invertebrate Cheops. But this time Hy says the gigantic market is really and truly there, no matter what red flags the naysayers raise about demand.*

HY HUNTER: I get that question every day, Bob. I don't think in your lifetime that we could ever grow enough worms to satisfy the demand to the garbage dumps alone for recycling. I really believe this, that earthworms are the salvation of mankind. Right now we're entering the earthworms and the enzymes into toilets, human toilets, so there would be no more sewage, which is remarkable. We also . . . in Australia, they've been experimenting with feeding contaminated waste, heavy metal, to earthworms, and they'll eat a certain percentage of it, and then they'll stop, and then they eat other organic material. And then they'll come back and they eat contaminated waste. And their excrement is pure. It's the finest fertilizer with no signs of, you know, hydrogen or atomic material at all that they've developed.

BOB: [interviewing] This enzyme will break down heavy metals and radioactive waste?

HY HUNTER: Not the enzymes, the earthworms. What do you do with contaminated heavy metal or materials, you know, that are . . . have been spiced with atoms or hydrogen bombs or something like this? I think that the worms can dispose of it, and we're working on that right now.

Earthworms neutralizing enriched uranium. The more you talk with Hy Hunter, blind visionary, the more you wonder what will become of all the people investing $2,000 and $5,000 and $15,000 at a pop and more, way more. Meet George Bodlak, as he drives me in his pickup to the Temecula, California, home of his very own, brand-new Ecology Farms.

GEORGE BODLAK, VERMICULTURALIST: I have been in construction as a builder of single family homes. I've been involved in manufacturing of after-market products. I have been involved in recycling of plastic waste. I made . . . I made a living. Unfortunately, in most of these situations, I end up working for the banks.

BOB: [interviewing] And why is this one different?

BODLAK: This one is different because the market is endless for the end product of our operation, which is the composting worms. The demand for worms is going to skyrocket. The golden rule, he who has the gold rules, and I feel he who has the worms is going to be in the driver's seat in the very near future.

His spread is on six acres now home to a mere 148 worm bins, each the size of a big footlocker. Soon, however, Ecology Farms will have 1,000 lockers full.

BODLAK: So the total capacity of the bin population is going to be close to 500,000 pounds of worms, as they fully mature and breed and propagate.

BOB: [interviewing] So how much money do you have invested in this operation to date?

BODLAK: Right now, about $50,000. And to bring it up to full capacity, it's going to be at least tenfold, ten times as much.

BOB: [interviewing] Half a million dollars.

BODLAK: Yes.

BOB: [interviewing] Is there a Mrs. Bodlack?

BODLAK: Yes, there is.

BOB: [interviewing] And what does she have to say about all this?

BODLAK: She thinks I'm nuts.

I wouldn't necessarily bet against George Bodlak. Some people will make money as worm ranching slowly takes hold, and it may well be him—or not. The point isn't whether this venture is finally the one that frees him from his bankers forever. The point is he's trying, daring to dream. Maybe, he says, it's an impossible dream, a futile, quixotic tilt at a windmill he mistakes for financial destiny. But maybe it isn't. And if it isn't, well, then . . . the worm turns.

BODLAK: To give you an example, when Henry Ford came up he was going to manufacture cars. Some people told him he's crazy because people were driving around in horse and buggies. So there is a certain amount of risk involved in every business. There are no guarantees that you're going to go into business and you're going to be successful. I believe that right now we're on the threshold of an industry that is going to explode. It's an industry that's badly needed. And I believe I'm in the right place at the right time. We know the market exists. We know the market is there. We know the need is there. We know the waste is there. All we know is we need the worms to make this work.

PART
3

Bobby Strikes Out

Wheel of Misfortune

Ready for some wholesome family fun? Complete this quotation from Buddhist scripture: "Who have not lived a holy life . . ."

A . . . are doomed to an unholy death."

B . . . may never enter the temple, even with their shoes off."

C . . . feed like rats and politicians on the goodness of others."

D . . . brood like decrepit herons in a pond where the fish have died."

The correct answer, believe it or not, is D, the business about decrepit herons in a stagnant pond. That according to *Familiar Quotations,* which dates the catchy proverb to the third century B.C. The other answers—shoes and politicians and unholy death and so forth—I made up just now. I swear. Here, try again:

In 1986, an Indonesian teacher named Sunardi sat motionless for fifteen hours. Why?

A. He was a contestant in the Indonesian Motionlessness Festival.

B. An emerald frond viper was coiled on his desk poised to attack him.
C. He was protesting a government regulation forcing teachers to stand at the blackboard for the entire school day.
D. Students in his punishment hall did not realize he was dead.

Answer: A.

Honest to goodness. It happened July 21, 1986, according to the *Guinness Book of World Records, 1989,* as Sunardi surpassed all previously recorded human achievement in the ultracompetitive sphere of motionless sitting. As for the other answers, they just came to me as I sat at my keyboard. There's no such thing as an "emerald frond viper," but it sounded real to me. And to you too, I'll bet. Odds are you were completely fooled, if not by the viper then by one of the other phony answers, which are designed to sound nearly as improbable as the peculiar truth, but with perhaps the slightest whiff of plausibility.

Kind of fun, isn't it, being bamboozled by these silly bluffs and sillier facts? Or maybe you beat the odds. Maybe you picked one of the right answers. Maybe you picked both of the right answers and are feeling pretty darned smug right now. Either way—and I can back this up with research—you probably want to try again. Okay. One more:

Fedorov, Konstantinov, and Garpenlov are Red . . . what?

A . . . Army generals convicted of high treason in the failed coup attempt against Gorbachev.
B . . . caviar. Three varieties of same. One from salmon, one from sturgeon, one from lump fish.
C . . . Wings. On Detroit's National Hockey League team.
D . . . heads, constituting *The Three Beet Heads,* Russian TV's slapstick answer to the Marx Brothers.

That was an easy one. Any hockey fan recognizes that these fellows are, yes, C, Detroit Red Wings. At least they were in 1991, when I came up with the question for my new television quiz show, *KnowItAll!*, billed as "the *other* game in Washington where players lie, dodge, and bluff their way through thorny questions they can't really answer." Because the three Red Wings were well known to such a large number of people, that particular question was never on television.

For that matter, neither was *KnowItAll!*

Despite several tens of thousands of dollars of investment by WETA-TV, a successful pilot, influential friends, official enthusiasm at the Public Broadcasting Service, and a concept demonstrated to charm viewers of all ages, my pet project did not take this fall season by storm as it was intended to do. Nor will it be a mid-season replacement. Nor, in all likelihood, will it ever be anything more than what it is now:

A. The most expensive videocassette in my collection.
B. The most painfully won bit of cocktail conversation I'd ever care to have.
C. A cautionary tale about tele-ambition.

The answer is D. All of the above.

I blame Steve Rosenbaum.

He's my pal the TV entrepreneur who produces two weekly regional newsmagazines, *Broadcast: New York* and *Broadcast: New England*, from studios in Saratoga Springs, New York. He's a relentlessly ambitious guy, always looking to expand his talents, opportunities, broadcast outlets, and, of course, revenues. By the fateful August day in 1991 when he phoned me about his latest coup, I had grown accustomed to hearing stories about his forays into the Big Time. One week a good meeting at Viacom. The next week a powwow with a top guy at Fox. Then maybe a deal producing a documentary for A&E. This call, however, was different. Steve had arranged to call on Phil Beuth, president of late-night programming at ABC.

"I told him," Steve explained triumphantly, "that I have an idea to transition from *Nightline* to late-night."

Impressive. For years, the network had struggled for a program that would interest the news junkies who watch Ted Koppel and the actual junkies who watch after 1 A.M. A show with L.A. deejay Rick Dees had been a disaster. And a test of six live talk/variety ideas, then in progress in Hartford, was not going well. Apparently, Steve said, Beuth couldn't wait to hear the Rosenbaum solution.

"There's just one problem," Steve said.

"Yeah? What problem would that be?"

"I don't have an idea to transition from *Nightline* to late-night. Do you, by any chance?"

Me? Why would I? Steve's the television guy. I'm in journalism, a columnist and critic for *Advertising Age,* where I earn a living basically by making fun of TV commercials. I also do radio as a commentator and roving feature correspondent for NPR, and had once futilely attempted to package a business news magazine show for PBS. But until Steve's call, I'd given scarcely a moment's thought to the midnight-to-1 A.M. slot on ABC. Yet, either because he has the utmost respect for my judgment and inventiveness, or because he was a desperate man, he was looking for help from me.

"What about a game show?" he asked.

"Look, Steve," I said, in exasperation, "I understand your predicament, but I'm in the middle of writing a column. I'm on deadline and I don't think I can be of any . . . *game show?*"

That quickly it came to me. Virtually all of it. The look: retro sixties, in the quaintly primitive fashion of *What's My Line?* The format: a bluffing game, like "the dictionary game" I'd played at parties, but with general information (not just word definitions). The cast: weekly regulars plus a guest celebrity. I even heard the theme music: a Henry Mancini number from *The Pink Panther.* It all came cascading forth. A bona fide epiphany.

How do these things happen? It had never occurred to me to fashion a game of any sort, much less a televised one, and here in the space of seconds a TV program was blossoming in my mind's eye, a spontaneously generating blueprint destined radically to change—i.e., spoil—the next year of my life. "I'll call you back in one hour," I told Steve, whereupon I knocked out my column and, in one remarkable burst of energy, committed breathlessly to paper ideas for a new kind of quiz show that was new principally by seeming thirty years old: "It's *What's My Line?* meets Trivial Pursuit meets *Liar's Club* meets *My Word* meets *Hollywood Squares* . . . It's spontaneous and outrageous and habit-forming. It's . . . *KnowItAll!*"

Steve loved the idea.

Problem was, ABC had an hour to fill, not thirty minutes. Thus did his Broadcast News Network staff begin kneading and expanding *KnowItAll!* to fit the space theoretically allotted to it. The result was something called *Equal Time America,* which was a talk show for the first half hour, after which the cast would reassemble elsewhere on the set to play a current events–filled version of *KnowItAll!* Please don't smirk. To you, with the benefit of objectivity and common sense, a talk/game show is clearly a ridiculous combination born of naked expediency. In the television world, where enough naked expediency can earn you obscene fortunes and a lifetime achievement Emmy, it is something else altogether. It is a Concept. Five days later, we were in Phil Beuth's office to unveil it.

Lo and behold, he was impressed. He was so impressed he took us—lowly us!—immediately into his confidence. With disarming candor, he spent an hour enumerating his problems as a programmer. Heady wine, that.

"I'm not a network," he revealed, "I'm a syndicator. I can't clear shows with my own affiliates." Turns out local stations aren't all that interested in what ABC serves up after midnight, because they can get better audiences, and more revenue, showing *Matlock* reruns they acquire themselves. Nothing personal meant toward us young folks, Phil said, but he'd just spent $1.6 million on six Concepts in Connecticut, and not one of them was likely to ever see the light of day.

Sure, it was the big brush-off, but we trundled off with smiles on our little faces. Phil Beuth, senior vice president of ABC, took us seriously! We were players! If we'd only hit on the idea a few months earlier, before he'd socked his dough in Hartford, we'd be . . . well, it was easy to imagine. Little did we know that Phil Beuth humors all pathetic, anonymous supplicants by telling them his problems.

"Did he say he was in the syndication business?" an executive at Arts & Entertainment cable network asked me, a year later.

"Uh-huh."

"Yeah, that's what he tells everybody."

And that's how, in five short days, I didn't achieve wealth and fame in commercial network television. Not achieving wealth and fame in public television took much, much longer.

If you've ever played the informal parlor game "dictionary," or its slick board game derivative, Balderdash, you already know the basics of *KnowItAll!* In them, an extremely obscure word is chosen and players anonymously write what they consider to be plausible-sounding definitions on slips of paper. The bluffs are mixed in with the correct definition, and then read aloud. Players then vie to discern the true definition from among the bluffs, with points awarded accordingly.

KnowItAll! is essentially the same, except that the questions aren't limited to obscure words, embracing instead all manner of esoterica. Hence questions ranging from the definition of "hippopotomonstrosesquipedalian" (answer: "referring to an extremely long word") to the technical description of Benjamin

Franklin's invention, the air bath (answer: breathing deeply while sitting naked in a window).

Unlike in the play-at-home games, *KnowItAll!* questions are posed by an emcee for a panel of four players (three regulars and a guest celebrity). Following each round of answers, contestants drawn from the studio audience evaluate what they've heard and try to identify the KnowItAll—i.e., the one panelist who has been supplied in advance with the correct answer. The KnowItAll changes from round to round, as does the difficulty of the questions. In the last round, called "The Big Lie," all of the panelists are briefed about the question and prepare minute-long tall tales designed to amuse and buffalo the contestants, the studio audience, and the viewers—all the panelists, that is, except the KnowItAll, who spins out a true tale designed to amuse and buffalo everybody. As you can see by now, the ease of contriving bluffs as improbable as the correct answers, while generating laughs in the process, is the heart and soul of the game.

Or would have been, had Phil Beuth only recognized the antidote to Rick Dees when he saw it.

For a couple of months after the meeting at ABC, I gave *Know-ItAll!* no further thought. But then, in late November, I came to my senses: You simply don't invest twelve or fifteen hours in something like a quiz show idea only to let it go after meeting one tiny obstacle, such as abject network disinterest. Maybe there was another more hospitable venue. PBS? Why not? Faced with competition from cable, the network was undergoing an excruciating public reassessment of its programming mission— a reassessment veering inexorably toward enhanced entertainment value. With a Washington spin, arcane information and its demands on the critical-thinking skills of contestants and home viewers, maybe *KnowItAll!* was just the ticket for the new PBS. Certainly it was worth a call to my friends at Channel 26.

In 1991, the vice president for news and public affairs at WETA-TV was Ricki Green. Ricki is an accomplished producer and documentarian with walls full of Peabody Awards, Emmys, and other hard-won trophies of a distinguished television career. Her executive producer and immediate subordinate at the time was Dick Richter, who had spent the greater part of his career at ABC News. Their boss was Richard Hutton, senior vice president and executive producer in charge of all WETA production. And I knew all of them.

How? From my previous failure as a TV wannabe, with a show-that-never-was called *BottomLine,* which was to be a weekly business news magazine, but which, after eighteen months of painstaking development in 1989 and '90, was judged by a mid-level PBS executive not to merit serious consideration. Never mind the gory details. Suffice to say I was well-enough acquainted with Ricki, Dick, and Richard to get them into a meeting on the basis of one phone call.

"I have another idea," I told Dick. "Nothing like *BottomLine.* This one has no substance. It has no redeeming social value. In fact, it's completely frivolous in every way. So, I'm thinking PBS will probably go for it."

"You may be right," he said. "What's your idea?"

And I told him everything. And he sort of liked it. And Ricki Green sort of liked it. And Richard Hutton, who turns out to be a games freak, sort of loved it. And on December 13, 1991, we all got together, along with Steve Rosenbaum and his lawyer and WETA's lawyer to talk about it. And next thing I knew, we had a general agreement to proceed toward a pilot.

Here's the part I won't bore you with: the part about writing scripts and quiz questions, about planning eight run-through games, about spending Saturdays in libraries poring over such dusty volumes as the *Dictionary of Mythology* for weird trivia, about trying to squeeze a production budget out of WETA, about working out kinks in the game format, about sitting in the U.S. Trademark Office looking to see if the term "know-itall" was already reserved by another TV producer (answer: no, though a trademark was issued for an independently published geography board game that never made it into general distribution), about taking sandwich orders for everybody at the run-throughs and fetching the food, about learning the elusive argot of TV production ("You don't know what you don't know," Ricki Green wisely, and correctly, and witheringly informed me), about dealing with lawyers in negotiating a contract with WETA, about still trying to squeeze production help out of WETA, and about a hundred other chores connected with transforming my quiz show epiphany into reality. But you should know about casting.

The emcee, from the very beginning, was Emil Guillermo, a fellow I knew from his brief stint as a weekend host on NPR. I feared Emil would be resistant (what journalist wants to be the next Wink Martindale?) but I also thought he'd be perfect for the job. He's quick-witted, has a great voice, and is sort of impishly handsome. Fortunately, when I phoned him about an audition, Emil latched onto the idea instantaneously. This is the advantage of epiphanies; they reveal absolute truth.

Casting the panel was trickier. If there were to be three regular panelists, and I were to be one of them (look, it's my bat and my ball), there remained two slots. One, I was sure, had to be Timothy Dickinson, of whom I shall say more presently. The other had to be a minority woman—this for all the good reasons of diversity and cultural representation, and for all the bad reasons of satisfying the gender/race bean counters at PBS. Thus did I consider it kismet when, out of the blue, I picked up my telephone one December day and found, on the other end of the line, Anna Perez.

Barbara Bush's press secretary, a total stranger to me, was calling to remark about something I'd written. Anna is professionally glib, funny, both Hispanic and black, and a woman. I quickly turned the conversation in another direction.

"So tell me," I said, "do you happen to remember *To Tell the*

Truth?" She remembered it all right. On December 17 we lunched at the Bombay Club. On January 16, 1992, she was on hand for the first run-through of *KnowItAll!*

On hand too was Timothy, a rumpled, heavyset English gent who at one time supplied columnist George Will with pithy quotations, historical references, and other bits of erudition. This would have been easy work for Timothy, who knows everything. Everything—from the day of the week of any date you give him to the origins of marzipan to the nitty-gritty details of the Peloponnesian War. Cobbling out a meager living as a freelance editor and consultant, he has no checking account nor visible assets, but possesses remarkable knowledge of the classics combined with keen wit and phenomenal memory. He's also a bit . . . shall we say iconoclastic? A disheveled fixture on the streets of Georgetown, he dresses in grubby striped trousers, waistcoat, bowler hat, and formal shirt often bedaubed with traces of his most recent meal. His hair is longish and unkempt flopping over his forehead. He looks, in short, like a refugee from *The Pickwick Papers.* A font of knowledge and a genuine eccentric: the perfect panelist for a quiz show trading on personality.

Thus, with my poet friend Miles Moore filling the seat of the guest panelist, we commenced the first attempt at playing *KnowItAll!* The culmination of a month of eighty-hour workweeks! The test of an epiphany!

Conservatively speaking, it was pitiful.

Marching orders were for answers to be brief. Pithy. Authoritative. In the run-through, however, they were typically long, tentative, and, worst of all, dull. Timothy, asked to supply the definition of "anacardic," launched into a fifty-second discourse on something to do with "the evacuation of Persia by the beaten army." His precise text I cannot be sure of because in addition to having total recall of material you and I don't really care about, he also has a tendency to mumble and swallow words in an already barely penetrable Etonian accent.

Later came the question: "A 'tormentor,' a 'wheel,' and 'stretchers' are found where?" To give you an idea of how the game is supposed to work, my response was, "In Madonna's rec room." That is what we in the TV business call a "joke," and everybody laughed, whereupon I quickly disavowed the answer and tendered my actual bluff: "Tools an artist uses to stretch canvas over frames." Between the gag and the real bluff, I expended about fifteen seconds. Timothy, by contrast, consumed ninety seconds in a flight of mostly unintelligible fancy about Copernican astronomy.

The whole game was supposed to last twenty-seven minutes, give or take thirty seconds. It ran to forty-eight minutes, or exactly one third my diastolic blood pressure. And yet . . . and yet . . . the thing was . . . fun? Yes, fun. The panelists, the contestants (my office mates), and the representatives of WETA all had a very good time. They were engaged by the questions, challenged by the bluffs, and amused by the repartee. Anna was particularly brilliant. Having signed on provisionally on the chance of becoming, as she put it, "the black Dorothy Kilgallen," she required no warm-up to assume the air of arch authority required to cheerfully, convincingly, charmingly lie through one's teeth. She had but one lackluster bluff, in response to the question, "Complete this quotation from Aeschylus: 'A great ox . . .' " The correct answer was ". . . stands on my tongue." Anna's bluff was, ". . . pulls a great wagon"— the triteness of which drew a derisive remark from Emil. But Anna was not about to concede the point. "Look," she retorted, "he didn't hit them out of the park every time."

Blaming the dull answer on Aeschylus! The woman was a natural. Timothy, on the other hand, struggled somewhat with the concept. Steeped as he is in ancient history and the literary classics, his answers tended to concern the Middle Ages. "The University of California at Irvine's basketball team is called what?" he was asked. The correct answer was "the Anteaters." Timothy's answer was: "The Isaurians."

The Isaurians? Sure, the Fightin' Isaurians of Irvine. That scans. Yet, when all was said and done, the single element of the game everybody seemed most to enjoy was . . . him. Nobody had the slightest idea of what he was talking about at any juncture, but still they found him fascinating, lovable, and hilarious. As we broke up for the evening, Ricki Green and I had little to say to each other, but there was something in her smile and expression I could read. It said, "Bob, this game is a diamond in the rough, but a huge and valuable diamond it is. In the coming weeks and months, together we will cut it, polish it, and make it sparkle like no gem has sparkled before!"

Sure enough, the next run-through went better, and the next better than that. Then, a critical test: our first live production of *KnowItAll!*, March 3, 1992, for approximately forty students at George Washington University. With pilot tapings scheduled for March 17—exactly two weeks hence—the GWU run-through was our first objective measure of how well the game worked with a live audience. Would they get into the game? Understand the rules? Enjoy the panel? Like the host? If the answer to all of those questions was "yes," the future of my brainchild was merely in doubt. If the answer to all of them was "no," well, thanks very much, Bob, you didn't win fame and fortune, but we hope you'll enjoy the home version of your game.

We did two shows. Both went . . . splendidly.

Asked to grade the game and participants in nineteen categories, the students were virtually uniform in their approval. On a scale of 1 to 5, they rated *KnowItAll!* 4.36 on "entertaining," 4.32 on "funny," 4.04 on "challenging." In the areas of capability, charm, and entertainment, the panelists as a group averaged 4.2. Thus spake the students! The young people! The future of public broadcasting!

Turns out that I misread that significant expression on Ricki Green's face. What I took to mean "this is a diamond in the rough" turned out to be, "Buddy, I am *outta* here." On February 5, the day after the second pair of run-throughs, Ricki quit WETA to start her own company. I was truly sorry to see her go. She had been an ally through two of my tilts at the PBS windmill, and wise counsel in both. Still, Dick Richter, who would temporarily fill her position, was on my side. And the big production boss, Richard Hutton, was utterly committed to the project.

For instance, a couple of days before the GWU test, he and Dick at long last assigned associate producer Kate Urbank to work with me. WETA also came up with a studio, director, and crew for the pilot shoot—although not on March 17. We had to push the date to April 10, the day before the vacation I'd planned for six months. No problem. (How difficult could it be to get four panelists and an emcee to radically change their schedules on virtually no notice? Hardly any of the participants were White House employees subject to the travel whims of the First Lady.) In any event, the extra few days of planning time looked like they might come in handy. In the five weeks after GWU, all we had to do was write two shows, design and build a set (for no money, because WETA couldn't come up with actual cash to build or rent furniture, flats, etc.), locate a Washington celebrity willing to be the guest panelist, recruit and assemble a studio audience, audition and hire an announcer, build the opening title sequence, locate and produce the Henry Mancini number I wanted for the theme ("It Had Better Be Tonight"), persuade the *Encyclopaedia Britannica* to donate two sets of books as prizes, finish negotiating the contract, and hire an outside producer to oversee the production. Among 100 other errands.

Which we succeeded in doing. Then WETA canceled our studio date again, in favor of a cash-paying customer wanting to rent it April 10.

This is where Steve Rosenbaum, who was my ever-more-frustrated adviser/partner in this venture, began to lose his patience. The combination of unilateral rescheduling, the station's refusal to spend real money on a set, and its too-little-too-late providing of Kate's half-time assistance had his blood boiling.

"Do you see what they're doing?" he asked, in one of our daily phone conversations. "Do you see what these people are doing?"

"Being a plodding, impoverished bureaucracy?" I replied, giving my WETA friends the benefit of the doubt.

"No. They're killing you with indifference. They don't care about this show."

"They care," I said. "They just don't have many resources."

"You just wait. They are incrementally compromising your idea. They are a malevolent force."

A bit harsh, I thought. The Evil Documentarians of Shirlington? Nah. But this difference of opinion on WETA's motives served us well in the contract negotiations, an episode so horrifying I won't recount it, except to make one observation: The station's naked greed and self-dealing was of astonishing proportions. It was opportunism, avarice, and arrogance on a mythic scale—exceeded only by our own. In a dispute over (strictly theoretical) revenue, we wound up in a nightmarish game of chicken that extended to ten minutes before an 11 A.M. deadline on Friday, April 10. Words alone cannot convey the tension, the harrowing, nerve-racking misery of that deadline day. Steve and I made it quite clear we were prepared to let the whole thing go up in smoke unless WETA conceded more compensation to us. We'd been invited to share in a meal, and we weren't about to be fed scraps in the kitchen—although, if we didn't have an agreement by 10:55 A.M., I, personally, was prepared to call WETA and say, "We'll take the scraps."

There was no need, however. At 10:50 A.M., the other side blinked. We struck a deal. The pilots were rescheduled for April 16, smack dab in the middle of my vacation. Here again, no problem. I made arrangements to fly in.

•   •   •

Henry Kissinger couldn't make it. Nor Jesse Jackson, nor any of the fifty-some Washington heavyweights we recruited for the guest slot. Hodding Carter and Jody Powell provisionally agreed, then ditched me. This left Christopher Matthews, the author/columnist/pundit, who graciously agreed to waive his dignity for the good of public TV.

It had been an obstacle-strewn path, but finally, thanks to an Olympian eleventh-hour effort by WETA, we had arrived. In mid-March, Dick had hired Consuelo Gonzalez, ex of ABC, to produce, and she was wonderful. With no budget to speak of, she crafted a cleverly cartoonish opening sequence (featuring the Mancini musical theme) and a mainly monochromatic visual look to suggest our black-and-white progenitors. The set, executed by WETA's Eric Schaeffer, was what you might call stylized minimalism—mimicking the stuffy, filigreed formality of a nineteenth-century parlor in simple, whimsical line drawings.

Kate Urbank, meanwhile, despite numerous scheduling changes, managed to fill the studio with a live audience and recruit four skilled, personality-filled contestants: a National Symphony personnel staffer, a retired French and Latin teacher, a housewife/student, and a Navy captain, in uniform, no less. By the time the music came up for the first show, everything that could be in place was in place. The only thing that could go wrong was . . . everything else.

It didn't.

The shows went smoothly. Seamlessly. Entertainingly. Wonderfully. Sometimes hilariously. Miraculously!

Chris Matthews was capable and charming. Anna was typically, persuasively engaging. Emil was affable, pleasant, and generally well in control. I was . . . well, modesty forbids. And even Timothy was almost succinct and on the hilarious verge of being coherent. Asked to name the landmark in the direct vista of Ferdinand Marcos's temporary Hawaiian tomb, he replied:

"The temple to Captain Cook as a slain god. This was felt to be obscurely appropriate, but the obscurity has defeated me so I shan't elaborate."

Later, the question was, "The Federal Aviation Administration is considering a rule change that would permit airline pilots to do what their military counterparts have done for years. What may they soon be permitted to do?"

My answer was: "Secretly bomb Cambodia," which got a nice laugh before I, as KnowItAll in that round, withdrew it in favor of the truth: "Sleep, on transoceanic flights." Timothy said something about giving name, rank, and serial number in case of capture. Capture? The audience roared.

Throughout both games, there was not only laughter, but gales of laughter and spontaneous applause. The bluffs not only fooled, but fooled completely. Despite having been cooped up in a poorly ventilated lobby for an hour waiting for our technical run-through to end, the audience was palpably enthusiastic and unequivocally won over. Shooting both shows took an hour and a half, after which the mood in the control room was a kind of suppressed euphoria. Entertaining! Informative! Challenging! Funny! We had succeeded on every score. And in exactly twenty-seven minutes each time. I flew back to Tennessee that night, visions of Emmy statuettes dancing in my head. Amid pirouetting dollar signs. Bob Garfield, heeeeere's what you've WON!!!!!

The euphoria, of course, quickly gave way to a more realistic assessment of the pilot episodes. Yes, as a game, *KnowItAll!* worked. Yes, the studio audience was won over. Yes, the cast—individually and as a group—worked well. But there were plenty of bugs to be worked out. Timothy was still largely unintelligible. There was no major Washington celebrity. A few of the set elements looked not so much minimal as amateurish. And, above all, the pacing was too slow, with the correct answer so long in coming that it was easy to forget what the original question was.

Nevertheless, of the six top WETA executives who filed written comments on the pilots, four were overwhelmingly positive. A fifth liked the game but emphatically thought it wasn't WETA's cup of tea. Then there was the one person who didn't bother to list detailed impressions, and instead scribbled her reaction in a note to Richard Hutton:

"Almost a parody of PTV [public television] . . .

"Not that engaging . . .

"OK to proceed if want to . . .

"I don't have instant reliable reaction . . ."

I'd have dismissed those remarks as careless and superficial, except that they came from the station president, Sharon Percy Rockefeller. Not THAT engaging?! Should I have worried? Richard Hutton said no. The only important words, he said, were "OK to proceed."

On this basis, we decided to do two things: (1) plan another pair of pilot episodes, and (2) show the first pilot to Mitch Semel, vice president of programming at PBS. The idea was to give him a chance to recommend changes himself—just on the off chance we might want to incorporate them into the next pilot. ("Bob, don't you think green would be a nice color for Emil's tie?" "You read my mind, Mitch." "Bob, don't you think the panel should be fired?" "What, those clowns? They're gone, Mitch." "Bob, would you be kind enough to lend me one of your mother's kidneys?" "Left or right, Mitch?")

This strategy was not without risk; the pilot had a lot of rough edges. While Mitch could not himself green-light *Know-It All!*—that would have to be a consensus decision, hinging largely on the feelings of Mitch's boss and PBS's top programmer, Jennifer Lawson—he could certainly kill it all by himself. So crucial was his positive reaction, in fact, that Richard Hutton and Dick Richter made another strategic decision: not to let me talk to the guy. Apparently they were concerned I might somehow submarine our chances, perhaps by making an intemperate remark, or a small joke ripe for misinterpretation.

Why would they be concerned about that? They weren't with me at the National Press Club on the day I ran into Jennifer Lawson at a reception and briefly mentioned my project.

"Well," she said diplomatically, "I look forward to seeing *KnowItAll!*"

"I hope so," I said, "because I know your home number. I know where you park your car. Basically, I will stalk you for the rest of my life. I swear I will. I swear!" Then I laughed diabolically, like Dracula sidekick Renfield, and excused myself.

I'm pretty sure she knew I was kidding.

As it happened, I was out of town on June 8, when Dick met with Mitch. But Dick faxed me a memo on Mitch's reaction, the key sentence in which was: "He liked it."

"He thought it might be good at eight o'clock," Dick reported. Eight o'clock! Family hour! Prime time! We set a late July date to shoot a second pair of pilot episodes, refining the game and otherwise incorporating Mitch's suggestions. Then as a practical matter, it would only be a question of impressing Jennifer Lawson exactly as we'd impressed him.

Ch-CHING!!!

The sound you just heard was cash registers going off in my head.

On July 9, 1992, Richard Hutton quit WETA. Three weeks thereafter, Mitch Semel quit PBS.

"No use panicking," I told Steve. "The show is exactly as good as it was in April. If Semel liked it, whoever replaces him will probably like it, too."

The sound you just heard was denial setting in.

The next few weeks were filled with the frantic activity of preparing for the second pilot shoot, preparations repeatedly frustrated by Dick Richter's preoccupation with the Democratic convention. As executive producer of *Washington Week in Review,* he was basically out of pocket for the duration. Scripts had to be approved, decisions had to be made, and our communication was reduced to dueling phone messages and—from me, at least—increasingly testy faxes. Meanwhile, I immersed myself once again in bizarre arcana. My reading matter for the summer was the accumulated intellectual achievements of *What's What?, Do Penguins Have Knees?, More of the Straight Dope, 2201 Fascinating Facts, The Bathroom Reader, Mrs. Byrne's Dictionary of Unusual, Obscure and Preposterous Words,* and the like.

Every spare moment was devoted to one aspect or another of *KnowItAll!* On airplane trips I skipped the in-flight meals and labored over a legal pad, adding to my forlorn list of fake ad-libs—cheap stalling tactics that I imagined to be a running joke for National Quiz Show Personality Bob Garfield on an 8 P.M. weekly TV event, but that were destined never to be delivered.

"Bob, define 'aprosexia.' "

"I'll take 'famous legumes for fifty,' Emil."

"Bob, what is an ASCOB?"

"Colonel Mustard, in the conservatory, with the candlestick, Emil."

"Bob, the Republic of Nauru's single export is what?"

"I refuse to answer on the ground that it may tend to humiliate me, Emil. Will this be on the final, Emil? You didn't say 'Simon Says,' Emil. Yes, Emil, Charlie Weaver to block."

Ominous signs were everywhere. The project's three greatest champions were out of the picture. Sharon Rockefeller was on the record as being un-bowled over. Twice more WETA canceled studio dates for the re-shoot. As the Democratic convention gave way to the Republican one, my key remaining WETA ally, Dick Richter, was virtually inaccessible. My partner Steve tried to warn me about impending doom, but I preferred to accentuate the positive. A woman named Kathy Quattrone had been promoted to succeed Mitch Semel at PBS. If WETA's interest was flagging, it would take only her encouragement to revive enthusiasm. Furthermore, word of *KnowItAll!* was leaking out to the game show world. A Hollywood "game doctor" called me, trying to get hired, as did the agent for the inveterate TV game host Art James.

Art James scrounging for work from me? How pathetic. How wonderful.

How futile. The summer of frustration came and went without a shoot of new pilot episodes. Finally—after a campaign of hectoring from bad-cop Steve Rosenbaum and good-cop me—WETA decided to show the original pilot shows to Quattrone, and sent her the same reel Mitch Semel had viewed so enthusiastically four months earlier.

"Frankly," Dick Richter wrote to her in the cover letter, "it is so different from our normal efforts that we don't want to travel down an unfamiliar road if the detour is not warranted." Ah, salesmanship, beginning another unendurable wait until Quattrone, learning the ropes as vice president of programming, finally got around to viewing the tape. In December. Dick got back to me with her commentary.

"She liked the panel, and she liked the humor of it," Dick reported. "She basically liked the game."

"But?"

"But she had a problem with the bluffing," he said. I didn't know what problem with the bluffing Quattrone had, but I knew from Dick's tone that it was not a small problem. After fourteen months of effort, fourteen months of highs and lows, fourteen months of divining hidden meanings from inscrutable executive utterances, fourteen months of gestation for a project that had very much become my baby, it was very clear to me that bluffing was going to have a material effect on my tax planning. That is, I was going to have to do less of it.

"What do you mean she had a problem, Dick?"

"She doesn't want the bluffing. She said, 'We can't have people lying on PBS.' "

"Has she ever watched *McNeil/Lehrer?*" I retorted darkly.

"She said maybe if the rules could be recast so nobody would have to give misinformation . . ."

"Dick, it's a bluffing game. It's about bluffing. To recast it would . . . would . . . would . . ."

He chuckled uncomfortably at the absurdity of the situation. It was over, and we both knew it.

"I understand," he said.

"So do I."

The endgame was grim formality. I wrote to Quattrone, reminding her that *KnowItAll!* wasn't supposed to be *College Bowl,* but rather "designed to be educational by demanding critical thinking, and developing listening skills." Sensing a desperate rationalization, she was unmoved. In subsequent weeks, WETA officially bowed out of the project, whereupon I immediately got in touch with Mitch Semel at Comedy Central cable network, informing him that the pilot he found so entertaining was now a free agent. "Uh," he said, "could you just remind me what it was all about?" Upon having his memory jogged, Semel referred me to his head of development, who found the show to be too much game and not enough comedy. The Arts & Entertainment network has expressed interest in *KnowItAll!,* in the event that three pure comedy shows it is testing all fail miserably, but nobody there is exactly badgering me to sign a contract.

The one person on whom I most pinned my hopes has, to the best of my knowledge, never seen *KnowItAll!* She, of course, is Jennifer Lawson. I regard this unfortunate circumstance as her loss, and PBS's. On the other hand, she may yet have an opportunity to see a wholesome, entertaining, family bluffing game on TV. Last summer, my wife and I were visiting Los Angeles, where we spent a day touring Universal Studios. There we had the opportunity to see the pilot taping of a real, live TV game show, featuring a panel of real stars. The game was called *Balderdash.*

We didn't go.

The Middle-Aged Man
and the Sea

The street was sun-baked already in the morning of the third day. This was the Costera M. Aleman, which is the principal boulevard, the strip of hotels and boutiques and al fresco saloons. Down the strip we walked, our eyes squinting against the brightness.

Acapulco is on the sea. The breeze rises from the surf, hovering like a *cometa,* which means parasail. Then it walks, gingerly, like a pale tourist in rigid new leather sandals, to the street. There, amid the vendors and beggars and *las turistas,* the zephyr softens the anger of the sun. With it comes the smell of last night's garbage, which here they dump into the sea. The smell is of rotten vegetables and of putrid red snapper. It crawls right up your nose and it is gross.

"Blanket, *señor?"*

The street vendor had a face of brown and hair of black. In the eyes he looked like the great Melido Perez, who pitches in the baseball. He pitches for the White Sox of Chicago, which is a sad and funny joke, for the White Sox of Chicago play now not like the White Sox in the days of Minoso and Aparicio, but like the Phillies of Philadelphia, in the days of Dalrymple and Herrera. This was after the great Sisler and before the great Montenez, who in the year 1971 knocked in ninety-nine. In the eyes Montenez did not look like this vendor, but like Montenez the vendor seemed indifferent as he displayed his wares.

The sun-beaten man held high his blanket and we too were indifferent. Two days we had been in Acapulco, and we had been molested by peddlers many times. On the day of our arrival we stopped at each encounter with our apologies, which were from our heart. To say no to a seller of cheap trinkets is to be filled with sorrow, for this is a country that is poor. To say, "I have for the beautiful Corona beer T-shirt no dollars" bruises the soul. But inexorably the heart hardens. Soon it is just, "No, *gracias*," and, eyes averted, moving on. On this morning of the third day, we said no to baskets and masks, hammocks and carriage rides, hats and mechanical rats. Also silver bangles and silver earrings and silver necklaces, the silver content of which was *questionable,* which means questionable.

"No, *gracias*," we said, but the seller of blankets was not content.

"Good price I give you. Twenty thousand pesitos, *señor.*"

"No, *gracias.*"

"*Señor,* you like this one, yes?"

Here is where I turned abruptly, taking the hand of Carla, my wife. Here, the waffled soles of my rigid new leather sandals squeaking upon the hot pavement, I encountered el Señor Capitan Jorge.

"Fishing trip, *señor?*"

"No, *gracias,*" I said, and I quickened my pace to move past him. The sun now was strong on my neck, and my breakfast of *huevos rancheros* was animated in my stomach. Yet this fellow stood before me, brandishing a binder of vinyl. The binder it was thick. The vinyl it was virgin. I turned my shoulder to pass him.

"Fish for marlin, *señor?*"

I froze. Marlin? In the blue waters of the Pacific, beyond la Isle de Rocquetta and the shoals of stone, there were marlin? What a thought! How these fish had fascinated me. How often I had imagined them, awash in foam, breaking the water, their ribbed dorsals glinting in the white morning light, their coarse blue skin firm against the gunwales. This fellow, the captain, wore a smile that said, "Yes, *señor,* I can show you the marlin. *Si, señor.* It is a fish of great majesty."

"Tell me about the marlin fishing," I said.

"You will enjoy, *señor*. Please, let me show you."

He opened the binder, revealing faded Polaroid photos taken at sea. In one was a woman, posing in triumph by a great large fish of blue. The marlin was like a carved sea god, its foil of a snout searching for heaven. The lady, her upper arms were like hams of Virginia. On her face was a grin.

"You see?" said the man with the binder of vinyl. "The woman caught the fish."

"She is bigger than me," I said.

"Yes, *señor*, she is bigger than you."

"But she has a beautiful fish, no?"

"*Si, si, señor*. You would like to go fishing?"

The man with the binder of vinyl had my attention, and it was clear from the smiling squint in his eyes that he knew. He displayed for me all of his photographs, each with a gringo fisherman and each with a fish. There were no pictures of him—of course not, he held the camera, did he not?—but in the photos were two sturdy young men.

"You tell me your hotel and I will pick you up at fifteen before six. The boat ride is very swift. At dawn you will be on the blue water. The cold water, yes? And there you will catch the fish. You will be home before the morning is done."

"Marlin?"

"*Si*, marlin. And yellowfin. You know, tuna? They are strong fish. They give strong fight."

"My back," I said. "My back is not very good. Do you have a harness?"

The man laughed.

"You do not need a harness. You will have my boys, Mario and Ricardo. They will help you land the fish."

The time had come. The man had closed his binder and was waiting for my question. It was time to ask the price. When I paused, he became bold.

"Very cheap, *señor*. Eighty dollars American."

Now I smiled at him. The game had begun. It was *la negociacion*.

In Acapulco, a tourist is advised to ignore the asking price. The place to begin is at half. Even in two days, Carla and I had learned this well. On the morning of the second day we went to the central market, where I found to my liking a pair of woven leather sandals.

"How much?"

"Thirty-five American, *señor*."

Ha! In fifteen minutes' time I walked away from the cobbler's stand with a new pair of sandals. The cost was $17 and inside I was full of laughter. Later that day, in a boutique on the Costera M. Aleman, where tourists are warned of the exorbitant prices of goods, I saw the very same sandals. In the fashionable shop, they asked for these sandals the outrageous sum of $16.

So for my encounter with the fishing captain I was more than prepared.

"Eighty dollars is too much," I said. "I will give you forty."

The man with the binder of vinyl shook his head. Gravely, he spoke.

"No, *señor*. The rigs they are very expensive, and I must pay my boys. There is also the cost of fuel and bait. The other men who call themselves captains, perhaps they expect to bargain. But this is my price. I can go no lower than seventy dollars."

I stole a glance at Carla, my wife. Already the seaman had dropped his price. This negotiation would be swift as a speed-boat, bouncing on the gentle swells where the water is cold. That is what my expression said and I was right. Only five minutes passed before I walked away in the arm of my wife, a deal struck. The next morning at 5:45, el Señor Capitan Jorge would call for me at my hotel and we would begin our expedition. The sun no longer flogged my flesh. Now it warmed my soul, for in my hand I grasped a receipt, from my boatsman and guide, for $70. I could not feel defeated. The peso, like my back, is very weak, and this was a good price for a morning of sport and the conquering of a powerful and regal fish. Come the dawn, the spray would be in my face and a marlin leaping wildly at the end of my line. All I would need to give the captain then was my undivided attention—and another 3,600 pesos, for a fishing license.

On the day of the eve of my expedition we were not idle. We went to the beach, where we said "No, *gracias*" to 1,000 peddlers. We walked through the Jardin Botanica, where we saw nineteen varieties of flora and Mexican teenagers in forty-two kinds of embrace. And we toured Gigante, a vast market that is super, where we bought bread, mustard, Pepsi, Corona beer, and loaf filled with olive for the sea journey. Then to our hotel, the Tortuga, which means "tiny bathroom." Stooped over a countertop, I assembled with the loaf filled with olive eight sandwiches, two each for Mario, Ricardo, el Señor Capitan Jorge, and myself. Then the hour grew late and it was time to sleep.

Carla kissed me on the forehead and asked me about the call of wake-up. I laughed, for a call of wake-up I did not need. El Señor Capitan Jorge would be my alarm clock—my alarm clock, my guide and, God willing, my photographer. These were happy thoughts and I drifted away.

As always, I dreamed. I dreamed of Connie Mack Stadium when I was a boy and the thick green grass and the orange dirt and the white bases, so white they hurt your eyes, and the sloppily painted slatted seats and the Longines clock. So many nights I have lived in that grandstand and in my dreams I have smelled the pine tar and spilled beer, and I have seen the foul balls lofted to me and I have caught them. One after another I caught them. Sometimes they rolled to me and I leaned, like a peasant gleaning grain, over the chain-link-fence rail and I gathered them. Soon I had so many that I thought I must be dreaming and always then I awoke.

A shrill sound filled my ears and disturbed my sleep. It was a moment before I recognized the sound of the Mexican phones, which are tinny in their rings. But that quickly I was wide awake. Ah, my alarm clock.

"Hello?"

"This is Jorge. You are ready?"

"*Si, señor.* I will be downstairs in five minutes. *Cinco minudo, por favor.*"

My limbs were heavy, but I climbed from bed at once to gather my things. There was my hat. Of course, my hat. There were my sunglasses and my windbreaker, my camera, and my block of the sun. Also the food and drink—How sweet will be the olives in this loaf!—which I tucked carefully in a thin plastic bag. I brushed my teeth and washed my face and hurried to the patio, where el Señor Capitan Jorge waited.

"*Buenos dias,*" I said.

"*Bueno.*"

A battered beige Toyota was waiting for us. A sun-darkened man, younger than Jorge but older than me, was at the wheel. He and the captain spoke pleasantly to one another in rapid Spanish. When they paused, I got the captain's attention.

"*El Señor Capitan,*" I said, hoisting my thin plastic bag of sandwiches and drinks. "*Tengo* sandwiches *y Pepsi y cervesa por los todos.*"

Yes, he could see that I had lunch for everybody. The captain seemed pleased and he smiled and gestured with an outstretched thumb. He and his companion then resumed their jocular conversation. They must have shared a joke, for they both enjoyed a hearty laugh.

Up the quiet strip and past the central marketplace we went. The Toyota pulled to the curb at the wharf and we climbed out. Down five rotted plank steps we stepped to the dock, where two young men in swim trunks were awaiting us.

"These are Mario and Ricardo," the captain said. "They will take good care of you. Just do what they say."

As Mario and Ricardo loaded the speedboat, mangy dogs with matted fur slept and skinny cats pawed nervously at a lump of frozen bait. El Señor Capitan Jorge, too, seemed restless, looking now at the boat and now at the street and back at the boat again. I wondered why we did not get underway. Then I realized the captain was waiting for me.

"You can get aboard now," he said.

"What about my license?"

"License?"

"My fishing license."

"Oh, *si*. Your license. Give me 3,600 pesos."

I handed him 5,000 pesos, but he could not change the bill so I told him to keep the rest. Then I boarded the boat. I could see that the captain was not following me.

"You are waiting for someone else?" I asked.

"No. I am not going. You are going with Mario and Ricardo. I am needed somewhere else this morning, but you are in good hands. They are good boys."

"They know where to find the marlin?"

"Oh, yes. They are good boys. Good luck, *señor*."

El Senor Capitan Jorge retreated up the plank stairs and into the shadows beneath the trees along the street. As he walked away, I noticed for the first time that he was carrying something. It was his binder of vinyl.

Mario started the boat. The motor whirred firmly as we chugged away from the dock toward the channel. The adventure was begun.

The sea was cast with hues of gold as we sped south along the coast. How the motor roared and the water's spray enveloped me. I sat with back to the bow, watching the wake unzip behind us like a *cremallera*, which means trouser fly. As the distant city awakened, we veered west toward the blue water. Mario and Ricardo prepared the tackle in silence, fixing heavy steel leaders to the thick monofilament line. Soon we were trolling. Perhaps we would have some yellowfin in the shallows before taking on the trophy fish.

It had been a long while since I caught a fish, a great fish. There was the carp, sleepy and roe-sodden, that I had pulled from the mud of the Allegheny. There were the three bluefish, small and angry, taken over six hours time in the Chesapeake Bay while all around me fishermen landed menacing blues by the cooler full. There were the sand sharks taken in the Delaware Bay, from the garvey with the motor with no power. I landed two such fish, two sinewy mockeries of sharkness.

Yes, but then there was the walleye—the walleye of which so many still speak. More than five minutes I fought this ten-pound fish from the bank of the river behind the cabin that is my father-in-law's. Still they talk of this great fish, but this was ten years ago and since then so little. After ten years without a fish, my heart told me I was finally and definitely *salao*, which is the worst form of unlucky. Perhaps today would bring my redemption.

As we motored to the blue water I fixed my gaze at the tackle. The rod was flexed against the drag of the water, and with each swell it arched still more. For an hour, though I knew better, my heart stopped at each gentle tug. I knew that a marlin would take the line and run with it as if possessed, yanking it off the spool in vast lengths to the whine of the gears. But what one knows and what one hopes are not always the same. In the second hour, the swells sometimes grew larger and the rod curled still more and still, sometimes, I started. But it was never a fish. Once I jumped from my seat to grab the rod and caught instead Mario's glance. He was smiling and shaking his head no.

By the time of nine o'clock my stomach felt empty and I pulled the sandwiches from the cooler. "I must eat now so that I will not have a failure of strength," I said to myself. I had put on the sandwiches not only loaf with olive but also cheese and French's, which means mustard. I wished I had bought lettuce, but when I put the sandwich in my mouth it was not unpleasant. The lettuce would have been better, but I chewed the food and was grateful it was not dead raw tuna. Mario and Ricardo were pleased with the sandwiches and we all ate greedily. At 9 A.M. we drank also Coronas. There was nothing else to keep us occupied.

"*Donde estan las fishies?*" I asked.

Mario shrugged.

At 9:30 still there were no marlin. At 10 A.M., there were no marlin and no more sandwiches. The beer was cold and good.

For all the time Mario and Ricardo stood, Mario at the helm and Ricardo nearer the bow. Sometimes they spoke in Spanish I did not understand, but mostly they were silent. They peered blankly into the distance, as if in a strange and familiar kind of sleep.

"*Mario, donde estan las fishies?* Where are the fish? Are there no fish?"

Again he shrugged.

"There are no fish," he said.

"Haven't they been catching fish?" I asked, realizing that his English, unlike my luck, was good.

"No, *señor*, not in March. In October, yes. But not in March. The fish do not bite in March. They are not hungry."

"That's not what Captain Jorge said."

"Captain Jorge? You mean George?"

"The captain. El Señor Capitan."

Mario laughed and Ricardo laughed. From the bow Ricardo shouted, "Did he tell you you would catch fish?" and he was grinning.

"Yes. Why else would I be here?"

Ricardo looked at Mario.

"Boat ride," Mario said.

At 10:30. the boat veered back toward the coast. I drank another beer, which dribbled down my chin. In my mind's eye I could see Jorge, in the heat of the Costera M. Aleman, and I thought of his binder of vinyl. Then I pulled out my camera and gave it to Ricardo.

"Please take my picture," I said, and I took the line that he had reeled in and dangled the bait in the sky and smiled for the camera. Mario, throttling up his pleasure boat, seemed amused. I had one more question but I did not ask it. I did not ask if there is such thing, in Acapulco, as a fishing license.

Spider Man

Oh, shut up.

You think you have me pegged, but you're wrong.

All right, so I was a few days past my thirty-ninth birthday, and I was in the minivan taking my kids to see *The Lion King*, and I happened to notice a little black convertible Fiat Spider 2000 sitting on a cul-de-sac with a "For Sale" sign in the window. So maybe I pulled over and gave it a quick scan and maybe jotted down the phone number, while my daughters—who represent the principal reason I didn't already own a little black convertible Fiat Spider 2000—sat in the back of the van fighting over a hairbrush.

Don't jump to any conclusions, okay? I happen to be perfectly content with my life. Just because a fellow happens to be in a dismal countdown toward middle age doesn't mean he is necessarily a pathetic, grasping, living cliché. Don't judge a man on the basis of coming home from an animated Disney feature and slipping out of the house with the cordless phone so he can dial a number undetected. It may be just a question of satisfying innocent curiosity without needlessly raising the hackles of a spouse, who could regard even the theoretical acquisition of a previously owned European ragtop roadster as extravagant, impractical, and juvenile.

To speak hypothetically.

So when a guy announces, "I'm going out for forty-five minutes," and doesn't specify where, you cannot infer surreptitiousness or even guilty feelings. Discretion, as someone once nearly said, can be the better part of candor. Saying "I'm going out for a test drive of a car I have no actual intention to buy" is simply asking for trouble. Nor can any smug outsider divine significance from the sight of a grown man sitting in the parking lot of West Springfield High School, trembling like a gearshift at high idle, in anticipation of a clandestine meeting with a 1980 sports car with 86,500 miles on the odometer. If, upon the arrival of the vehicle in question, the fellow should happen to leer at the sexy little Mediterranean as if she were a centerfold and caress the gleaming brown-black body like something out of *Naughty Flight Attendants,* you can conclude nothing about him—which is to say, about me.

I am not ashamed to say that, upon achieving my fortieth year, I happened by sheer chance to become quite enamored of a hot little sports car. All right, enamored to the point of considering making an offer for it. But that doesn't mean what you take it to mean, and believe me, I've heard it all. Roll your eyes all you please. I am not going through anyone's idea of a midlife crisis. A sports car is a sports car. It is not, repeat *not,* the dead-rabbit test for male menopause.

Look, I've seen people on a collision course with the fifth decade before, and I'm not one of them. Take my older brother, for instance. When Josh turned thirty-nine, he was a bit dispirited—more or less in the way that Van Gogh was a bit dispirited. The idea of turning forty seemed to terrify him, partly because in our family the term "midlife crisis" is not glib pop psychology so much as giddy actuarial optimism. Garfield men, going back at least two generations, have the blood-lipid profile of a nice flan. Also the annoying habit of dying at fifty-one. For most people, the years between forty and fifty that they so love to whine about constitute the prime of life. For my brothers and me, there looms the very real possibility that our forties constitute the home stretch.

So maybe I'm even within my rights to have a little crisis of my own. With a wife, two kids, two car payments, and mortgage the size of Dan Rostenkowski's stationery budget, I fully understand this is the moment when I'm expected to do something irrational and bold—like risk marital and financial ruin on a ridiculous entanglement with a young woman, for the purpose of assuring myself I am still young, vital, virile, and manly.

But I can't be bothered. For one thing, my back is acting up. Secondly, I already know I'm extremely manly. Just the other day, when a guy cut me off in traffic and I accelerated like a maniac just to catch up with him and curse him out, my wife assured me, "You are such a man." This was not the first time she's flattered me with such a spontaneous compliment, so I don't think I have to prove anything to anybody by latching on to any of the multitude of hot babes who I'm sure are just hanging back waiting for me and my potbelly to emit the right signal. Also, I have no patience for this hapless, hypothetical mistress's incessant and pitiful pleadings for me to get a divorce. Can't she see that you just don't snap your fingers and break up a happy marriage of seventeen years?

In any event, my wife, who pays all the bills in our household, has informed me that even if there were a younger woman out there with designs on my arthritic body and unfunded tuition liability, I can't afford her. "Unless you use your lunch money," she said.

So my thirty-ninth birthday came with no emotional *Sturm und Drang*—until the fateful Sunday not long ago, when I stopped on the way to *The Lion King* to admire a handsome black Fiat 2000.

"Are you gonna buy it, Dad?" Katie asked.

"Oh, I doubt it, dear. I'm just kind of curious. It sure is beautiful though, isn't it?'

"Uh-oh," Allison said. "Mom's gonna be mad."

Which I thought was harsh. Carla and I may have a different sense of our overall automotive requirements, but she knows full well I have never indulged myself in any major purchase, unless she'd count a few pieces of artwork or a $90 set of used golf clubs. Furthermore, it is Carla, of the two of us, who is preternaturally considerate of the other's wishes and desires, who unfailingly anticipates my needs, and who goes to sometimes astonishing lengths to make life more pleasant. She is, in short, the dream spouse. Kids sometimes aren't willing to give credit to a parent, but I knew that if Carla knew a Fiat 2000 Spider in the driveway would make me happy, a Fiat 2000 Spider in the driveway would make her happy too.

Arachnophilia for me. Arachnophilia for her.

"I CANNOT BELIEVE THIS!"

This was the moment when the rumination phase of my fantasy purchase was over, the negotiation phase was about to commence, and I was first introducing Carla to the idea that I was about to give the two of us a tremendous amount of personal satisfaction. Oddly, my dream spouse was uncharacteristically subdued in expressing her overwhelming happiness. If I didn't know her better, I might have interpreted her incredulity as contempt. Not that she lashed out exactly—she didn't say much at all, but her lips tightened and she stared at me in a way that almost seemed to betray disgust, as well as certain preconceived notions about men and their pitiful clinging to lost youth. The situation seemed to demand drastic action.

"Admit it," I said preemptively. "You think I'm a jerk and I shouldn't be doing it."

Carla was caught off guard by this brilliant dialectical maneuver, in which, by exaggerating the negativity of her reaction, I forced her to be defensive and conciliatory. Actually speechless, she glared at me a good moment before she gathered her thoughts enough to reply.

"I think you're a jerk and you shouldn't be doing it," she said, adding thoughtfully, "I bust my backside around here clipping out coupons and saving pennies and paying for vacations out of the household budget, and you're gonna go out and pay $3,000 for a toy?"

Or, put another way, arachnophilia for me, arachnophobia for her.

"No," I said. "I'm not going to pay $3,000 for anything. The guy's asking $3,000. But I'm not going to pay him $3,000. The thing has 86,000 miles on it. But the body's in great shape. If I can keep it good condition, it will actually appreciate in value. It's only a few years from being considered an antique."

Carla was now looking at me, more or less the way Mama Berenstain Bear looks at Papa during one of his fatuous misadventures. "Is there," she inquired skeptically, "room for the children in this antique?"

Room for the children? What does that have to do with anything? The object of a little Italian roadster is to *not* have room for the children.

"There's a back seat in it," I said, telling exactly 50 percent of the truth. If the driver and passenger are more than 4-foot-6, there's no room in the back for anybody burdened with one or more legs. Nor are there any rear seat belts. To take the kids anywhere, seating would have to be configured as follows: Katie sitting in the front and Allie lying face down in the back, weighted down with cinderblocks. Carla, of course, would have to follow behind in the van.

Happily, when the next day I spoke to the owner and offered $2,500, pending "a few things working out on my end," and he accepted, my wife seemed somewhat mollified. At least, she used the word "idiotic" only twice. That same night I called the owner back to sew up the deal and take possession of the car.

"Well," the guy told me, "the thing is, since we spoke somebody else offered me $2,900 and they're picking it up at nine o'clock in the morning."

"What are you saying?" I asked. "Are you saying you sold the car to somebody else?"

"I'm saying that somebody offered me full price, and you were still trying to make up your mind."

"Make up my mind?" I sputtered, trying to maintain composure. "I did make up my mind. I offered you $2,500. You accepted it, and I told you I'd make final arrangements tomorrow, and we aren't even at tomorrow, and now you're reneging."

"You never gave me a deposit."

"You never asked for a deposit."

"It's just that I've been through this before," he said, sounding somewhat abashed by this disgraceful last-minute turnabout. "Someone shows interest and says they want to show it to their mechanic, and it's the last we ever hear from them."

"But you are hearing from me, just like I said you would."

"Well, the other couple is giving me the full price . . . actually, less a hundred dollars, because I just found out that the windshield wipers don't work. I'm sorry, but we have to protect ourselves. And that's what we're doing."

And just that quickly my car, my roadster, my destiny began to slip away.

Yes, my destiny—since 1972, when I was a senior in high school. Though I strained to affect a bohemian image back then, I was still very much steeped in the preoccupations and desires of many generations of teenage boys before me. I speak, naturally, of cars, sports, and girls. In the third category I mainly opted out, due to a crippling lack of self-confidence and a complexion like the Sea of Tranquility. Cars too were a burning desire dismally out of reach. My father was sick (he died in December of that year), and what money I earned as a pharmacy delivery boy and weekend flower arranger was socked away for college. I spent a lot of time with brochures and buff books, but the closest I ever got to my fantasy car was Ashley Botnick's Fiat 124 Spider.

I refer to the dentist in the apartment below us, who vroomed in and out of the parking lot every day with a *popitapopitapopita* sound that affected me like pheromones. As soon as I could afford one, I pledged to myself, I would get me a Fiat Spider. Maybe in five years, after college, when I had a job. Until then, though, it was like my complex, three-tier relationship with girls: stare, speculate, wait.

Then, one day, out of the blue, a miracle occurred. Our doorbell rang, and when I answered it, there on our threshold stood Ashley Botnick, DDS. He was holding a key fob, pinching it between his thumb and forefinger, with a tiny ignition key dangling in my face.

"Want to drive the car?" he asked.

Want the Phillies to win the pennant? Want your skin to clear up? Want to violate all standards of moral decency with the tight-sweatered girl in your biology lab?

"Uh, sure," I croaked because it would have been unseemly to fall to my knees.

Considering how overwhelmed I was at the time, it's funny how the details have faded in the two decades since. Was he going on vacation? I'd have to say yes, although my memory on the subject is indistinct. Twenty-two years later, I couldn't say how many times I took his car out, or how far, or with whom. I remember only driving down Levering Mill Road in Bala Cynwyd, Pennsylvania, moving through the gears and knowing that the experience was changing my life.

It's difficult to explain the visceral joy of this sort of motoring. Speed has nothing to do with it. The 1970 Fiat 124 had an engine of 1,438 cc's. It went 0 to 60 in approximately October. But it was *driving*. The engine's vibration was like a heartbeat, the handling so nimble that physics were neutralized. And the feel of the road under the tires was sublime, like a massage. Relaxing. Stimulating. Life-affirming. And, above all, sensual. Sedans by and large are designed to defeat sensation. A roadster is a conductor.

Now don't be getting that knowing little smile again. A lot is made of male fixation on sports cars and the supposed inverse relationship between car flashiness and masculine endowment. There's even been a Hyundai commercial on the subject, the premise of which is that a Corvette is a phallic extender, a 400 horsepower prosthesis, and that a humble Hyundai therefore is a mark of . . . well, you get the idea. And you may well buy into it, because the theory of overcompensation is not uncompelling. When you see a fellow in a Ferrari Testarossa, perhaps you are within your rights to smirk. But not when you see a fellow in a roadster, which is tiny and typically underpowered, if you follow my drift.

Anyway, twenty-two years came and went with my Spider pledge unfulfilled. A series of external forces—namely, poverty, spousal practicality, and the children—militated against my dream. The closest I got was in 1978, when I acquired my second post-college car: a used VW Super Beetle that cost $1,700. That car did have a stick shift, which was a minor consolation, but not much in the way of horsepower or what the car buff books call "road manners." It was like driving around in a barber's chair, the principal difference being that a barber's chair, I believe, has a better defroster.

And so it went, with economics and pragmatism outweighing desire. After the birth of Katie, our first child, out went the Super Beetle and in came a used 1977 Plymouth Grand Fury Brougham, which was the size of the *Queen Mary*, but with a slightly longer turning radius. This car was basically the reason Chrysler almost failed. Then, in various pairings of two came the Plymouth Horizon, Dodge Caravan, Dodge Lancer, Plymouth Voyager, and VW Passat—the last two of which constitute our current fleet. The Passat is a great car, sort of a poor man's BMW, a European performance sedan that breaks just often enough to keep me from taking it for granted. But it ain't a roadster either.

Which brings me back to that late-June expedition to *The Lion King*. It was only then, long after my brief encounter with the Ashley Botnick-mobile, that my dream stood a chance of becoming a reality—and now my destiny car was about to be given to somebody else.

Apparently. There was no way I could be sure there really was another bidder. All my instincts told me to call the owner a few choice names and slam the phone down. But lust won out over pride. The phantom other party had offered him $2,900, so I offered him $2,900 too, and said I'd come pick up the car right this minute.

"All right," he said.

All right! The Spider of my dreams was going to be mine! I

broke the good news to Carla, and she was so excited she couldn't even smile.

"Let me see if I have this right," she said. "You offered $2,500 for the car. You found out the windshield wipers don't work, and now you're buying it for $2,900. Is that correct?"

"That is correct."

"Oh," said my adoring life partner. "You are one shrewd businessman."

Still, Carla consented to drive me to pick up the goods. It sat in the owner's garage, gleaming under the fluorescent light. As the seller fumbled with the title and the owner's manual, I wrote the check. Then I asked him to show me a few things, such as how to open and close the convertible top.

"Very simple," he said. "See these latches under the sun visors? Flip them down, and just pull it back. See?" And he did just that, tucking the collapsed top into a well behind the back seat. "And to close it, just reverse the process."

Which he also did, attaching, flipping, and locking the right-hand latch, and doing the same thing with the left-hand one. Except the left-hand one didn't lock; it sprang right back up. So he flipped it down again, firmly. And again it sprang back up. That's when he went for the hammer, an ordinary claw hammer that had been nestled under the front passenger's seat.

"Sometimes you've gotta . . ." Tap. Tap. Tap. He was hammering the driver's side latch to center it in the metal groove atop the windscreen. ". . . just line it up—see how it lines up here?—and tap it a few times, and then pull it down and it should stay." He did, it didn't.

Tap. Tap. Tap. Tap. "Okay," he said, tapping the latch for a third try, "it's gotta be dead center or it won't stay." Pulling firmly down on the top with his left hand, he wielded the hammer with his right and tapped, tapped, tapped. This time it held.

"Do you want the hammer?" he asked. "I'll give it to you. I have another one."

The Pentagon should be so lucky. When I buy a $2,900 Manual Fastener-Percussion Device, at least my vendor throws a car in with it. At this stage I glanced back at Carla, who stood with her arms folded, an eyebrow cocked. Anyone who thinks *The Berenstain Bears Go on a Picnic* is the last word in ritual male behavior leading to abject humiliation wasn't there for Papa Bear Buys a Spider.

Finally, with the ragtop in place, the guy asked for one last time to back his baby out of the driveway. I obliged, delighted to once again hear the car's throaty purr, somewhat less delighted to see half a dozen oil spots on the garage floor. The now previous owner got out of the car and saw me staring at his greasy floor.

"That's fourteen years of oil spots," he said, reassuringly. Then, absently, he pushed the driver's door shut.

Whereupon the left convertible latch popped open. So now at 10 P.M. in this man's driveway, I got to tap, tap, tap it myself.

"This is just surreal," I muttered.

"Well," the guy said, "this is a sports car. It's all part of the experience."

Another part of the sports car experience is the nearly unprecedented opportunity it affords a person to give large sums of money to gentlemen with grease under their fingernails. Fiat, it is said, is an acronym for Fix It Again Tony—although this clearly does not apply in my case because my mechanic's name is Pete.

I picked up my car on a Tuesday night. Wednesday morning, on my way out of town for a few days, I dropped it off at Pete's to have the windshield wipers repaired, brakes checked, and to get a general appraisal of the car's condition. Many people, of course, go through this exercise before they make major purchases, but in my view that takes away all the drama. Sure enough, when I returned on Saturday, drama was awaiting.

When I pulled into the driveway from the airport, Carla was standing there with the telephone. Pete was on the line.

"I'm finished with your little piece of . . . car," he said.

We quickly ran over to Pete's, where he was pleased to tell me the body, engine, and transmission all were in good repair. He put on rear brake pads and was able to locate a brand-new windshield wiper motor. All for only $608.95. Or, computed another way, in four days, from the time I got the previous owner to accept $2,500 for the car to the moment I pulled out of Pete's, I had spent an additional $1,008.95 and driven the car exactly five miles. But then I got to drive it home, the long way, along the winding two-lane Pohick Road in Burke, which my Spider clung to like a monorail. The top was down. The wind was in my hair.

Funny thing about the wind in the hair situation. You'd think it would blow the hair straight back, the way I comb it, creating no hairstyle interruption. But it doesn't work quite that way. For aerodynamic reasons I can't begin to understand, the windscreen deflects the oncoming stream of air in such a way as to create either a vacuum or a swirl, the effect of which is to blow my fairly coarse hair forward and backward at the same time. Coming to a rest at a stop sign, I looked as if I had just done a headstand in a blender. Henceforth, I decided, I would do my convertible motoring wearing a hat.

Other than that, and some minor cramping in my right foot from depressing an accelerator positioned much farther forward than it is in our sedan and minivan, the road home met and exceeded all of my expectations of the roadster experience. It was sensual. It was bracing. It was sublime. And when I puffed into our driveway, I knew it was all worthwhile. Carla was waiting for me inside.

"Well," she asked. "Any blondes wink at you?"

"Maybe," I said. "There was this one lady and she may have been winking at me—or, possibly, squinting, to see what was the matter with my hair."

"You should have hung the repair bill on the outside of the car," my wife said. "That would have impressed her."

All right, so she wasn't yet quite sold on this purchase. I didn't blame her. Most women do not understand the allure of the roadster, though many a college girl runs around in a convertible Golf Cabriolet, and there are countless Mazda RX7s and Camaros and Nissan 300ZXs out there with women at the wheel and vanity plates on the order of DZ BLND. Yet I suspect— indeed, I am certain—most bought these cars for reasons utterly apart from the ones that motivate men. Nothing to do with cornering. Nothing to do with pushing the tach to the red line and hearing the engine rev to a scream. Nothing to do with the zenlike convergence of man and machine. To the degree women appreciate convertibles, it is for one reason and one reason alone. It is the very reason Carla cited when she offered her first positive statement about my Spider. It was the word she used when I left the house and headed for the car on the first day I was to drive it to work. The car, she finally conceded, was "cute."

Cute?

No, a puppy is cute. A toddler is cute. Lambchop the hand puppet is cute.

A roadster is a gift from God, a gift giving man—and I do mean man—absolute control.

Work was uneventful, and I was happy to escape at about 7 P.M., to get back home. In my new baby. It was one of those scorching, humid July evenings. As I backed out of my parking space, it began to drizzle. No problem. I pulled back in, reached back and yanked on the handle of the top, in order to pull it over my head and into place. At that moment I experienced, conservatively speaking, the most excruciating pain anyone has ever felt. It was my right shoulder, which, miraculously enough, was not dislocated. Simply wrenched. But now the drizzle was a steady rain, so I had to ignore the pain. I hopped out of the car and from the outside pulled the top up. The right-hand latch snapped perfectly into place, and then I doubled back to the driver's side, where the latch chose not to cooperate. I pulled down on the top with all my might, aligned the center latch pin with its corresponding socket and flipped the handle. But it would not stay down. So I reached under the seat to use my $2,900 hammer. Tap. Tap. Tap.

Bingo! It held. Hopping back in, I pulled out of my space and, within three minutes, I was heading south on the Shirley Highway.

Funny thing about summer rains. It can be pouring down in sheets, as it was this day, and still be 90 degrees, as it was this day. Inside the tiny car, with the windows and top up, I was sweltering. What air I had was so damp the windshield was fogging like a bathroom mirror. So I opened the vent window, deflecting the airflow right at the windshield. This accomplished three things:

(1) getting some oxygen into the chamber

(2) moderately defogging the windshield

(3) directing a steady flow of water down the edge of the vent window and onto my left trouser leg.

Then I hit a bump, and the left convertible latch popped open. Now water was streaming in from above as well, and the onrushing wind seemed to grab at the loosened top, tugging it backward and putting strain on the right-hand latch. As I sped down the highway, with rain soaking my lap, I feared that the whole convertible top would be ripped right off the car. So, handling the steering wheel with my right hand, I used my left to pull downward with all my might, forcing the leading edge of the top to seal against the upper edge of the windshield.

Then my right foot began to cramp. A lot, for the next thirty shoulder-aching, top-gripping, thigh-soaking minutes—all in all, one of the more sensual half hours of my life. When I got home, I pulled into the driveway, inching as close as possible to the Passat, so that Carla would be able to pull the van out of the garage. But then I realized that it could rain again tomorrow, so I backed the Fiat onto the street, got into the Passat, backed it onto the street, got back into the Fiat, pulled it into the driveway, got back into the Passat, and pulled it behind the Fiat, inching it as close as possible in case Carla had to maneuver past it. It was like an automotive version of the fast-shuffle con game favored by New York street grifters: three-car monte.

Finally I latched and hammered the ragtop, locked the doors, and walked into my house. Allison was the first to hear me come in.

"Daddy! Daddy!" My adorable nine-year-old ran down the hall and, nearly before I could drop my briefcase, jumped happily into my arms. "Oooh. You're all wet."

Then, as I put Allison down and doffed my windbreaking softball cap, Katie emerged from the family room.

"Hi, Dad. Hey, you're soaked. OOOH. That is major hat hair."

Then, as if on cue, Carla walked into the hallway too.

"Hi, hon," she said. 'it's a shame it's raining out there."

"Oh, yeah? Why is that?"

"I was kind of hoping we could take a spin in your new car."

"In my car? You were? Why?"

"I don't know," she said. "It's kind of fun."

"Fun? Are you saying you're actually glad we bought it?"

"Well," she said, grabbing my wet cap from the newel post where I'd hung it and tossing it in the closet, "it's awfully cute."

"It's cute," said my sister-in-law, Dee, as she and my brother Josh eyeballed the Fiat for the first time. "What's the hammer for?"

I patiently told her the exact truth: that it was for an extremely delicate mechanical procedure she could never even conceive of performing, so never mind the details. Then my brother had a question.

"Have you broken it yet?"

Have I broken it? "No, why?"

"Oh," he said, "I was just wondering, because you broke the other one so quickly."

The other one? *What* other one?

"The dentist's Fiat. The one you drove in high school. When he had the heart surgery?"

Heart surgery? Oh, yeah. Heart surgery. Dr. Botnick didn't go on vacation all those years ago. He went into the hospital, for a bypass operation or something.

"At the Mayo Clinic," Josh reminded me. "And he let you use his car."

"Right. And I fell in love with it. I've been thinking about it for twenty-some years."

"And you stripped second gear."

Stripped second gear? What in the world was he . . . wait a second. Second gear. Upon a moment's reflection, I remembered that Josh was right. Ashley Botnick went to fix his coronary arteries, and I broke his transmission. Almost immediately, come to think of it. Maybe on the second day I had the car. No wonder I could only remember one little spin down Levering Mill Road. The memories were still fuzzy, but one other detail came rushing back to me too. All of a sudden, I recalled that twenty-two years earlier I had found the wind playing havoc with my shoulder-length 1972 locks. So I wore a baseball cap, and wound up with a case of major debilitating hat hair.

So much for destiny.

Still, there was nothing Josh could say that would make me less appreciative of my own personal Fiat Spider. I'd say now that I'm rather more appreciative—appreciative, for example, of how smooth riding the Passat is, insulating me as it does from those annoying bumps in the road. To say nothing of a roof made of a space-age hard material called "metal" that stays magically affixed to the windshield no matter how fast the car is going.

Yes, my fortieth year and my little automotive indulgence

have been truly transforming. Whether it was the experience of driving, or the exercise of analyzing it, I have been forced into confronting my ascent into middle age—a confrontation that has inexorably led to a conclusion. And that conclusion is this:

FOR SALE. *Sleek, Italian 1980 Fiat Spider 2000. Ragtop plus mint-condition hammer. 87,000 miles. $3,508.95, or best offer. Feel the wind in your hair.*

The Haunting of Aspen Grove

Sometime before 1750, a man named Fitzhugh built a cozy, three-bedroom farmhouse on his 21,996 acres of land in what is now the city of Fairfax. The estate was called Aspen Grove. Then came the American Revolution. Then came the War of 1812. Then came the Civil War. Then came the Spanish-American War.

Then came the mortgage interest deduction.

Then, not quite a year ago, came a minor psychotic episode in which I staked all of the money I had, plus four times as much that I didn't have, for the privilege of owning a charming piece of history. I did this even though it was a colossal financial gamble based on a ludicrously optimistic presumption of future earnings. I did this even though the intervening centuries have seen historic Aspen Grove trimmed back by approximately 21,995 1/2 acres and 100 percent of its aspens. I did this even though the house itself provides less living space than the cookie-cutter tract house we'd lived in happily for nine years only five miles away. I did this even though I'd been warned from the very outset that the place was haunted.

Haunted. By a ghost.

But I did it anyway, and the results have been something on the order of *This Old House* meets *The Amityville Horror* meets *The Money Pit*—ghoulies and ghosties and long-legged beasties and things that go bump in the checkbook. It has been a terrifying combination of unforeseen expenditures and strange, ghastly, ominous, alarming events that have rattled my family like so many lengths of heavy-duty, phantasmagoric chain, and for the next 4,000 words I'm going to whine about it.

Yes, I am, and you can hold on right there because I know what you're thinking: *This clown buys a fancy old house that a billion people around the world would love to own, and he's complaining, the pig. People are sleeping on grates in this city, people in Florida and California and the Virgin Islands have seen their homes flattened in a matter of seconds by hurricanes and earthquakes, and this oblivious, self-centered, latter-day Mr. Blandings thinks anyone cares about his petty little problems? He can kiss my Aspen Grove.*

Okay, now, settle down. Settle down. This isn't about feeling sorry for me because Aspen Grove don't have enough aspens to suit me. This is about feeling sorry for me because, like everyone else who ever bought a house in the history of real estate, I'm a complete sucker and moron and self-deluding fool. In a moment, I'm going to tell you what I spent $435 on and about the brown bilge trickling down my siding and about my daughter's brush with death by cabinetry, and in all probability, I will start getting condolences pouring in from Bosnia.

On the other hand, don't even bother sticking around if you're waiting to hear about major calamity, about how the whole place tumbled into a sinkhole, or how some claim on the title from a disgruntled plumber three owners ago has tied me up in a nightmare of litigation. As this story went to press, those things hadn't happened. Yet. What did happen was everything else.

Everything else.

1) Excitement
2) Skepticism
3) Denial
4) Satisfaction
5) Remorse
6) Revelation
7) Terror

These, of course, are the seven stages of home purchasing, and I don't deny being excited, on a warm evening back in April, the first time I saw Aspen Grove. It was all very much of a surprise to me, because I had begun my day in Los Angeles, and, upon arriving in Washington, had expected to grab a cab directly home from National. But Carla insisted on picking me up at the airport.

"Don't bother," I'd told her on the phone from California. "I'll take a taxi."

"It's no bother," she said.

"It isn't? You're not dragging me to Pentagon City Mall again, are you?"

"No, I'm not dragging you to Pentagon City," my wife replied, sounding a bit peeved that I'd suspect, beyond her characteristic thoughtfulness and generosity, some sort of ulterior motive. There was a brief pause before she added, "But there is one stop I may want to make."

"What kind of stop?"

"You'll see."

About 3,000 miles and seven hours later, from the front passenger seat of our aging Voyager, I saw. I saw, perched upon a Fairfax hill—smack in the middle of a subdivision of fancy townhomes—an old white house with four towering columns supporting an imposing front portico. The front lawn sloped gently eastward into a sprawling labyrinth of shoulder-high boxwoods, covering in all about two acres. Lush shrubbery surrounded the building, weaving between it and the white-frame detached garage along a flagstone path. On the far side of the garage, just before the 200-yard borderline of woods, was a wide flat lawn. Around the other side of the house, an enormous and stately black walnut tree shaded the southwest corner.

Like all first-time visitors to Aspen Grove, I went a bit slack in the jaw. I know now that its emplacement, on the crest of the hill, presents a visage rather grander than what a flatter perspective reveals. The pretentious columns do nothing to blunt that effect, and, of course, I had no way of knowing that the boxwoods, and most of the lawn, are on the subdivision's common property. So all I could do was what all of our subsequent visitors have done when they first eyeballed the place. I stared at the portico and laughed.

I hooted, actually, because we are not portico sort of people. We are beige aluminum siding sort of people. At that very moment, in fact, we were the proud owners of a whole mess of beige aluminum siding, just over yonder in Burke Centre. Aspen Grove? I mean, *please*. People who drive old Volkswagens and older-still minivans and who shop for clothes at Marshalls do not belong in a house with a proper name.

To the manor born we were not. Both my wife and I went to Penn State, for crying out loud, where I spent approximately the same amount of time throwing up as Ivy League undergraduates, but not once in a blue blazer. I have a mezuzah on my doorpost and Vibram soles on my shoes. No one in my family has a last name for a first name. The only dwellings I'd ever been in with a name were Mount Vernon, Monticello and a summer beach rental a few years back which had been dubbed by its physician owner, if memory serves, Tetanus II. I did toddle up to horsey country once, but that was to witness the federal raid on Lyndon LaRouche, and I got lost on the way. In short, I have no more business living in a house with a name than Ethel Kennedy has hosting a Tupperware party at Hickory Hill.

And I guess that's why I was excited. I knew my wife had found our dream house. I knew we didn't fit in it. I knew we couldn't afford it. And I knew that therefore, no matter how lovely the place was inside, I wasn't going to have to move.

My wife, of course, had different ideas. She'd become aware of Aspen Grove by reading the local shopper, one of those prestige journals whose feature stories tend to lavish attention on the interests of large advertisers, such as real-estate companies. In the third week of April, the big news was that Aspen Grove was on the market. The cover story, no less. Carla had a copy in the van.

"Look at the facade," the puff piece puffed, "and the music and images from *Gone With the Wind* come to life. . . . As soon as the door is open, the stage is set. You expect to see Scarlett O'Hara flitting about."

No, what I expected to see was a Realtor flitting about, and I was not disappointed. The listing agent was waiting for us in the kitchen, a large and well-appointed kitchen, indeed. A center-island Jenn-Air range. Hmmmm. Very nice. Trash compactor. Spacious pantry. Burglar alarm. Not one but two bright sunrooms. Soon enough I'd all but forgotten the silly columns, which had been installed in the 1950s to pouf up the primitive Georgian facade of the home like some sort of low-rent Tara. Once inside, my attention turned to Aspen Grove's bona fide dream-house qualities: nine-foot ceilings and elaborate dentil moldings throughout; beautiful heart-of-pine random plank flooring aged to golden honey tones; a huge formal dining room with a fireplace, wainscoting, magnificently carved mantle and solid brass 16-candle chandelier; an equally splendid living room; a vast master suite with a fireplace and, in the master bath, Jacuzzi and huge stall shower; a large basement with ancient, exposed log beams still covered with bark; and all about the house—courtesy of its four fireplaces—a pleasant smoky aroma such as has wafted inside Aspen Grove's walls for centuries.

It smelled faintly of smoke here when Franklin and Jefferson labored over the Declaration of Independence. It smelled faintly of smoke when Mason and Dixon surveyed the Pennsylvania-Maryland border, when Lewis and Clark forged west to explore the Louisiana Purchase, when Lincoln and Douglas debated the future of slavery, when Grant and Lee met at Appomattox Courthouse. Aspen Grove was redolent, in short, of history itself.

Since its deeding to Lt. Col. Fitzhugh, the place had changed family hands a mere thirteen times in two and a half centuries. In the 1860s, a Quaker family named Sagar is said to have used the house as a station of the underground railroad, secreting escaping slaves in what is now a hidden cedar closet-behind-a-closet. During the Civil War, the house was occupied variously by both Union and Confederate troops as a bivouac and a hospital. Ruddy stains in the dining room floor—according to "History of Aspen Grove," a thirty-six-page scholarly pamplet by historian Wendy Nicholas—are from the blood of wounded soldiers. Uniformed in gray and in blue, they slept in the house, ate in the house, lived in the house, died in the house—resting, for the most part, in everlasting peace. But one tortured spirit dwells in Aspen Grove yet today, a soldier searching eternally for a pair of boots left behind. Or so the legend goes.

Even without such a colorful history the house was truly magnificent, and priced at what struck me as a tremendous bargain—not much more expensive than the townhouses that surrounded it. But it was way out of our price range. Way, way out. For us to buy this place, several things would have to happen. The sellers would have to slash the asking price. We'd have to sell our house at top dollar, even as identical models were languishing on our street unsold for months. Interest rates would have to plunge. And a 250-year-old dwelling would have to pass all sorts of scrutiny from building inspectors, structural engineers and so on.

I looked at Carla and smiled. "Nice place," I said. Then I looked at the real estate lady and shook my head. "Sorry, not in a million years." This is the skepticism phase of home buying.

The next thing that happened was interest rates began to

plunge. The next thing that happened is the real estate woman brought buyers to our house offering top dollar, even though our house was not listed for sale. The next thing that happened was a clean bill of health for Aspen Grove from an army of inspectors and contractors. The next thing was a fateful bit of calculus: The house was many, many tens of thousands of dollars more than we could afford. What if we made an offer that was only several tens of thousands of dollars more than we could afford? After a while, we'd grow into the mortgage payment. Sure, we'd have to scrimp for a year or two—or seven—but the place had been so thoroughly renovated when the townhouses were built that at least we wouldn't have to sink a lot of fix-up dough into it.

Stage 3: Denial.

And so, contingent on some minor repair work being done by the seller, we made an offer. Approximately 1.9 seconds later, the seller accepted.

"When I presented the contract," the listing agent told us, "everybody cried. This was to be their 'forever after' house."

They cried; we toasted our marvelous good fortune. The job change that had deprived them of their dream house had furnished us with ours. There commenced the "satisfaction" phase of home ownership, the period of optimism, delight and nervous expectation as the buyers await mortgage approval and a sufficient appraisal. At this stage we were too pleased with our accomplishment to understand that Aspen Grove was soon to be our "forever after" house, as well: a huge investment followed—hauntingly—by expenditure upon expenditure upon expenditure, forever after.

Was it some sort of omen when, on the day of settlement, I excused myself from the lawyerings to use the bathroom and strode, with confidence and a lively gait, into a coat closet? Maybe not, but from that moment forward things began to happen. Unexpected things. Costly things. For instance, immediately upon settling I hurried to my new dream house and scrambled up a ladder to repaint the downstairs. The beautiful moldings were all painted in Williamsburg blue, and we wanted them white. I had a week before moving to do the job, so I wasn't concerned about time—until, after the third day of dabbing a brush between the thousands of teeth in the dentil molding, I realized I was only 20 percent finished. With time running short, we had no choice but to call in a real painter. But only one man could do the work right away. When he came to bid the job, he took one step into our living room and began to laugh.

"Hah!" he said, in a thick Greek accent that did nothing to conceal his contempt. "This ees not how you paint."

For the next few days, he shook his head, clucking and snorting about my workmanship, and showed me how to paint. All I had to give him was $2,400.

It was a tense week. On the day of the move, with the van still in our driveway, we got no visits from our new neighbors, but the president of the community association got four calls of complaint about our kids' tasteful, built-by-Grampa wooden playhouse. The girls complained, too, about the authentic, historical honey-toned pine flooring in their rooms. They wanted carpeting. And the house was hot. Very hot. The AC was cranking, but when we retired for our first night in our dreamhouse the bedroom must have been 80 degrees. The loose louvers of the air vent quaked and rattled. Walnuts, from our stately, ancient black walnut tree—in an eerie preview of our autumn—were dislodged from their stems in the gentle breeze and thereupon onto the tin roof the tree overhangs. Bamp. BAMP. Carla, who was still in the middle of studying for final exams in graduate school, lay in bed contemplating what we had gotten into. Exhausted, overwrought and worried, she began to cry.

Stage 5. Remorse.

"Did we make a mistake?" she sobbed.

"No, sweetheart," I said soothingly and unconvincingly, "of course not."

In a few days, I assured her, when exams were finished and the house was more organized, we'd have a whole new outlook. But I lay awake, too, for the longest time. Rattle, rattle. Bamp, BAMP. And what was that I smelled? Smoke? Was that the same pleasant whiff of history I'd been so enchanted with? It isn't very pleasant at 4 A.M., when you're busy staring into the dark fretting about the biggest financial commitment of your life, and you don't know whether you're smelling that charming smoky aroma of American history or the children in flames.

Was it the next day we were awakened, at dawn, by a rodent six feet from our heads? It was a squirrel, or squirrels, digging around the fascia beneath the roof and just above our window. The rotten fascia. The fascia that was the entrance to squirrels' nests and birds nest in at least four places around the house. The fascia that would have to be replaced at heaven knows what cost. And so on, and on. After the first hard rain, the basement flooded. ("Is the basement wet?" I'd asked the listing agent. "It *has* been wet," she replied. Is. Has been. These are semantics. But when the rains come, it *is* Waterworld.) We're just now debating whether to go with the sump pump, at $1,300 installed, or the full-fledged waterproofing with concrete excavation at $3,800. Meanwhile, the hot water heater proved to be old and inadequate. The new one was $750. The tubs didn't drain properly. The plumber took $100. The closets in the master bedroom had no lights in them. $230.

Stage 6: Revelation.

After a few days, the house did cool down. I fixed the rattling AC vent. I stuffed the rotting fascia with steel wool and covered the holes temporarily with boards. The boxes were gradually unpacked. A few neighbors stopped by to welcome us. Carla and I both got some sleep. By the time a month had passed, Aspen Grove was no longer the new house. It was beginning to be home. And home, of course, is where . . . the electric bill is mailed.

Four hundred and sixteen dollars. $416. Four one six.

Here is what you can buy with $416. You can buy 10 boxes of 25 La Aurora handrolled Dominican cigars. You can buy a 27" color television with stereo Surroundsound. You can buy lunch, at a Capitol cafeteria, for the entire U.S. Senate. Or you can run power to our house for thirty days.

For what earthly reason it costs that much I could not imagine. Our old dead-of-summer electric bills ran to $225. But, of course, maybe there was no earthly explanation. As gradually became apparent, the best explanation might well have been an otherworldly one: the ghost. The bootless Civil War ghost who, as the household sleeps, tiptoes from room to room barefoot and does something in his tortured afterlife that he could never do when he was alive. He uses electricity.

That's correct. A voltergeist.

I know, I know, there's no such thing as ghosts. But who ever heard of a three bedroom house with a $416 light bill? It's one thing to face the one-time squeeze of an unanticipated capital expense. It's another matter altogether to pay blood money, month after month, to Redi Kilowatt. Under pressure like that, the imagination runs a little wild.

A week or two later I was at LaGuardia Airport, just about to catch the shuttle back to D.C., when I called in to check voice-mail messages. There was only one, from my daughter. I cannot begin to describe the sobbing hysteria of the delivery, but I can relate the text in its entirely: "Daddy! You've got to call home right away. Something horrible has happened. Oh, Daddy, call right away!"

I called right away. The line was busy, as, of course, it would be, if my wife and other daughter were lying in a pool of blood and the paramedics were tying up the line to call the coroner.

So I phoned the operator and managed to break into the line and get through.

Carla answered. This was good news, for I reasoned that if she was answering the phone, in all probability she wasn't dead. Indeed, she was quite intact and so were both the children. What was not intact was a pair of kitchen cabinets. While my fourteen-year-old was home alone, standing but a few paces away in horror, the cabinets had for no apparent reason ripped from the wall and fallen six feet to the floor, smashing all of our wedding crystal to several thousand glistening leaded shards. One moment all was normal, the next moment a strange crackling noise, the next moment a horrendous crash. Sixty seconds earlier, my daughter had been standing directly beneath them. No wonder she was so terror stricken.

This news made me very happy. After all, I'd been anticipating more than broken glass. On the other hand, the children were quite shaken. Everybody enjoys a charming little ghost legend. But hardly anybody wants to be crushed to death in the Fairfax edition of *House on Haunted Hill.*

"Don't worry, sweetheart," I told my rattled teenager, "it couldn't have been the ghost."

"Why couldn't it, Daddy?"

"Because cabinets aren't plugged in."

Beep. Beep. Beep. Beep. Beep. Beep. Beep.

It was 6:15 A.M. on a frigid December Sunday. I stared at the burglar alarm panel, with greenishly backlit buttons, like fragments of a Timex Indiglo. Yes, it was definitely beeping. Loudly. Insistently.

There was no reason for it to be beeping, however, because it wasn't hooked up to anything. We hadn't bothered contracting with an alarm company, for fear that false alarms would create a nuisance for us and our neighbors. And after their nettlesome reaction to our playhouse, we had no interest in being a nuisance.

"What's the command code?" I asked Carla.

"We don't have a command code," she said.

I didn't think so. So I randomly pressed buttons for a few moments hoping it would shut down as spontaneously as it has acted up. No such luck. Well, it was just a little beeping. We could live with it for a day until we could get an alarm company to check out the situation. Still, with equal parts bewilderment and disgust, I trundled to the basement and began poking around the control boxes. First I checked the circuit breaker, in case a power interruption had somehow set the thing off, but all the circuit switches were in place. No outage. Then I looked into the alarm boxes themselves, where I found a tangle of wires and no apparent method for disconnecting them. I didn't want to rip them out, on the theory that they are set up to make such tampering fruitless, but I did disconnect the terminals of the back-up-power drycell.

I believe that's when the siren went off.

The siren, attached to the front of our house. A loud and shrill siren, blaring, for all the neighborhood to enjoy, like a soprano sax in your eardrum. At 6:30 on a Sunday morning. Luckily our nearest neighbors are nearly forty feet away. The two naval officers across the street must have been particularly delighted.

Pearl Harbor: the Reenactment.

That's when I started ripping out wires, for all the good it did. Turns out they are set up to make such tampering fruitless. Carla immediately tried to call the police, but couldn't get through. Our phone was dead, presumably because the alarm system was trying to automatically dial up the security company that we don't have. But the police soon showed up anyway, called by the neighbors. I went out to meet the cop, who after asking for my picture ID (in case I was that barefooted, half-dressed, tousle-headed, police-hailing, middle-aged burglar that has so terrorized Northern Virginia) entered the house. I explained the situation, about the weird beeping, about the fact that the alarm wasn't hooked up, about the dead phone.

"Why didn't you just call your alarm company and have them shut it down?" he asked.

"Because we don't have one," I said. "We just have the hardware. It's not connected to anything. And our phone is dead."

"All right," the officer said. "I'll radio the dispatcher. They can call the alarm company."

I looked at Carla. She shrugged. And the siren wailed.

The dispatcher didn't know what to do, so the policeman radioed for assistance from another officer who knew more about alarms. Meanwhile, I stuffed wads of toilet paper in my ears, grabbed a stepladder from the garage and headed for the portico. There I struggled with a moldering sheet metal screw and, after three ear-shattering minutes, reached the wires to the siren and tore them free. The noise stopped.

By then the second cop had shown up, and he too stared, bemused by the tangle of wires in the alarm control box.

"Where's your circuit breaker?" he asked.

"It's over there," I gestured. "But I've already checked. None of the breakers is tripped, so that isn't what set it off."

He insisted on looking anyway, and, as I stood there rolling my eyes, he checked every single switch.

"What about this one?" he asked.

"Which one?" I replied with disgust. It was perfectly in position. What could he possibly think was amiss with it?

"This one," the officer said. "The one that says 'ALARM.' "

Oh, *that* one. He flipped it to the left. The beeping from the panel in the kitchen stopped.

And fortunate it was, because now that I was no longer running current through my burglar alarm, in December my electric bill plummeted to $405.

WHACK! DIE! DIE! DIE!, YOU FILTHY BEAST!

Any house can have a ghost. How many houses have a ghost and marauding gargantuan flies from hell?

WHACK! There. Got another one.

Apparently a few weeks ago, an animal somehow got into the basement and died. Probably by drowning. And there, in the earthen portion of the cellar, hidden in the crawlspace, maddeningly out of my flashlight's view, it putrefied, no doubt crawling with maggots, unseen but ever-present, fouling the air, wafting up the stairwell and assaulting us whenever we opened the door. This lasted for a month. Then, just the other day, we opened the basement door and a hundred flies flew out. And, over the next week, a thousand flies. Big, fat, indolent flies, like jumbo pitted black olives with wings. They head for windowpanes, where they basically cross their legs, light a cigarette and just hang. Until I whack them, with a rolled-up *History of Aspen Grove*. One after the other. Whack. Whack. WHACK! Oooooh, it is something to experience. When they fall to the sill or the floor, you can actually hear the tiny thud. Is that one now? It is! To the manor born, eh, you miserable insect?! You can die there, too. WHACK! Thud. The honey-hued pine planks shudder. And so do I. Shaking like a leaf. The great white hunter is trembling.

Because he is cold.

As I write this, it is late January and about twenty-three degrees outside. Luckily, I'm working indoors, where it is a balmy sixty-six. That's because we're really cranking the heat pump. Yes, the heat pump—that amazing invention which doesn't cool your house very well in the summer, then, miraculously, thanks to heat-exchanger technology I don't begin to understand, doesn't heat it very well in the winter.

It's an old house. It's a cold house. My last electric bill was $435 —$435!—and I'm freezing my butt off.

All right, once again, I know what you're thinking: It would be foolish, for a house so old and porous, to try to use a heat pump.

Duh. That's why the people who remodeled the house ripped out the old oil furnace and installed two heat pumps, one to heat the lower level not very well and one to heat the second floor not very well. On a pure BTU-per-unit-cost basis, we could more efficiently warm our home with a fireplace fueled by bricks of tightly bundled $10 bills. That December electric bill cinched our bid for Virginia Power's Customer of the Year, narrowly edging out the Norfolk Naval Shipyard. This thanks to our distracted founding fathers, who were so busy experimenting with democracy that they forgot to invent fiberglass insulation. Never mind Franklin and Jefferson. To hell with Lewis and Clark. Where in the name of God were Owens and Corning when I needed them?

Here again, but for Stage 3 denial, we probably would have been prepared for something like this. When we looked at the previous owner's utility bills, they did seem a bit high—not this high, but enough that I asked the listing agent if they were cold in the house.

"They were *last* winter," she said.

Oh, *last* winter. *Last* winter, when it was ten degrees for two weeks in a row. Not every winter, was the implication. Just *last* winter. Hey, how about *this* October. And *this* November. And December and January. Suddenly I'm understanding what happened to our ghost. If he was fool enough to take off his boots inside, he deserves to be dead. Probably of pneumonia. And now, stuck in an all electric house for all of eternity, this spectral, amp-sucking prankster from beyond taps into any stray line of current he can find in the vain hope of taking the chill out of those old bones.

For all the good it will do him. By mid-December the place was just too cold to stand. So, before Christmas, we brought in a heating contractor to solve the problem—and he found one right away. The upstairs heat pump was installed without the auxiliary heaters that are supposed to kick on when the heat-exchanger becomes too inefficient. Our unit was equipped for two. It had none. But they're going right back in this week— along with a heating vent in the master bathroom, which until now has been unheated and uncooled. Total cost: $600.

"I've never seen anything like this," the contractor said. "How can you stand it when it gets cold?"

"Strength of character," I said. "Anyway, we've only been chilly for a few months. The previous owners must have suffered for five years."

"Five years?" the HVAC man said. "Try thirteen years."

Silly me. I hadn't asked the housing inspector how old the heating system was. I'd assumed, foolishly, that the two heat pumps were part of the renovation five years ago. In fact, they'd been part of the renovation in 1982. So . . . if they're that old . . . we can expect them to last another . . . how many years?

"Ummm, hard to say. It's possible they could make it until next winter," the contractor said. "Or they may quit tomorrow."

Luckily you can replace them for only $4,000.

Apiece.

Stage 7. Terror. Yielding anxiety, paranoia and bitterness.

Is that Scarlett O'Hara I see as the front door swings open? Fiddle dee dee. Slam it shut, you energy-wasting tramp.

But it's funny. Comes a time when there is also a Stage 8. And that is called "contentment." There's no set time for this to occur, but it does. It always does. For us it arrived during the Blizzard of '96. Like other Washington-area homeowners, we were buried in snow and ice, and all but frozen in fear of how the house would take it. I myself alternated between praying for a power outage, to keep my electric bill down, and for the structural integrity of the portico, shaded as it was by a flat roof holding approximately 3,000 cubic feet of snow.

Here's what happened: the roof didn't cave in. In fact, nothing went terribly wrong. The old heat pumps pumped. Water run-off didn't come sloshing beneath the ice-dammed gutters down our interior walls. The burglar alarm, finally connected to a service, didn't trip by accident. And those fireplaces worked like a charm. The worst damage came from that old walnut tree.

The last of its leaves, trapped in the gutters, colored a nasty, snow-melt sluice that channeled behind the gutters and ran down the exterior white siding like sewage. Very Stephen King. Very staining. Very unsightly.

Not supernatural, however. Notwithstanding the quaint folklore, I'm not fully prepared to certify Aspen Grove as a haunted house. Yes, some mysterious phantom had been haunting us, but I'm not sure it was a soldier with no boots. I think it was more like a remodeler with no pride. The missing heater fits right in with the kitchen cabinets, which had been installed with a total of six drywall screws, only one of which was embedded in a stud. The truly mysterious question was how the things had held up for five years.

The new ones will hold. And they'll be toasty warm, by golly, because the heating problems—with the installation of two ten-kilowatt auxiliary units—have just been taken care of. And so will the basement, and the fascia and the walnut-stain streaks and everything else that crops up. All it will take is money, which we're short of, and time, which we have in long supply. What the storm reminded us of is that Aspen Grove didn't get to be 250 years old by being a bad house. It is a good house. It is a lovely house. In many ways, it is a breathtaking house. Those mantles. Those ceilings. Those floors. The landscaping. The portico. The history. It is not a nightmare property; it is our dream house after all.

Why just the other day I got a small arcing problem on the circuit breaker fixed for a mere $225. And now I can sit and write with true peace of mind, letting the smoky aroma of history envelop me, filling my nostrils and my heart and my mind and . . . whoops.

Gotta run. As God is my witness, one of the new heaters is on fire.

Jews Don't Hunt

*Call me Reuven. I have endured untold trials. I have suffered the
stings of disdain and recrimination from a dark and malevolent
world. I have let fall into imbalance the very life-giving humors of
my body—all in my search of the elusive Great White Tail. And
now, as dark befalls the valley of the shadow of death, the climax
is upon me. Here I stand, somewhere (I know not precisely where)
in the woods, face-to-doe-eyed face with the demon. The only question now, as I raise my Winchester 30–30 against my quarry, is
who will triumph.*

All right, so that isn't the *only* question. Maybe there's one other
little matter. Such as: What the hell am I doing here?

The fact is, nobody calls me Reuven. The last time anybody
called me Reuven was nineteen and a half years ago at my bar
mitzvah. "Reuven ben Shmul," the rabbi said, "read now from
the Torah." I refer here to the holiest of Jewish books, which
chronicles thousands of years of history without one passage—
without one single sentence—involving a Jew in the woods
with a loaded gun.

Verily, Jews don't hunt.

I don't mean to mislead you. This is not a religious distinction; it's a cultural phenomenon, like the aversion to pastrami
on white with mayo. Such a sandwich is in all likelihood kosher,
but to any right-thinking Jew, it's repulsive. Yet many a gentile
will walk into a deli and order such an atrocity without com-
punction, which only shows that people of different upbring-
ings have widely divergent notions of what constitutes right
and wrong. And so it is in the world of sport. For the same rea-

son you don't find many Mormon fight promoters or Episco-palian stock-car drivers, you simply don't see many Jews in tree stands looking for woodland fauna to blow to kingdom come.

My particular predicament, however, arose out of not one but two cultures. I'm a nice Jewish boy from Philadelphia mar-ried to Carla, a nice Catholic girl from Pittsburgh. Even via the Pennsylvania Turnpike, our respective families are about 280 light-years apart.

Carla's father and her four brothers are all avid hunters. For years they have leaped at every chance to drive three hours to mountainous northwest Pennsylvania so that they might tramp the woods in search of game. My family knew no such activity. Our most rugged wildlife adventure was a head-boat trip in the Barnegat Bay, during which I personally landed one flounder and threw up nineteen times.

At the risk of sounding insecure, I'll admit to being a bit con-cerned about the image I project to my in-laws. How could I not be? Nobody wants to be regarded as a citified, tenderfoot wimp—even when one (I speak entirely hypothetically) obvi-ously is. But the comparison between my background and theirs, in terms of relative machismo, is unsettling indeed. White-collar executives though they now may be, all my broth-ers-in-law had worked their way through school by building cooling towers. They would be sixty feet in the air, tools strapped all over them, shouting, "Hey, yo! Send me up a rivet gun!" Any one of those guys can build a house with his bare hands.

My after-school job was for Floral Fantasies, designing cen-terpieces. "Hey, yo! Send over three spider mums and some baby's breath!" The most elaborate thing I ever built with my bare hands was the pulpit arrangement for the Feinstein wedding.

As I said, these guys have been liquidating grouse, squirrels, and whitetail since they were knee-high to a baptismal font. I never so much as donned a flannel shirt in anger.

That's not to say I didn't have the opportunity. For as long as

I've been married, I've had a standing offer to join the in-laws at their deer-hunting camp. This is an annual post-Thanksgiving rite of male bonding in which ten or so grown men repair to a cabin to not shower while fantasizing about Bambicide and consuming their weight in red meat and beer. The three days of revelry culminate in opening day, when everybody hustles into the woods under cover of darkness and, for eleven solid hours, tries not to freeze to death.

That, anyway, was my experience two years ago when I succumbed to a decade's pressure and tagged along. In borrowed clothes, with a borrowed gun, I clambered around the woods with the real hunters hoping against hope that I wouldn't do something stupid, like get lost or shoot my father-in-law.

As it turned out, I didn't shoot anyone or anything. I never even saw a buck. But something very strange did happen. I had a good time. Though I came to suspect that *hunting* is a gentile word meaning "stepping over logs," I thoroughly enjoyed the whole experience. The only troublesome aspect was dealing with my parents and brother. They were horrified that I would even consider such an expedition, and they weren't entirely satisfied with my explanation that I was just browsing.

Alas, when last fall I announced I would be going hunting again, there was no fooling them. My mother didn't actually say anything—a woman can't communicate effectively when she's sobbing in her room—but my brother had certain questions concerning "the wanton slaughter of innocent animals." That was fine with me, for it enabled me to enlighten him on certain key aspects of the sporting life.

"Number one, it's not as easy as you think," I said, affecting an authoritative tone. "Deer are fleet-footed and cunning animals. I'm told most disappear out of target range the moment you yell 'Stop or I'll shoot!' Second, this isn't wanton slaughter. The woods are overpopulated with deer. If there isn't an annual deer harvest [a word I'd picked up from my in-laws], they'll die an agonizing death by starvation and along the way will destroy woodlands by gnawing at tree bark in search of food. Third, speaking for myself, I'll shoot only if provoked."

There's something about soft-spoken reason that affects the most hostile interlocutor. My brother was amazed at how thoroughly I'd thought it all out. "Unbelievable," he said. "I *cannot* believe you're going to kill a defenseless animal."

Perhaps I wasn't making the impression I'd hoped for, so I opted for a change of rhetorical direction. This time I spoke of pastoral beauty, of the frosted stillness in the snowy woods, of the sweet laurel in harmony with the towering hardwoods, of the forest's serene quietude broken only by breathtaking songbirds or the gentle, whistling winds.

That didn't work, either.

"So if it's so beautiful, why don't you go into the woods with a camera and no gun? Huh? Why do you have to kill anything?" he asked.

Once more I explained it all patiently. "Look, it's kind of like fishing," I said. "You can fish all day and not catch anything, and it'll still be a good time, because the liberating part is the total concentration on the problem at hand. While you're busy monitoring every minor nudge on your line and trying to envision the terrain and activity beneath the hull of your boat, you're not giving a moment's thought to the car-insurance bill you have to pay by Thursday or else sell one of the children. But if, say, you have a line out without a hook on it, you're not going to be concentrating on anything because you can't possibly catch anything. All you can do is sit there daydreaming, like how you'd rather have a stroke than go to work tomorrow."

To which my brother, stunned finally by the clarity of my logic, responded, "I can't believe you're going to slaughter a deer for no good reason."

I would have argued longer, but I had to get my gear packed and hit the road. Besides, I wasn't so sure he was wrong. I had bought the intellectual argument for deer hunting, granted, but that's very different from squeezing a trigger, killing an animal, slicing into its flesh with a knife, pulling out its guts with your bare hands, and dragging the carcass to a butcher where it will be cut into venison steaks that everybody will rave about, but nobody will actually like.

Which brings me to Bully Hollow, a cold-water creek between two mountains six miles north of Tidioute, Pennsylvania, which in turn, in case you're a bit hazy as to where this village is located, is fifty miles west of Kane. As expected, the hunting camp was as congenial and relaxing as could be. The weekend began with the annual beer-and-cussing orgy at the Crazy Eights, a neighboring cabin inhabited by cheerful, middle-aged roughnecks. Played on an accordion, washtub bass, and washboard, the country-and-western and polka music sounded great. I myself handled bass during "Oh, How She Lied," creating on my thumb a blister the size of a hyla crucifer, an amphibian species I identified on the handy wall chart titled "Frogs of Pennsylvania."

The ensuing two days were passed consuming two kegs of beer and $240 worth of meat. (I certainly didn't let my congenital cholesterol disorder deter me. What's the use of cleaning rifles and swearing if you stick to some sissy low-fat diet? So I had conversations like this: "How do you like those pigs' feet, Bob?" "Delightful pigs' feet, Dad.") Meantime, the veteran hunters exchanged charming stories of trips past. My particular favorite involved a man driving a black Jeep up a logging road. Seems somebody mistook him for a bear and killed him. Ha!

But there in Bully Hollow, all of that was behind me. This day had been all hunting and none too fruitful. In the morning we sat for hours in a freshly clear-cut logging site, hoping the deer would be feeding there on the fallen brush. No such luck. The only wildlife I saw was a starling. Or perhaps it was a sparrow. Or a jay. Maybe it was a condor. I'm not sure. As I watched this bird flitting from branch to branch, my brother's words burned in my head: "Man is the only species that kills for sport." After five hours of sitting, I was ready to kill just for something to do.

Later we moved on to a more densely wooded area, but still no deer. Two years earlier under similar circumstances I had felt relieved; on this trip I was bitterly disappointed. As I stood peering into the thicket for any sign of movement, I envisioned a ten-point buck. My mind's eye paid no heed to the fact that a deer's head would clash with our drapes.

Twice more we changed our position. As no Garfield had ever done before me, I rode in the bed of a pickup truck, rifle in my frozen hands. (Before the trip began I'd gone out to buy gloves, remembering how quickly and thoroughly immobile your hands can get in the cold. I couldn't find any ordinary gloves to suit me, but I did find—for $38.99—a nifty Glove Component System. The GCS had a nylon outer shell and a three-ply inner lining for warmth and durability. Indeed, the GCS would have been a real boon, had I only been able to fit the stubby, multi-ply forefinger through the trigger guard. So in the pickup I sat, my hands stiff in my old One-ply Wool System.)

At 4 P.M., with less than an hour of daylight remaining, I broke off from the others. We were maybe two miles from our cabin, high on the ridge overlooking the hollow. I thought it would be fun to work my way down the mountainside, hang a right, and follow the creek home. This I did. Only, when I got to the creek, after twenty minutes of rugged falling down, I noticed it ran not to my right but to my left. This presented two possibilities. Either I had simply miscalculated the relative positions of the ridge, the creek, and the cabin, or I was lost in the forest just before nightfall. If the latter were true, the only question was whether I would starve, freeze, be shot, be eaten by a bear, or be hog-tied and raped, à la *Deliverance,* and left to die. Any way I looked at it, it spelled major embarrassment.

"Aha!" I said aloud. "*This* is why Jews don't hunt."

I did then what I had to do: I followed the creek downstream, figuring that it would either get me home or somewhere else with gentiles who knew what they were doing. Dusk was falling. There was no point panicking, but I walked briskly along a muddy hiking path, huffing and sweating and feeling generally stupid.

That's when I saw the deer.

Two of them. Maybe a buck and a doe. Maybe two bucks. They'd come down the hill to the creek and were crossing back and forth as if unsure of where to go. I froze, no more than fifty feet away. Ever so slowly I raised my rifle. My Winchester had no scope, and I was having trouble seeing for sure: Were those antlers or not? The deer were in shadows. Should I shoot, or just ask them for directions?

For the longest time I kept the deer in my sights. Ten seconds, 15 seconds. Finally the larger one looked right at me. My finger was on the trigger.

Are those really antlers, or just twigs? Can I really kill this beautiful animal? What if I'm lost; how will I get the carcass back to camp? What if I miss and hit the doe? What if I step a few feet closer. . . .

Whoosh. The deer were gone. No shots fired. No wanton slaughter for Reuven.

As it turned out, this whole drama was played out 400 yards from the cabin. I strolled right in for some beer and pepperoni. Then I took my cholesterol medicine. Then I took a shower.

The Journalism Life

NEW YORK—My Trip to New York City: I took a trip to New York City for my Work. My Work is to write Articles for Newspapers.

It is sometimes very fun, like the time I talked to the robber in jail. The robber had once got cornered by policemen and blew some of his own brains out with a gun. It was fun when I was talking to him and he accidentally confessed to killing a man when he still had 100 percent of his brain. Other times, like the time I stood ankle-deep in latex paint after a train derailment and later in the same week somebody threatened to kill me, my Work is not fun and is quite annoying. On my trip to New York City nobody threatened to kill me, but it was mostly not fun and sometimes quite annoying.

On my trip to New York City I met a lady magician and a man with fifty-four Statue of Liberty pins on his lapel and I interviewed a lady who dresses in leather and ties men up and whips them and makes them bark like dogs. I enjoyed that part of the trip. The lady did not make me bark like a dog. The part of my trip I didn't like was the part where I lost my wallet and my notebook with seventy pages of interview notes and got stranded at LaGuardia Airport.

Also, part of my Work was to interview a man named Barry who has $300 million and bought a castle in Southampton, Long Island, and wanted to make it even more impressive with a cupola and other geegaws but some people there threw a Fit. They threw a Fit partly because they do not like cupolas and partly because Barry is a Jewish person and they are not Jewish persons and partly because he does not wear madras trousers and partly because they wish they had $300 million to put geegaws on their castles. I knew this would make an interesting Article for Newspapers, but when I got to New York City, Barry said he did not wish to be interviewed. I said it is just as well because I probably would have just lost the notes anyway, but he did not know what I was talking about.

The reason I got stranded at LaGuardia Airport was because it was raining and New York Air's airplanes did not want to come to New York. This made me sad because my car was in Washington. I was eager to be in my car and drive to my house and talk to my little girl. My little girl is four and a half years old and everybody says she is so Smart and she was so Smart that during my trip to New York City she took a key and jammed it in an outlet in the wall and melted part of the key and got a shocking surprise. The lucky part was she was not seriously hurt, but I wanted to be with my little girl and remind her about safety and also possibly beat her within an inch of her Life.

The lucky part about being stranded in LaGuardia Airport was at least I didn't have to pay for my air tickets. I didn't have to pay for my tickets because New York Air gave them to me for free. New York Air gave me the tickets for free because it felt bad from the last time I was in LaGuardia. The last time I was in LaGuardia the planes also didn't come and I was stuck there all night so I couldn't fly all the way to Washington because of the curfew.

On that trip I met a man who was not only a hostage of New York Air but was once a hostage of Shiite Moslems in Beirut and escaped by tying bed sheets together and scaling down a wall. The man told me at least the Shiites served food, which I thought was funny and I laughed only he didn't laugh when I asked him if he had ever stood ankle-deep in latex paint.

On my trip to New York City this time I did not meet any Beirut hostages in the airport so I decided to go to the train station. I went to the train station and the train they wanted to put me on was called the 125 and this made me sad. This made me sad because the last time I rode the 125 it stopped dead in New Jersey and had no ventilation and it was July. I did not want to be stuck in New Jersey, because the lady magician and I had driven together to Tenafly, New Jersey, where she did magic for twelve mortgage bankers and we got lost on the way and I didn't want to be stuck twice in New Jersey and once at LaGuardia in one trip to New York City. But I got on the train and went to Washington and did not get stuck.

When I got home and my wife asked me how my trip to New York City was I told her about the man with fifty-four lapel pins and she told me that did not sound like an interesting Article for Newspapers and I told her I'm considering a new line of Work.

PART
4

Success, and Other Outcomes

He Is the Egg Man

Thanks to the miracle of modern catering . . . CHING-CRACK-BLUUP . . . he is often in two places at once, especially on weekends. Because of his remarkable heritage . . . CHING-CRACK-BLUUP . . . he can be liberating eggs from their shells at a bat mitzvah in Adephi, Maryland, while at the exact same moment be here at a small party in Rockville doing the very same thing.

"I get excited about my work," he says, without pausing from the steady, concussive discharge of his duties, "and I don't know what it is to this day. You can ask me the question and I really can't give you an answer. But I just get excited."

The excitement doesn't show. In his floppy chef's hat, pleated tuxedo shirt, bow tie, red apron with black piping, black pants, and black Reeboks, he is all business. Again and again he shifts his weight, reaches for an egg, wheels, and CHING! hammers the edge of the stainless-steel bowl, CRACK, cleaves the shell, one-handed, then BLUUP, unceremoniously dumps the contents into the bowl. Again and again, CHING-CRACK-BLUUP, he cracks them here, he cracks them there, he cracks those eggs most everywhere. Except, at the synagogue in Adelphi, it's happening by proxy, which is the luxury of having fifteen employee namesakes and at least as many steel bowls. Here, in Rockville, in the dining room of William and Marty Triplett's spacious apartment, with fourteen dozen eggs to his right, a four-burner propane stove to his left, stands a busy, solitary figure: none other than David Model himself, the peripatetic (or is it ubiquitous?) Scarlet Pimpernel of short-order, the man they call Mr. Omelette.

"I look at an egg the way some people look at a good written paper," says Mr. Omelette, twenty-eight, curly-haired and not entirely unegglike in build. "I look at an egg as being very versatile. Eggs are in everything. And I look at an egg to be light, fluffy, and very sensitive. I look at it, you can't make an omelette without cracking any eggs."

Over in the Tripletts' living room, there are twenty revelers, highballs in hand. Host and hostess mingle with family and old friends. The festive conversations produce something more than a murmur and something less than a din. Here in the dining room, the salad has long since been tossed, the cream cheese and butter long since scored with a fork for luncheon elegance. The containers of fillings—mushrooms, onions, lox and ched-dar and mozzarella cheese—are lined up in a tidy row. Now is the time, before lunch is served, for Mr. Omelette to finish doing what Mr. Omelette has to do.

Like a hunter who professes to so love wildlife that he must shoot it with a rifle, Mr. Omelette expresses his lifelong affinity with eggs even as he shatters one after another. With perhaps four dozen forlorn yolks floating in a dense lake of albumen, he absently pours a cup of cold water into the bowl.

Look out! He's got a whisk!

Mr. Omelette attacks the plump, delicate yolks, and they hemorrhage instantly. The albumen lake becomes a vortex, a roiling yellow cyclone. The love of Mr. Omelette's life . . . battered.

In an era of dignified titles incongruously attached to inanimate objects, it might be easy to confuse somebody named

Mr. Omelette with somebody named, say, Mr. Mattress or Dr. Vinyl. Make no such mistake. Dr. Vinyl is a Colorado Springs polymer-restoration specialist who entered the glamorous field of vinyl repair only after abandoning a dead-end job as a singer/guitarist with Stud Buzzard and the Swingin' Sirloins. Mr. Mattress, the 545-pound Baton Rouge, Louisiana, bedding store proprietor, is selling Posture Rest Royals and bargain twins only to subsidize—coincidentally enough—his singing/song-writing career. ("Oh, I can't see the forest for the trees / I spend all my time loving in the street / But I'm so glad that she's my woman, instead of a tree / Because she sees, she sees the real me.") "It's something to do," Mattress says. "It's income."

As for the good doctor, if it weren't for the rigors of the road-house life, he'd still have a stake in the Sirloins. But the hours and the uncertainty of living gig to gig, he says, were "real tough. It's just not a very healthy atmosphere." So he switched careers for the sake of Mrs. Vinyl and the two Vinyl children.

In other words, impressive titles or no, these men acquired their personas by default. Not so Mr. Omelette. His adopted name was his destiny.

While other little kids in Lido Beach, New York, grew up preoccupied with the New York Mets and Bruno Sammartino and *The Brady Bunch,* young Master Omelette worked in his father's deli, visions of knishes dancing in his head. Ed Kranepool was the furthest thing from his mind. He was thinking: dairy.

"I grew up basically in the food business," he says. There was little doubt how he would spend his life, "since I was very, very young—about eight, nine, ten years old."

Oh, maybe he didn't have a precise fix on omelettes that early. It wasn't until he was a teenager that his father, Mr. Omelette Sr., founded the business on Long Island. But what this boy knew about blintzes in the third grade would make your head swim. As his father's business evolved, so did the junior Omelette's interests. From retail delis in Brooklyn and Long Island, to pastry manufacturing, to the dairy catering business, he found himself immersed in and enchanted by food preparation. By the time he enrolled at the University of Maryland in 1980, majoring in marketing with a minor in foods, his field of study had become a mere formality. By his junior year, with the Alpha Epsilon Pi fraternity house as his base of operations, his legacy was realized, his peerage fulfilled, his destiny achieved. Like his father before him, he became Mr. Omelette.

And that means *became* Mr. Omelette. This is not just a trade name, some sort of casual *nom de spatula*. It is his identity, the very yolk of his being. From ovum to frat man and back to ovum, he has become one with his omelettude. Or so it appears. He wears a 14-carat gold chain with the Mr. Omelette logo—a grade-A large egg sporting a chef's hat and a grin. His vanity license plate reads MR OMLET. He IS the eggman, goo-goo-goo-joob.

"My friends don't call me David," he says. "They call me Mr. O. I just like it better. It becomes my personality. I have a four-foot doll that runs off electricity, and the spatula and whisk go up and down.

"This is what I know," he says. "This is what I was taught to do."

Luncheon could be served at any time, but one of the Triplett's children hasn't arrived yet and the hostess prefers to hold off. At various times Mr. Omelette has been poised in front of his portable stove—exactly, no doubt, as one of his fifteen junior Mr. Omelettes is now poised in Adelphi—only to cut the gas when nobody came in to eat. At 1:36 P.M., he is a trifle uneasy.

"They'll probably get started in two, three minutes," he says. "I guarantee, in two minutes she'll say, 'Light it up!' "

Ninety seconds later, Marty Triplett walks in to give him the green light—which is attributable either to the caterer's sixth sense or to the fact that this is the sixth year in a row Mr. Omelette has done this party. The sixth year, and perhaps the last. The Tripletts are elderly people, and are thinking about moving into a Methodist Church–run retirement home.

"I may do this one more time before we move," the hostess says. "Methodists don't drink . . . I'm an Episcopalian."

Mr. Omelette smiles with satisfaction. This delightfully candid exchange fits right into big theory about the catering business, which seems to have three principal elements: 1) Don't forget to bring the eggs; 2) customers don't like it when you scorch their dining room tables, so you can just imagine how annoyed they'd be if you set fire to their homes; and 3) the personal touch is everything.

"I want to know everyone's name on a personal level. I wouldn't change that for $10 million right now," he says. "My business is more than going to somebody's house and making omelettes. Our slogan is 'We're more than just omelettes.' "

So, then, what is he? What is Mr. Omelette besides omelettes? Well, he's also waffles, crepes, fresh fruit, pastry and hors d'oeuvres. He's someone who has himself cooked omelettes for Speaker of the House Tom Foley; curvaceous TV star Heather Locklear (ratatouille and cheese filling); strategic arms negotiator Max Kampelman; and bookstore-chain owner/gargantuan hair possessor Robert Haft. He's someone who personally prepares and packs every order for every party over which he and his fifteen chefs preside.

"To put it all in one word," he summarizes, "value, reliability, and service."

Omelette and his wife, Jennifer, take this credo to heart. They are kept busy catering, he says, 500 parties a year, which is why he is regularly firing up stoves at several venues at once. All this from a standing start in 1983. They insist that they don't want to grow more, that the catering business loses its charm when the proprietors must delegate responsibility to managers and lose personal contact with the clients—and in that sense the universe is being only too cooperative. Mr. Omelette is feeling the effects of economic recession—the high-priced omelette orgy has given way to the $9.95-per-diner economy job. But even more menacing is the dreaded NCP:

National Cholesterol Panic.

Mr. *Omelette,* for crying out loud! In this day and age, that's practically an epithet. "You lousy artery-clogging son of a knish peddler! You . . . you . . . you omelette dealer!" Down in Baton Rouge, Mr. Mattress certainly fears no such recriminations. Locally, Mr. Muffler and Mr. Topsoil aren't saddled with that sort of excess baggage. Maybe in the universe of anthropomorphic trade names, Mr. Vacuum, Mr. Mulch, and Mr. Garbage USA don't exactly exude romance, but at least the surgeon general isn't mounting a crusade against them. Maybe Mr. Faucet doesn't offer nine zesty fillings the way Mr. Omelette does, but then nobody's calling Mr. Faucet lethal.

You want a business challenge for the nineties? Position yourself as a silent killer. Mr. Omelette. Why not Mr. Dioxin? Only, so far, for Omelette, it hasn't been a problem. He swears he turns business away. It seems that for every cholesterol-crippled chow hound with HDL-LDL totals in the low four digits who must order at restaurants from the special Flavor-Free menu and who generally lives on the Modified Feedlot Diet, there are thousands of people who do not regard an omelette brunch as an atherosclerosis theme party. On the other hand, Mr. Omelette didn't struggle through four years of marketing courses and twenty years of hands-on, egg-cracking, propane-burning experience to summarily dismiss one of the great dietary trends in culinary history.

"I'm not real book-smart, but I'm basically street-smart," he says. And, therefore, he's always pleased to whip up an egg-white omelette, and therefore, also, he's ticked. "I think that the media—this may be an insult in your field, but you talk about cholesterol, I gotta have something to fight back with—the media has to have something to write about. And cholesterol, I think, the people are overreacting toward it."

Yes, the anti-egg media bedevils him. But what he regards as the prejudice of the medical community positively makes him crazy.

"I don't get along with doctors all that well." Like that time, not long ago, in the restaurant. Mr. and Mrs. Omelette walked into one of their favorite little eateries, and who was sitting at the next table but the family podiatrist, Dr. I'm So Important Removing Bunions and Selling $250 Orthotics to Everyone Who Passes By That I Dare Not Acknowledge Such a Lowly Being, who ignored him. Then, as dinner progressed and the pastry cart was wheeled around to the foot surgeon, Omelette overheard something that to this day he cannot believe: The doc asked, "Do you have any desserts without eggs?"

"I mean," Omelette says, shaking his head, "what kind of [expletive] is that?!"

As the Tripletts' guests file into the dining room, Mr. Omelette tends two and three burners at a time, and if the rush were large enough, he could do four at a time. It all happens so quickly. He ladles the batter into the sizzling Silverstone aluminum pan, quickly rims the pan with a rubber spatula to define the omelette's edge, plops in the fillings, folds over the edges with the spatula, shakes the pan side-to-side, and—short-order style—flicks his wrist, sending the omelette somersaulting skyward before landing upside down in the pan. It takes exactly one minute. One after another, each guest makes a point of admiring his masterpiece, before cutting it up and eating it.

The time is now 2:15 P.M. There is a lull, and the caterer takes advantage of the opportunity to lift up the hinged surface of his stove. Inside: bits of egg flotsam and mushroom jetsam, cheese detritus and rogue onion. Mr. Omelette commences removal. "I don't want to brag about it," he says, "but this stove gets a lot of crumbs of omelette debris, and I try to keep it clean."

Nobody ever said this business is pretty. And, speaking of nasty little housekeeping points, nobody ever said Mr.

Omelette has the monopoly on eggcentric catering. When asked about competition in the area, he allows, with a shrug, as how "There's a guy in Baltimore," which is almost the whole truth.

There happens, first of all, also to be a woman in Baltimore—royalty, no less—by the name of The Omelette Queen. As for the guy, he is Ralph C. Harrison, a.k.a. The Omelette Man, who has served the Baltimore-Washington metroplex for the past twenty-six years. Macy's builds next to Gimbels and all that, but Harrison says he hasn't determined whether competition stimulates overall omelette demand or simply cuts into his business. "Actually," he says, "I've never had any feelings about him either way."

Mr. Omelette, naturally, isn't much impressed with the man who was doing omelette luncheons while little David Model was still in diapers. To him, it isn't a question of experience. It's a question of pedigree.

"I mean, anybody can make an omelet," he says, as the guests begin arriving for seconds and . . . CHING-CRACK-BLUUP . . . he prepares more batter. "Anybody can come in here with a chef's hat and a smile. But it's got to be in your blood. I mean, if an egg can think, I can think like an egg."

A Whorehouse Christmas

CARSON CITY, NEV.—The kitchen looks so darn festive. Jasmine, Raven, Heather, Vanity, all the girls have pretty red stockings hanging between the twinkling, decorated tree and the black-hosiery vending machine.

It's Yuletide at the Sagebrush Guest Ranch, and, really, is there anything quite like Christmastime in a brothel?

Just look at Desiree, the new girl. Even though they made

her change her *nom de boudoir* ("Yesterday I was Courtney, but there was this other Courtney"), she's like a kid knee-deep in presents. Not that Santa visited her, but—ho, ho, ho—a lot of other fellows have.

"It's my second day and I've made probably a grand," says the excited rookie. "You know what's so cool about it? The money. It's so easy."

Absolutely. You dress up in your Victoria's Secret special, cantilever your bosom over your bodice just so, and have meaningless sex with total strangers. No nasty street corners to haunt. No cops bothering your evening. And it's safe for everybody, because condoms and regular blood tests keep Nevada's legal brothels 100 percent disease-free.

What's more, as Desiree's colleague Traci puts it, "You meet some very interesting people."

The Sagebrush is one of four such meeting places in an X-zoned enclave seven miles east of town. Just as Gimbel's was near Macy's, The Kit Kat, The Moonlight, and Kitty's guest ranches are in one brightly lit cul de sac, where gentlemen can patronize experienced professionals, free of worry about robbery, AIDS, or embarrassing arrest.

Owner Jim Fondren made a fortune building mini-warehouses before diversifying into maxi-whorehouses. The place looks like a sprawling motor lodge/girl's dorm. Traci, Desiree, and all the residents are independent contractors who pay board, plus a percentage to the house.

Ring-a-ling. Ring-a-ling.

Are those sleigh bells? Oh, it's the door chime. Customer on the way. "Line up, ladies!" exclaims the parlor hostess. Time to go to work.

Suddenly to the parlor we hear, the click of high heels as the hookers come near. "I'm Traci," says Traci to an incoming guy. "I'm Lisa," says Lisa. (Is it she he will buy?) "I'm Colby." "Diana." "Vanity." "Raven." A veritable feast for the pulchritude maven.

The customer, a presentable-looking young man, demurs on his selection pending the ingestion of multiple beers at the parlor bar. He's about to spend between $30 and $200, and he doesn't want to come to a hasty decision. He may choose the conventional service or something more exotic, perhaps a naked Jacuzzi followed by an exclusive video screening of *Oil Wrestling.*

No matter what he winds up with, of course, the hired help will never let on that, for her, it's all mechanical, routine, and basically boring.

"It's kind of repetitive work," says Traci, who swears she's about to quit the profession. Indeed, thoughts of a New Year leave a lot of Sagebrush women considering their futures. Courtney says she's off to Hawaii in February. Kathy, who has a college degree, is talking about going for her master's. She was a meagerly paid hospital social worker who, at the age of fifty, took a drug-abusing client's advice and put her miraculous body to work for serious money.

"I came up for two weeks on Easter vacation," says the statuesque divorcee. "I left with $2,700 in my hands. I had never *seen* $2,700 in my life."

Formerly a talented amateur, she turned a hobby into a big-bucks career. But the holidays have her thinking that maybe now is the time to take the money and run. Kathy has grown children, and two years is a long time to conceal a double life: "I'd rather take death than have my family know I'm a prostitute."

Well, that's the thing about Christmas; it can get depressing. Take Diana. She hasn't had a customer in a week, and every unrewarding line-up gets more discouraging. Lisa, meantime, has customers galore, but with them a dark mood that won't go away. At twenty-one, she's been a prostitute for a full third of her life. She has a two-year-old daughter by her late business manager, a junkie who shopped her to rich sickos before he died of an overdose.

"I hate what I do," Lisa says. "Sometimes I wonder why God put me on Earth."

Concrete Benefits

What is worth in anything
But so much money as 'twill bring?
—SAMUEL BUTLER, 1663

His story is about a nightmare of protracted litigation. It is about a decade of frustration, about the entrepreneurial spirit, and about the bankrolling of institutional liberalism. It is even largely about cement. Mostly, though, Frederic Lang's story is about the significance of wealth.

Samuel Butler only pondered; Fred Lang has it all figured out. First he turned an arcane idea into a fortune. Then, having seen the money, having caressed the cashier's checks with his meaty hands, he is doing with it precisely what you would not expect. He is giving it away. All of it. Four million dollars. Or perhaps twice that amount. Or three times. Away.

How does it come to pass that a sixty-eight-year-old retired Du Pont Co. working stiff should come upon such a windfall? It came to pass because Fred Lang is an inventive engineer who devised the best, cheapest way to reinforce structural concrete. He patented his invention—a plastic-sheathed lubricated cable—started his own manufacturing company to produce it, then watched helplessly as one large competitor after another began infringing on his patent. Now, after devoting eleven years and most of his assets to fighting the infringers in court, he is fresh off a pair of stunning triumphs—triumphs that have finally enabled him to reap the financial rewards of his ingenuity.

So far, the sum is $4 million. By the time his patent runs out five years from now, it could exceed $30 million. Even after his lawyer and the Internal Revenue Service take their bites, Lang could accumulate something like $10 million for his efforts.

Except that he doesn't intend for the money to accumulate. He's already begun to redistribute it: to organized charities, to engineering research and development, to consumer- and environmental-interest groups. He insists he won't stop until every last nickel has been contributed in some way to the greater public good. Fred Lang is a man of noble thoughts, noble thoughts and concrete ideas.

Seldom-pondered fact: concrete is brittle. If it weren't reinforced, the concrete in roads, bridges, parking garages, and nuclear power plants would do what your patio has probably long since done: crumble, crack, and slowly disintegrate. So, reinforced it is.

The best technique is called "prestressing." Imagine holding a deck of cards between your forefingers. If you press too lightly, the cards will slip and fall to the floor. If you increase the pressure, they'll hold in place. Prestressing uses steel to apply that inward pressure to concrete. The most common method is to stretch steel cable between two fixed anchors, called "deadmen," on either side of a mold, then to pour concrete over the steel. When the concrete dries in its mold, the steel is cut free of the deadmen. As the steel in the new slab tries to snap back to its normal tension, the effect is to compress the concrete from the outside, thus strengthening it.

The problem with that method is that it must be done at a casting yard equipped with deadmen and stretching equipment, then the slab is transported to the construction site. A cheaper, more convenient alternative is a technique called "post-tensioning," wherein the concrete is poured into place at the job site. Instead of prestretched steel, the concrete is poured over hollow tubing laid across the mold. Steel is threaded through the tubing and, as the concrete dries, stretched with a hydraulic jack. It's then fastened on either side of the slab to small, flat anchors, which compress the slab between them. For many applications, post-tensioning offers all sorts of advantages, but it also presents all sorts of difficulties: 1) Water and gas tend to seep inside the tubing, corroding the steel. 2) Wire heavy enough for the job tends to be too inflexible for coiling, making transport of the material an obstacle. 3) Seven-wire, helically wrapped cable mitigates that problem, but the pressure of the concrete squeezes the paper or plastic tubing into the grooves of the cable, making it impossible to stretch and move the cable freely in the tube as the slab hardens.

In 1970, having taken early retirement at Du Pont to go out on his own, Fred Lang solved all three problems. He took a seven-wire cable and coated it thickly with grease so that the lubricant more than filled the grooves. Then he took a machine that uses melted plastic to draw out seamless tubing and extruded a plastic jacket over the grease-coated cable. He thus created a strong, flexible tendon—a freely moving cable within a jacket—that virtually excluded water and air. He called it Langstrand and filed for a patent.

"I thought I'd invented the better mousetrap," he says, "and the world would beat a path to my door,"

No such luck. Sales were slow, and the only path beating was done by his competitors, who rushed to their own extruders and began producing Lang's invention by the millions of feet.

Frederick Lang is sitting in the office of his 193-year-old stone farmhouse in Landenberg, Pennsylvania, a mile from the Delaware border. He's hunched over a butler's table, smearing horseradish on a half of a cracker, to which he's about to add a chunk of canned salmon. He'll dispatch the cracker presently, but first he'll pause to chuckle at a visitor's question, something about "obvious solutions" and why didn't somebody else think of it first.

"You can ask why somebody didn't invent the lightbulb

before Edison did," scoffs Lang, making it quite clear that the line of inquiry is academic at best and stupid at worst.

He pops the canapé into his mouth. No dainty nibbling, no crumbs, no wasted effort. It is easy to see that this large white-bearded man has no difficulty reducing things to their simplest form. As his thirty-four-year-old son, Chris, puts it, "He does have a way of getting right to the heart of the matter."

Take the infringement case. Never mind that "prior art" in post-tensioning had previously (but separately) introduced a seven-wire cable, a grease-coated cable, and an extruded jacket, thus muddying the legal waters. Never mind that the odds against bankrolling a suit to the end against deep-pocketed adversaries were tremendous. The fact was, the infringement was unfair.

"These guys didn't realize what a crime they'd committed," says Lang. "Intellectual property belongs to the inventor and there should be respect for this."

So, in the summer of 1972, three months after his patent was issued, he prepared to move against the first major infringer, Prescon Corp. of San Antonio, Texas. Before he could act, though, a civil engineer named William F. Kelly moved against him. Kelly was claiming to have invented the tendon a year earlier than Lang and was fighting Lang's claim before the U.S. Patent Office. The case and a subsequent appeal dragged on through the Patent Office's tedious, antiquated bureaucracy until September 1976, when Kelly's claim was thrown out. In the interim, however, Prescon and a dozen other infringers produced more than 100 million feet of Langstrand. That December, Lang filed against Prescon in U.S. District Court in Wilmington, Delaware. Then came another detour, this one lasting three years. Lang's lawyers suggested he go back to the Patent Office with a "reissue" petition, a new process of affirming a patent's validity outside of court at considerably less expense. The theory was, with a successful reissue in hand, Lang could go back to federal court and demand a summary judgment. By mid-1979, he had the reissue and rushed back to federal court for satisfaction.

Judgment denied.

It was March 1980. Lang had spent eight years and $250,000 since getting his patent, and he was exactly nowhere. His lawyers cheered him with the news that it would cost him another $400,000 to continue fighting, and they'd appreciate it if he'd show his good faith by signing away his house as collateral. Lang took the only reasonable course: he fired them. Then he stood before U.S. District Court judge Murray Schwartz and pleaded for a sixty-day suspension of proceedings. He wanted to sell his patent to a corporation with the means to continue the fight. Otherwise, he told the judge, "I just can't see this thing through."

In the beginning, the battle had been something like sport— "a great time." As Lang stood before Judge Schwartz, though, the fun had given way to hurt.

"I was in the depths of pain and suffering," he says. "I felt I was being cheated by the system and cheated by my lawyers, who couldn't get me more justice at lesser expense."

Granted the extension, Lang went to Atlantic Richfield Co. and Hercules Corp. in Wilmington, trying to sell the patent. He would have unloaded it for $40,000, but he found no takers. What he did find was a new law firm, Lemer, David, Littenberg, Krumholz & Mentlik of Westfield, New Jersey. In conjunction with Patlex Corp., a patent-enforcement and technology-development company, the law firm agreed to take the case on contingency. Lang's cost: 40 percent of the patent.

Legal maneuvering began again in June and lasted for twenty-one months. In March 1982, ten years after the patent was issued, the trial finally began. One month later Schwartz ruled in Lang's favor. The lawyers immediately filed against a second big infringer, VSL Corp. of Los Gatos, California. In proceedings as swift as the Prescon case was slow, Lang came away with a second huge victory. Then came a succession of settlements with thirteen other infringers worldwide. Suddenly, Fred Lang was a rich man.

This is a situation he is in the process of remedying. He's turned his manufacturing company, PIC Inc., over to his four children. (Chris runs it; the others are in different lines of work.) They'll also inherit his house and remaining land.

The rest goes.

It goes to: champions of land-planning conservation (Audubon Society), consumerism (Public Citizen), technical innovation (International Human-Powered Association), civil and human rights (Amnesty International, Mother Jones Tax Defense fund), social and human services (Salvation Army Mobile Kitchen, Delaware Rape Crisis Center), and an array of other efforts.

Not the least of these, by the way, will be the promotion of Langstrand itself. "The first thing I'm going to do is make Langstrand appreciated," he says. "I'm going into marketing for the first time in the life of the product."

Langstrand is used in 5 percent of structural concrete applications. By increasing that to 15 percent, Lang figures to serve civilization by facilitating types of construction once thought to be economically unfeasible. By introducing his invention into road construction, he figures to save a lot of taxpayers' money. Meanwhile, the vastly increased royalties will be thrown into the same philanthropic pot.

Occasionally, Lang says, his philanthropic finger will also point to individuals—those who are quietly engaged in some small selfless enterprise Lang regards as heroic. "I want to give a vote of confidence to what they're doing," he says. His vote, of course, comes from his checkbook.

Today, in the way that some people scribble out a $10 check to the Heart Fund, Fred Lang is unflinchingly signing away $10,000 to Essential Information, a new Ralph Nader–inspired public-interest group. The significance is not lost on Nader, who has known Lang since 1967. "I think he's just burning with the ambition to do good," Nader says. "He's really quite unique. He's kept his convictions as he's won his court victories, and so as he's improved his material status, he keeps advancing his sense of civic responsibility." He surely does. The $10,000 check is enclosed along with a letter Lang has written to Essential Information, an organization devoted to obtaining and disseminating government-held data for the public good.

"I have some thoughts on information I consider essential, which I shall discuss with you from time to time," he writes. "One of those items is presented here." He then talks about "rate of U.S. debt increase" and "rate of income-tax receipts by the Treasury"—statistics he'd like to see printed at least weekly by the media.

"I'm not looking for the random spenders of my money," he says in conversation later. "I want to be a participant wherever my money goes, at least to some degree."

Yes, Lang is giving away all of his money, but nobody ever said there would be no strings attached. That he'd want to exert his influence is only natural, and it is also a heartening clue: maybe Fred Lang really is of this world.

"He's not the world's greatest philanthropist, and he's not a crackpot," says Lang's son Philip, Chris's twin. "He's just an incredibly driven entrepreneurial person who also has very strong moral values."

Indeed. Though he spent twenty-nine years in middle management at Du Pont, Lang always had been an entrepreneur at heart. He realized that as early as 1935, as a twenty-year-old thrust by his own enterprise and by external events into the managership of an ice company in Fulton, Missouri. "I loved it," he says. "I've always wanted to be a leader. My greatest moments were when I was leader of the pack."

Nonetheless, once out of engineering school at the University of Missouri, he opted for the security and opportunities of a big corporation. In 1940, he joined Du Pont, where his engineering ingenuity and leadership potential served him well. He got all the right promotions, all the right bonuses. But he also got restless.

"I found," he says, "that the Du Pont Co. couldn't harness my energies to my satisfaction."

So he dabbled in any number of side ventures. He raised cattle (successful), bought a tuna company (unsuccessful), bought metal wall studs and resold them as fence posts (successful), and plotted to haul fresh water to the Caribbean in giant plastic bags (unsuccessful). His biggest enterprise was real estate. The 150-acre Delaware County farm he bought in 1946 for $18,000 plus the 100 acres next door he bought for $18,000 in 1955 have proved a steady source of income. Whenever he's needed cash, he's subdivided and developed the land. It thus saw him through the start-up of PIC, a divorce, four college educations, and eleven years of lawyers' fees. It also became the stakes in his first David and Goliath battle, a five-year struggle beginning in 1963 between him and Colonial Pipeline Co., controlled primarily by Gulf Oil Co. and four of the other six major oil companies. Colonial wanted to exercise the right of eminent domain on a portion of Lang's property and lay a natural-gas pipeline there. Lang had other ideas.

"I couldn't understand how Gulf Oil could take my land against my will," he says. He headed for court. As he waged his legal effort, though, construction continued, and he noticed that the installation of the pipe was a haphazard affair. Suddenly, a second issue was born, and Lang found himself at the center of a nationwide controversy on pipeline safety. It was then that he first met Ralph Nader. Since then, to a large degree, Nader's causes have become Lang's causes.

The eminent domain action was a loser in court, but a turning point in Lang's life—"his first crusade," says son Philip. Never before had he had a firsthand look at the darker side of economic power. Never before had he tasted the sweet nectar of activism. And never before had he so antagonized his superiors at Du Pont. By 1968, the man who had once been on the fast track most assuredly was on the outs. So when he couldn't convince the company to pursue development of an idea he had—to extrude a plastic jacket over a grease-coated wire—there wasn't any promising Du Pont future to keep him from leaving the company to pursue it on his own.

"I always felt I wanted to change the world," he says. "I was eager to be in charge and be a big participant in what was going on. At Du Pont, I was one of many, many participants. I decided to feel more important than I could feel there."

Thus he embarked on his odyssey. If he had known at that time, he says, what he knows now—"that it would take eleven years and so much trial and anguish"—he wouldn't have attempted it. But then, he points out, he didn't know it.

The only question that remains is this: Why, having spent more than a decade of his time and more than $250,000 to get what is rightfully his, would a man proceed to turn around and give it away? The answer has a lot to do with civic-mindedness and Christian charity. It also, once again, has to do with the significance of wealth.

"For my invention to appear important," Lang says, "I have to be paid money for it, because that's the measure of importance in America. Once I've got it, I can give it back."

Shot by Cupid

NEW ALBANY, MISSISSIPPI—Down here it's been referred to as the St. Valentine's Day Love Spat Massacre.

The St. Valentine's Day part is because it happened on February 14. "Love spat" refers to the fact that Robert Green and

Cassandra McWilliams were quarreling. The massacre part makes reference to the portion of the quarrel where Robert took a .32 and shot Cassandra four times in the head.

"She pull a gun on me, and we got tussling," Green recalls, "and I pull it away and shot her . . . [It was the] first time for something like this. Most times before I just get up and leave."

This time he got up and summoned an ambulance, as he was feeling very badly about what he'd done. His anger had turned to fear and remorse—but then to hope when Cassandra began to speak to him, asking why blood was gushing out of her head.

Yes, she was conscious. What they should call the incident is the St. Valentine's Day Love Spat Miracle, because despite the four gunshots at point-blank range, Cassandra survived. She wasn't even seriously injured. Somehow the bullets stopped at her skull.

"I guess I didn't want to die," she says.

For one thing, she had plans that dying would have interfered with. The twenty-year-old woman has three children, and by the time the shooting took place she had pretty much set her mind to getting married—which is precisely what she did. She got married.

To Green.

"We were going together for three years, and it was just time," says the new Mrs. Robert Green.

After courting him for so long and bearing his twin boy and girl (now two years old), Cassandra was not about to let a matter so trivial as aggravated assault and attempted murder get in the way. So she marched into the authorities and pleaded with them not to send her intended to jail. "They told me I was crazy," she says.

"She forgives and forgets," concludes Rodney Shands, Union County prosecuting attorney. "We said, 'You can't get shot four times and drop charges.' That's a pretty serious offense. It's not open season on humans."

Shands points out that "These were not graze shots. They

were right up their under her skin against the cranium . . . He didn't have to shoot her if he got mad at her. He could've wrestled around with her a while."

But Cassandra was insistent, and the justice system obliged her. Green's eight-year sentence was suspended. Four months after the shooting, the two ran off to Alabama and got hitched. It was a June wedding.

If only the future were bright. This may be a love story after a fashion, but the hearts and flowers are absent. Robert and Cassandra are feuding again. They're sitting together now in their crumbling, three-room block-and-clapboard house, but lately Robert, twenty-four, has been staying a half-mile away at the crumbling block-and-clapboard home of his parents.

He has no job, no prospects. She has a pair of two-year-olds, who now are sitting on a ragged sofa playing silently and solemnly with, as their toy, an old sandal. The place is immaculate but tattered and bare. *The Young and the Restless* is playing on a black-and-white TV. The only thing hanging on the wall is a framed Alabama marriage license.

Married life, says Robert, "has had its ups and downs." This particular down, much like the one on the day he shot her four times in the head, concerns his proclivity for carousing. Another down came a week ago when he was hauled in by the sheriff. "They caught me trying to transport liquor across the county line," he explains.

That is significant because Union County is dry, and as the sheriff tried to impress upon him, such indiscretions could cause the judge to reinstate his eight-year sentence.

"I didn't know they could," Robert says, and on that point, prosecutor Shands concurs. Evidently nobody explained to Robert Green that in a world of laws, infractions are cumulative.

Says Shands: "He told the sheriff he thought he just wasn't allowed to shoot folks in the head."

Jerome the Pig

WOMAN: [from the cab of a pickup truck traveling down the highway] I have always loved the name Jerome. I mean, since I was eight years old, I just love the name Jerome, and I always thought at that time, if I'm ever married and I have a son, you know, his name is going to be Jerome. . . .

This is the story of a pig, and the woman who loves him. The pig's name is Jeffrey Jerome. The woman is Victoria Herberta, and for the umpteenth time this year, she's making the three-hour pickup truck ride between Houston and San Marcos, Texas, to visit her beloved hog.

VICTORIA HERBERTA: [still in truck] I'm the only mommy he knows, and he's like a son to me. I mean, he's like a child. So what I've been doing, I come to San Marcos. I stay thirty days at a time, go back to Houston for four or five days, which he will not eat during the time I'm gone . . .

This has been going on for a year, ever since last October 31 when Jerome—all 700 pounds of him—was exiled from the city of Houston. The charge: being a pig.

MAN: Section 6-dash-11 of the City Code: the keeping of swine and goats, which are prohibited, with the exception of milk goats. That's the particular ordinance, and it just says where you can have these kinds of animals and where you can't.

That's Dr. Robert Armstrong, chief of animal regulation in Houston, a man who in Victoria Herberta's view falls somewhere between Simon LeGree and Oscar Mayer. It was he who, upon learning that Ms. Herberta was keeping a pig within city limits, enforced the century-old law. But what began as a routine pig eviction has become a Texas cause célèbre. Dr. Armstrong didn't realize that Ms. Herberta is not your typical fifty-year-old pig-owning housepainter. And he didn't know Jerome is not your ordinary pig.

HERBERTA: No, he's no ordinary pig. You know, he's got very good heritage, being the son of Priscilla. He's done a lot of good work. I mean, I've taken this animal and I've done good with this animal.

She's done well with all of her pigs. Jerome's mama, Priscilla the swimming pig, became internationally famous after saving the life of a drowning retarded boy at nearby Lake Summerville. This was in 1984, a hot July day when an ordinary outing with twelve people and a swimming pig would change Victoria Herberta's life. Press interviews, talk show appearances, even a Priscilla the Pig Day in Houston.

HERBERTA: It was really something. I wasn't expecting it, because all I wanted was a pig to have as a pet and to raise as a pet and live in obscurity, you know, and just enjoy my pig.

That's all she ever wanted, but the universe wouldn't cooperate. Six months after Priscilla's water heroics, Herberta's pride and joy overdosed on backyard morning glories, and was retired to the farm in a porcine stupor. This left Herberta temporarily pigless, until, two pigs later, Jerome came into the picture. He lived with her from July 1987 to last fall, a period through which Herberta devoted her mother love to Jerome, and her leftover human compassion to the area's homeless. Most of her meager housepainting income went to feed needy men and women. Her purple frame house—the one with the antique signs and the giant hog on the porch—was a conspicuous oasis for the down-and-out. Whether the procession of hungry visitors angered neighbors, Herberta doesn't know. But somebody complained to the city, and all of a sudden she was being cited for an illicit pig.

HERBERTA: They had to admit that he was totally clean. His quarters were clean. He had absolutely no odor. And I took them around the yard and there was no excrement or no urine in the yard.

Didn't matter. Jerome was still a pig. Swine non grata. Herberta engaged a lawyer, but that was no help. Dr. Armstrong's department was burdened by the tragic and overwhelming daily duty of putting down stray animals and protecting the health of an irresponsible public. In that unpleasant context, the problems of a woman and her pet pig seemed trivial. Armstrong's only concession was to let Jerome remain at home for one last hurrah: a charity fling, a Halloween party for the homeless. Then it was to the farm.

Now that may seem like a fitting venue for a pig, but that presupposes that the pig is a pig at heart. Jerome—terrific, radiant Jerome—is some pig, Herberta says, by virtue of being not very piglike at all.

HERBERTA: He's humanized. All he knows is human companionship. He is totally afraid of other pigs. He will never, ever adjust to being a farm animal. I mean, he sees another pig— even his own mother—and he screams, and he runs and hides. He's terrified.

Not that the farm is inhospitable. Owner Ada Davis, who trains all the diving pigs for the nearby Aquarena Springs amusement park, has made her home Victoria and Jerome's home. When Herberta stays on the farm, Jerome does fine. But when she leaves, he goes . . . well, he goes hog wild—crying, squealing, laying in ant beds, starving himself. And it tears his owner up inside. After a year of living with her pig three weeks out of four in a 14 x 14 pump house—a tiny farm outbuilding with neither toilet nor kitchen facilities nor even hot water—Herberta can no longer bring herself to leave, and no longer afford to stay. There's no work for a fifty-year-old housepainter in rural San Marcos. Unless the city of Houston relents, she says, she'll have to put Jerome to sleep—if she can bear the agony of doing it.

HERBERTA: [choking back sobs] I don't really know. I don't want to live without him, and I don't think he deserves that. I just don't think he deserves that.

Nor is she alone in that sentiment. Jerome's fate has become the focus of a campaign by concerned Houstonians, an eclectic assortment of citizens led by an unlikely advocate. She is Caroline Farb, the city's highest-profile socialite—she of the Christmas Food Basket Program and the Cancer Challenge Telethon, of the notorious $20 million divorce settlement and the 2,000-square-foot bedroom closet. Can it be that Caroline Farb, owner of the sprawling River Oaks mansion called Carolina, is now Houston's foremost champion of wronged hogs?

CAROLINE FARB: Well, I'm not interested in all pigs. I'm interested in this specific pig, because he has done a lot of good, and he is truly a ham-bassador.

The effort has include a Save Jerome billboard, a letter-writing campaign [music begins to fade up from background] and even a specially recorded song called "The Ballad of Jerome."

SONG: "This is the ballad of Jeffrey Jerome. He feeds the people without any home. Collects the food, all in cans, and takes it to his homeless fans. Ohhhhh, ohhh Jeffrey Jerome [fades under]. . . ."

Unfortunately for Farb and her volunteers, the campaign has been a bust. Attempts to pass special legislation have failed in City Council and the Texas statehouse, on the principle that legislative exemptions for specific barnyard animals constitute bad government. As for Dr. Armstrong, the law is explicit, and because it all began with a citizen complaint, unavoidable.

ARMSTRONG: Either say it is a pig, or it isn't. It is in the city, or it isn't. That's how you enforce ordinances.

But that sways Victoria Herberta not one whit.

HERBERTA: You tell me rules are rules, and I will tell you rules are made to be revised and amended. Look at the amendments to the U.S. Constitution. And also we've heard that there is an exception to every rule, and I am sure that the mayor and the City Council—every member of City Council—at one time or another in their life has had a rule bent for them.

[To the sounds of the truck on a dirt and gravel driveway] *At last the ride is over, another separation ended, another happy reunion.*

HERBERTA: [slamming truck door, walking around the vehicle as geese and ducks are heard in background] Have to watch the rocks and the mud. . . . I seeeeee you! Yes I doooo! How's my little pumpkin, huh? How's Mr. Swoonie?

There's nothing quite like the feelings between a pet owner and a pet, even if the pet is a snorting third of a ton of highly saturated fat. [Jerome is heard panting and snorting]

HERBERTA: Look at my pretty boy! Look at Mama's boyyyy! [animated snorting] Hey! Heyyyy!

Sitting in the old pump house, Herberta pulls out snapshots of Jerome the way some people show off their grandchildren.

HERBERTA: Okay, this is Jerome when he was ten days old, just a little ol' bitty handful [laughs]. Okay, now here he is when he was about three months old and I was teaching him to pray. He knows how to pray. And here's his Halloween party. Here he was dressed like the Vampig, in his cape and orange feather tutu. And this is where we had over 1,000 people show up. This is his birthday cake, shaped in a pig face. The inside is dog food and the outside is cream cheese. [laughs]. And here's a picture . . .

[With her continuing to show off snapshots in background] *What will become of Herberta and Jerome is still uncertain, but something has to give. She's sold virtually everything she owns to sustain herself this past year. Her only asset is her house, against which the city has placed tax liens. With no solution in sight, now she's just a lady with a pig, enjoying whatever time the two have left together.*

HERBERTA: [to the pig] You're gonna get a treat! Yeah, you're gonna get a treat! [she rustles the cellophane wrapper of a muffin] Come on! You want a snack? Huh? [pig noisily gobbles muffin from her hand] That good? That's a bran muffin. Yeah, Mom give you a treat. Say, "Oh, I like that!"

Bowling in the White House

One way to think about what goes on in the nation's capital is this: the federal government is a trillion-dollar pie, and every day, people from all around the country come to Washington to fight for a slice. Many represent the so-called special interests— the tassel-loafered lobbyists Ross Perot likes to grouse about. But what if one person, one lowly citizen, wants to take on the whole monolithic bureaucracy all by himself? I offer this parable of political influence in Washington.

It all started a few Saturdays ago when, in the car, on the spur of the moment, the Garfields decided to have some wholesome family fun. Bowling! Why not? We headed for the local bowling center, but when we arrived, we found this notice taped to the door: "No open lanes today. Tournament play only." Talk about aggravating. And what made it particularly distasteful to me was knowing that a few miles away sat a perfectly good bowling alley that nobody was using—not leagues, not the public, and most of all, not us. It was built by no one other than Richard M. Nixon and has been maintained for more than twenty years by taxpayers like me. It just didn't seem right.
[sound of phone ringing]

WHITE HOUSE OPERATOR: White House.
BOB: Hi, this is Bob Garfield, I'm recording this for National Public Radio and I'm trying to reserve the White House bowling alley for some Saturday coming up soon.
WHITE HOUSE OPERATOR: [no response—sound of dial tone]
BOB: Hello?

Somehow we got disconnected, so I called right back. This time, the operator rang me through—to somebody.

BOB: [on phone] What I'm trying to do is reserve the White House bowling lane and, for some reason, they switched me here.
WHITE HOUSE STAFFER: To Media Affairs [laughs].

BOB: Right, yeah.

WHITE HOUSE STAFFER: Probably because you said you're with National Public Radio.

BOB: Yeah, is there an Office of Bowling Affairs that I could call?

WHITE HOUSE STAFFER: [laughs] Ah, who knows? Let's see here. [looks through directory] Gosh, you know, I don't have a clue who would handle that. You know what? Let's do this. Can I ask a favor of you?

BOB: Sure.

WHITE HOUSE STAFFER: You call the main number, right?

BOB: Yeah.

WHITE HOUSE STAFFER: Don't tell them that you're with National Public Radio.

BOB: Uh-huh.

WHITE HOUSE STAFFER: Just tell them that you're a person . . . that you want use the bowling alley and see if they have some clue because I don't have a . . . good directory here. The switchboard has a whole, huge directory. They'll have a better chance, I think, of figuring out where to send you than I will. [end of call]

I didn't do that. It wouldn't have been right, but I did dial the switchboard and I told them one more time who I was and what I wanted. Finally, this time, I was switched to . . .

WHITE HOUSE STAFFER: [answering phone] Administrative Office.

Administrative Office. It was here that the odyssey truly began, a telephonic tour of what seemed like the entire executive mansion. It was almost as if there was no policy in place for dealing with routine bowling requests.

3RD WHITE HOUSE STAFFER: Just a minute and let me give you the number for Communications, sir . . .

4TH WHITE HOUSE STAFFER: Let me give you the number for Scheduling . . .

5TH WHITE HOUSE STAFFER: I'll have to take a message and have someone get back to you . . .

6TH WHITE HOUSE STAFFER: Facilities Management is 2335 . . .

7TH WHITE HOUSE STAFFER: OK, the White House bowling alley. OK, hold on, let me see if we have . . . handle it . . .

8TH WHITE HOUSE STAFFER: Hi, I don't know, but let me get you in touch with . . . possibly, someone who can. Hold on.

BOB: Okay, thanks so much. [Pause. Then a dial tone as the line is disconnected]

Lesson number one in dealing with the White House: Just because they're nice to you doesn't mean they can actually help. The string of phone calls and referrals landed me for the fourth time back in the Press Office, where a deputy press secretary named Lorraine Voles finally told me the last thing I wanted to hear.

LORRAINE VOLES: Bob, the deal is that the bowling alley is for the president and his family, and people that bowl there do so at the pleasure of the president.

Lesson number two in dealing with the White House: it pays to be Barbra Streisand. The only way to get into the White House bowling alley—the only way—is to be invited by the president, the first lady, or Chelsea.

[sound of phone ringing]

WHITE HOUSE OPERATOR: White House.

BOB: Hello, may I speak to Chelsea, please?

WHITE HOUSE OPERATOR: Who's calling?

BOB: Uh, this is Bob Garfield from National Public Radio.

WHITE HOUSE OPERATOR: Well, she's not available.

[Instrumental of "The Impossible Dream"]

*Faced with the callous indifference of the executive branch, I did
what thousands of Americans in the same situation do every day.
I phoned my congressperson. This time I managed to wade through
the aides and factotums to reach Congresswoman Leslie Byrne herself. Alas, like thousands of Americans, I sensed that my elected
representative possibly wasn't taking my concern entirely seriously.*

U.S. REP. LESLIE BYRNE (D-VA): [hearty laughter]

*It turns out that I'm not alone. Her office gets a lot of constituent
requests from Northern Virginians looking to hobnob with the
president. Some people want to go jogging with him; some want to
deliver baked goods; some want to babysit Socks. But, of course,
these pathetic presidential groupies and their transparent schemes
to one-up their neighbors had nothing to do with my very real need
to grace the White House with my explosive hurls to the pocket.*

REP. BYRNE: Given that it's part of the private quarters, it will be
    difficult. Now, there are people who get into the private
    quarters, so I'm willing to give it a try.
BOB: Great, great, well, I appreciate it. Not to be accused of
    horse trading or anything, but if you can pull this off . . .
REP. BYRNE: [laughs]
BOB: . . . I have a long memory.
REP. BYRNE: [laughs]

*I also had a sneaking suspicion that a freshman member of Con-
gress wouldn't have the clout to get what I wanted. It was time to
call in some big guns.*

[sounds in restaurant]

1ST WAITER: Come on, Mr. Nader, we've got you right here.

Why not Ralph Nader? If ever there was a Washington giant slayer, it's him. So I asked him to Duke Ziebert's, the Washington power spot, for lunch. I had the crab cakes.

RALPH NADER: [ordering his lunch] Let's have some side dishes, okay, 'cause . . . the cole slaw, sliced tomatoes with onions, potato salad.

Side dishes! Saving more than four bucks versus a veggie entree. See what I mean? The guy knows every angle. He sank his teeth into the tomato and onions and then he sank his teeth into my problem.

NADER: You work by analogy and principle. Every week, President Clinton invites about ten corporate executives—big-business types—to lunch. That means they're using the food in the White House and utensils in the White House and the tablecloths and the chairs in the White House and all those are taxpayer assets. The bowling alley's a taxpayer asset. Let's approach it politically. One of the biggest sports in this country is bowling. It has, probably, 40 million practitioners. They all vote. What has President Clinton done for bowlers?

What Ralph told me—I call him Ralph—what Ralph told me was to get pragmatic, to contact my natural political allies, the bowling leagues, to get them involved in lobbying, write-in campaigns, demonstrations, the works. He took a bite of potato salad and leaned across the table.

NADER: Without naming him, I know the PR person and the chief lobbyist for the bowling leagues. Do you want me to put you in touch with him?
BOB: I want to bowl.
NADER: I'll see what I can do.

The *magic words in this town. Lunch cost me* $49.12, *but I considered it an investment.*

NADER: May ask you that, if you do bowl with the president in the White House, that you ask him to return my call?
MAN: The easiest way to do it would be . . . and the quickest way to do it . . . we have a publication that goes out in about two weeks to every one of our members—about 2.7 million members.

I took Ralph's advice and phoned Darrell Dobbs, head of the American Bowling Congress.

DARRELL DOBBS: Ah, we could certainly put something in that. Simultaneously we'd go to the proprietor groups and as the bowlers are signing up for their fall season, to get them to sign some sort of petition. I would be within, I would say, thirty to forty-five days, we could have a bunch of signatures for you if that was the way we want it to go.
BOB: Thirty to forty-five days?
DOBBS: Yeah.
BOB: I was kind of looking to next weekend.
DOBBS: It'd be very, very difficult to contact all our people by that time.

Thirty days! I wanted to bowl in the White House, not make a career of trying. I needed fast action. I needed instant gratification. I needed America's number-one, top-of-the-charts political strategist. To get me into the White House, I needed the guy credited with getting Bill Clinton in the White House.

JAMES CARVILLE: [answering phone] Okay, this is James.

James Carville, political miracle worker, who said that to book the lane, I'd have to get the president's attention, do something that would help him sell his programs, or, really, do anything that might catch his eye.

CARVILLE: You could feign some illness, say, that, you know, that your last request is to, you know, throw a bowling ball down the thing, you know, like the kid used to do in Babe Ruth, you know. You could move to Arkansas and hurry up and develop a relationship with one of his lifelong, childhood friends that come to Washington from time to time. If you could find some single woman that's a friend of Mrs. Clinton's and start dating . . . do you have any looks? Do you have any kind of social ability or something like that? Maybe you could try it out.

But, in fact, Carville said, had I wanted to do things the way they are really done in Washington, I was getting started about two years too late. To extract favors from the White House, one needs long-term relationships, which means making campaign contributions, volunteering during the primaries—in short, accumulating political capital. Unfortunately, I have no political capital. And therefore, Carville said, my prospects were . . .

CARVILLE: . . . pretty pitiful, unless you were an early contributor and had some relationship with people I doubt if there's much that you would do right now. One way is you get an undecided senator to vote for the president's budget plan [laughs]. You could probably get an invitation if you [laughs] if you got a leaning-against a vote for us, you'd probably get to bowl and play tennis, too.

And so, last Thursday, with the tax package and President Clinton's entire economic program then apparently riding on Senator David Boren's swing vote, I made a call to Capitol Hill.

BOB: [on phone with aide] I know the senator has this key vote in the Conference Committee on the tax package and I was wondering if it was too much to ask for the senator to hold his vote hostage pending me being invited to bowl at the White House.

BOREN STAFFER: You know, I think the person you need to talk to is the press secretary here.

[As "The Impossible Dream" again swells] *It was frankly nauseating how uninterested, how monumentally uninterested Senator Boren's aide seemed in my proposition. And, for the first time, I truly despaired of ever rolling a ball on the raw, blond boards of the White House lanes. Every path seemed to lead to a dead end. I even tried to exploit my one meager personal connection: my friend Gwen, whose sister Marian's husband, Jack Kaplan, is best friends with Jack Doppelt who was the graduate school professor of Hillary Rodham Clinton's aide Lisa Caputo. But that didn't pan out either and I was just about ready to give up. Then, driving dejectedly to work, I heard an interesting news report.*

NEWS ANNOUNCER: The task of finding Senate votes was made more difficult yesterday when Oklahoma Democrat David Boren announced that he would vote no.

Well, I thought, that was very nice of him. And sure enough, the next thing I knew . . . [sound of bowling ball rolling down a lane, then ball hitting pins and children cheering] *Yep, me, my wife, my kids. Bowling in the White House. Look, I'm not claiming Senator Boren actually did my bidding. I'm not claiming I extorted recreation favors from the president. All I know is my family and I were escorted through the Rose Garden, into the executive mansion, where, down a corridor from the kitchen, awaited our holy grail. It's a single lane—AMF circa late-sixties—trimmed by the ugliest brown and bluuugh carpeting you have ever seen. There's no bank of vending machines, no pro shop. But there is a nice selection of shoes. I wore a set of tens, which may, at one time, actually have shod a president of the United States. Or, maybe, Bebe Rebozo. The Clintons, I'm told, haven't exactly haunted the place.*

The only evidence they've ever set foot in the room is their bicycles, which are stored—inconsiderately, I don't mind saying—along the edge of the alley. On the other hand, there was no waiting. The president, thankfully, didn't bother us and we didn't run into any league play. Furthermore, Ann Stock, the social secretary of the president of the United States, gave my daughters Katie and Allison a bowling lesson. In heels, no less.

ANN STOCK: Take your hand and release it so that your hand goes like that to the center pin. [sound of bowling approach and ball rolling down the lane]
KATIE: [sound of pins falling] Yes! [laughter]

Now that is putting people first. And it just goes to show, in this great nation of ours, no matter who you are, no matter how humble your beginnings, no matter how politically unconnected you may be—just as our parents and teachers always told us—you can wind up in the White House. All you gotta do is ask. On tape. For the record. On a national broadcast network.

BOB: [to Ms. Stock] I just want to thank you very, very much for opening up the White House to me and my family. We had a wonderful time. I just want to thank you.
STOCK: You're welcome. I'm glad you enjoyed it.
BOB: Now, about that state dinner . . .

The Serum Cure

In, 1984, Allan Manny watched his father die of lung cancer—oat-cell carcinoma, to be precise—and it was slow and agonizing and horrible. The end finally came in August, inducing for the Mannys the sort of anguished relief peculiar to families who have witnessed prolonged suffering in someone they love. The relief lasted eleven months, at which point Allen Manny learned he had the very same disease.

The next day, the Decatur, Georgia, promotions consultant was admitted to Atlanta's Veterans Administration hospital for chemotherapy, the same chemotherapy that had failed to help his father. Then came the radiation, the same radiation that had burned and scarred his father in the brutal months before his death. For Allan, too, it was no use; the cancer promptly spread to his neck, bone, and brain. By March the VA doctors had thrown in the towel. He was sent home until such time as he absolutely needed to check back in and expire.

"My cancer is what's known as terminal," he says. "It's a question of, 'when he stops walking, we bury him.' "

But Manny, fifty years old and vigorous, has other ideas. He and his wife, having borrowed to the hilt, have scraped up enough cash to reach Tijuana, Mexico, where, on April 2, in a small hospital called Centro Medico del Prado, he is taking the serum cure.

They've heard of the treatment through an acquaintance in Georgia. The information was fuzzy, but tantalizing, and reports of remarkable remissions in the many previous patients have given them the straw of hope they are so desperate to grasp. They know little about the medical nuts and bolts—the researchers who developed it are in Panama somewhere—but it clearly is no mere scheme. A fellow in Maryland has even offered to subsidize the cost for them. So here they are, in the care of Dr. Jorge Estrella, the physician who now stands by observing closely as the treatment gets under way.

The ice-blue contents of an IV pack are dripping steadily through a narrow tube into Allan's arm. The needle has been in place for fifteen minutes, and he has winced with every drip.

"Right now as I'm sitting here, my stomach is burning more and more," he says. A moment later he is bolt upright. "Oooooh!" The pain is coming in waves.

"I don't think I've ever had so much pain in my life as since

I've got this cancer. Everything concerned with it is pain. I think maybe dying's easier . . . You know what would be the pits? Going through all of this and dying anyway."

Phil Duda is not the single most organized man in the Inventors Club of America Hall of Fame. Here he is in his Panama City bungalow talking about the hand-held laser weapon he designed, and nothing is where he can find it.

"Hon," he asks his wife, Cindy, "do you know where the laser crystals are?"

Cindy is exasperated. "What?" she replies. "Right off the top of my head?"

Never mind. Phil comes up with a ragged circuit board and shows off the guts of a different weapon—a sonic gun, which, he says, "will rip you apart from twenty miles away." Then he's rustling around in an old wooden army trunk, shuffling through notes and schematics on all manner of arcane technology. There's his earthquake-prediction monitor, his DNA-mutating growth compound, his toxic-waste detoxifier, and, of course, his laser-in-a-flashlight. This, like his sonic gun, Phil says, he has built but disassembled, lest it fall into the wrong hands.

The laser was particularly easy to fashion: "You've got your titanium-tungsten wire, your electromagnets, your beryllium, your ruby crystal . . . and you have your high- and low-intensity in the laser. Then you have your electromagnetic solenoid cells to get your E-M field." Then, *zaaaaaap*.

Meet Philip H. Duda, thirty-six, inventor, U.S. Air Force supplies master, rock collector, Boy Scout leader, electronics wizard, biochemistry hobbyist, and Father of the Serum Cure. With the help of his friend, colleague, fellow non-com, and fellow rock collector Brian McDonald, Duda formulated a theory of what causes cancer and what cures it.

"He's not an ordinary person," says Alexander T. Marinaccio, founder of the Atlanta-based Inventors Club of America, an organization devoted to helping the little guy on the street develop, patent, and market inventive ideas. "He's a super genius. If you called him a genius, you'd be insulting him."

Alex Marinaccio is a man I encountered by chance. Seeking some innocuous information on patent development, I found his name in a reference guide and was surprised when he responded to my phone call in this fashion: "Are you calling about the Inventors Club or the cancer thing?"

I assured him I was calling about the club, but after I disposed of my routine question I added, "By the way, *the cancer thing?*"

"Yes," he said firmly. "We have the cure for cancer. We are curing cancer in seven days for the average person."

Marinaccio went on to describe Phil Duda and his work in Panama, about a serum that "strengthens your immune system," about a medical development so big, "I've been approached to go on TV, but I don't want to." Several days later, I received the formal announcement on the subject. On Marinaccio's Inventors Club letterhead—over the signatures of Duda, McDonald, their wives, Cindy and Barbara, and a doctor named Luis Olivares—came this earthshaking news:

"We are ready to report that we have cured many terminally ill patients. The cancer serum is an effective cure of leukemia, cancer tumors, and cancer of the lung, pancreas, intestines, colon, blood, and bone. We are ready to offer the treatment to cancer patients at this time.

"Since the development of the serum, 100 percent of the patients undergoing treatment have been cured. The results of our research show there is *no* pain, *no* surgery, *no* chemical therapy, *no* radiation.

"Terminally ill patients are advised to submit their medical records for review by the Medical Research Scientist in Panama. Upon acceptance into the program, patients will be notified to meet with the Directors and Staff members for full consultation.

"Treatment will last seven days for patients who enter the

program. Those who have multiple health conditions (i.e., diabetes, heart ailments, etc.) will be treated for an additional period of time, up to thirty days. However, our facilities are limited to provide service only to patients with the ability to walk.

"Daily expenses incurred during the visit to our medical research center pertaining to food, lodging and travel are to be provided by the patient. Air fare is an additional charge. It is necessary to obtain a thirty (30) day visa.

"There is no charge for the treatment; however, donations will be accepted to further research and cover the cost of supplies."

Phil Duda and Brian McDonald, thirty-eight, met in 1979. Both were clerical non-coms at a Massachusetts air base, but what brought them together was a mutual interest in rock collecting.

"I've talked to many peoples and groupings and folks about stones," Phil says.

Their acquaintance blossomed into friendship, through which they discovered still more in common, not the least of which was a fascination with electronics. A tinkerer himself, Brian was taken with Phil's various inventions. They covered the gamut, from the long-range antenna that netted Phil election to Marinaccio's Hall of Fame, to a contraption designed to neutralize unwanted radiation ("Dow Chemical was interested," Phil recalls. "You have a firm that a Dr. Nakamas was involved with in Japan. You have a German firm—what was that individual's name? It began with an *N*").

Another convergence in their lives was a tragic one. Both had loved ones ravaged by cancer: Phil's former fiancee, mother-in-law, and son; Brian's father and father-in-law. So one day in 1980, the Dudas and the McDonalds, now close friends, decided to act. With all their combined skills ("A point of interest," Brian says, "Barbara is an R.N."), they could see no reason why they couldn't find the cure that had eluded medical science for all of history.

The first thrust was something on the order of Andy Hardy Goes to Harvard. Barbara and Cindy each spent two hours a day at the Harvard Medical Library "for three or four days" and photocopied what Brian describes as thousands of documents. They searched in particular for spectrographic studies of tumor tissue, but they went after anything remotely connected with Phil's hypothesis that cancer "was in a parasitic cell frame." At home, Phil and Brian pored over the material until, sure enough, they found what they were looking for: a pair of anomalous findings in two unrelated studies each noting with some puzzlement an observed change in blood type within a tumor. That is, the blood type of the blood found within the tumor was different than the subject's blood type. In each case, Phil says, the researcher discarded the observation as a clinical oddity and went about his research business. But to Phil, this was the smoking gun.

What if cancer were triggered by a virus that invades dormant cells, making them biochemically susceptible to the further invasion of ambient nitrogen, which in turn affects the chemistry of the blood cells passing through it? What if that change was a momentary mutation of the blood cells' sugar chain, the determinant of blood type? It was all so simple, so fetchingly simple—and likewise the treatment. After several more brainstorming sessions, Duda once again stumbled on the obvious. If blood within the tumor was different from the blood elsewhere in the body, the tumor could easily be dispatched. All one needed was a two-step procedure: 1) Administer argon, an inert gas, to serve as a benign replacement for sinister nitrogen molecules, and 2) intravenously pump blood antigens specific to the tumor blood type—blood antigens in the form of commercial blood-type testing reagent. This, Phil surmised, would clot the blood within the tumor while leaving the rest of the body alone. The tumor, deprived of oxygen and nutrients, would quickly die and slough off like so much dead skin.

"Understand, we're not miracle makers," says the Inventors

Club chief scientist, as he sits in the living room of his base housing/medical research center, between the wall with the Madonna and child and the wall with the painting of the mule deer. "We were able to put together what everybody has missed. . . .

"We've got cancer done now. It's just more of what I call clean-up. Now we're off on leukemia—we found out that there's three different types—[and on] cystic fibrosis, muscular dystrophy, multiple sclerosis."

Allan and Jackie Manny would really prefer to be elsewhere. This is all so mysterious and unnervingly new. Dr. Estrella seems to know what he's doing, but they'd still rather be across town at the Gerson Clinic, where the daughter of the late Dr. Max Gerson continues his legacy of dietary therapy. Theirs is a regimen of fruit, vegetable, and liver juices combined with coffee enemas and other natural "detoxifying" agents. But the Mannys haven't nearly the funds to swing the Gerson Clinic, which Jackie says costs $294 a day. As it is, they've checked out of the $49 per night Hotel Lucerna across the street from Estrella's office in favor of a $19 per night motel near the racetrack—this so they'll have the money to eat.

"We borrowed from parents, brothers, sisters, friends, anybody else," Allan says. "After a year [with cancer] you run out of money if you ain't working."

His course of treatment is serum injections for two days, argon gas for two days, injections for three, gas for two, and so on for fourteen days. This is day ten and, unnerving novelty or no, their optimism hasn't flagged. For weeks Allan was unable to hold down food, or even fluids, a problem they attribute to the ravages of chemotherapy and radiation. But after two days here, he was able to hold down a fish-and-salad dinner. And he got a rare full night of sleep. "We're very happy," Jackie says. "We're looking forward to being excited."

By now the sleeplessness has returned, as have the problems with eating, and during the serum treatments the pain gets more intolerable with every dose. "I cramp up like a woman going into labor," Allan says. Yet his grotesquely swollen lymph nodes seem to be receding, and the coffee colonics Jackie gives him at the motel help mitigate the cramps.

"I've got a good feeling this will cure me," he says. "Either I'm getting worse or I'm getting cured. Something is happening."

From the moment Alex Marinaccio encountered Phil Duda, he felt big things were possible for the young inventor, and when the cancer serum surfaced, Marinaccio backed him all the way. There was no significant money involved, but to the degree that the serum was promoted in the United States, Marinaccio was unstinting in his support. Apart from the cancer-cure announcement, Marinaccio's two crucial contributions were to interest Marie Steinmeyer, an Atlanta advocate of cancer-patient rights, and Arthur Fellner, a Lutherville, Maryland, real estate broker. Both were attracted by the plausibility of the theory, and both worked hard to locate prospective patients.

"Our basic philosophy is we want this to be for the benefit of all mankind," Fellner told me in late November 1985, "not the type of people who want to soak people and get rich on it . . . My philosophy is, let's try what we can on it and get some documentation. But I don't want to wave a flag and say it's The Thing and spread it all over until we get some evidence on it."

Duda and McDonald, Fellner said, are "Naive individuals. They haven't had the experience with how to go about these things."

Strictly speaking, neither did Art Fellner. A sixty-year-old former construction management executive, he is well-regarded in that field. But for the past two years he has been out on his own trying to make it big as a real-estate wheeler-dealer. Until recently, his principal enterprise was Atlantic 4 Properties Corp., a Myrtle Beach, South Carolina, brokerage firm. His deal-making, however, has involved him in myriad other opportunities, from the sale of used jumbo jets to Hawaiian shopping centers. It has been a rugged two years; nothing has come through yet. But, for Fellner, the big payoff is perpetually imminent.

"We've got a lot of things just around the corner," he told me last February after having described a killing he was about to make in gold refining. "We have a system that can extract more gold from a ton of ore than anyone else can. . . . We have a system where we can get 5,000 to 6,000 ounces out of the same ton of ore. We're going to set up operations in Arizona."

In Texas, he said, he's sitting on 4,600 fifty-five gallon drums of ore worth $1.5 million per barrel. He bought the whole she-bang for $12,000 ("Now, the guy who sold it didn't know the value of what he had").

Moreover, Fellner said, a guy in Seattle can extract even more gold by recovering "gold vapor" lost in conventional refining. "My God, you can see it coming out of the chute as if you were pouring water." And the same guy has figured out a way to take worthless "low-valence" gold—gold molecules missing an electron from their outer shell—and turn it into pure precious gold. "It turns out to be the purest gold ever assayed," Fellner says. "We know of a spot where there is a trillion tons of this stuff. If we just go to work on that, we can treat people with every disease in the world and not charge for it."

Maybe Art Fellner is not the world's most experienced promoter, but he isn't afraid to dream out loud. Not only would he recruit patients for a full-fledged research trial, he promised Duda, McDonald, and Marinaccio, he'd bankroll the whole affair himself. Fellner's plan was to treat at least fifty patients with various forms of cancer, then, miraculous results in hand, spring the news on the conventional medical world—a group which thus far had dismissed the serum cure as the ravings of medical incompetents.

•   •   •

The first of the patients referred by Fellner was to be Barbara Canady, a forty-year-old Virginia Beach, Virginia, tanning salon employee with four children, a partially disabled husband, and a seven-year history of cancer. It began with a tumor in her eye. After the eye was removed, the cancer still spread to her ovaries and now had metastasized to her lungs. On the eve of her trip to Panama, Canady told me she knew the researchers there were sincere. I asked if she was concerned that, however well-meaning they were, they might also be very wrong.

"I have thought of all of this," she said. "I really prayed about it. It seems everything that has happened has worked out for me to go down there. I hope and pray I have a success story to tell you when I get back."

Her oncologist, Dr. Saul Yanovich of the Medical College of Virginia, was very disappointed to hear of her plans.

"Maybe they [Duda et al.] are well-intended, but extremely naive, and they are going to hurt a lot of patients in my point of view. . . . I'm not trying to sound arrogant. They may mean well, but emotionally these patients are going to be crushed. They get to a foreign country, are promised the moon and the stars. . . . Today it's Panama. Next time it'll be the Bahamas. Then Hong Kong. Soon you'll see a whole migration of people [spending money] going from place to place [searching for alternative cures]."

Yanovich was articulating one of medicine's two chief misgivings with so-called "alternative treatments." The other— that those with conventionally treatable malignancies might forego or delay potentially saving therapies while off chasing quackery—did not apply to Barbara Canady. Conventional medicine offered little to her.

Doctors had told her that neither drugs nor radiation alone would help her. They held out one small hope—an experimental bone-marrow transplant in combination with megadoses of chemotherapy—but they discouraged her from taking it. The treatment offered about a 10 percent chance of some success, but it was expensive and she, with no health insurance, would have to share in the cost.

"I have really talked to some cruel doctors who put death in front of you and are really cruel to you," Canady said, sobbing. "Now do you see why I'm going to Panama? If these doctors have put together a cure, it's sent from heaven above, let me tell you."

A day later she was in Panama, and by then she was developing some misgivings of her own.

"I really expected things differently," she said. "I expected a clinic, for one thing. I didn't expect treatments in a motel room. I really expected more professional treatment than what I saw. I just had a lot of mixed feelings while I was there."

And there were other problems. Dr. Rosa Britton, director of the National Oncology Institute of Panama, had been approached by Duda and McDonald for help and now, much to their chagrin, was raising a stink. She threatened, in fact, to have them deported. So for forty-eight hours Canady's first treatment was delayed. Finally, on a Friday morning, she and her husband were sequestered in their room at the La Siesta Motel waiting for Duda, McDonald, and their physician colleague Olivares to arrive. The Canadys took to their knees, in the narrow space between the bed and TV, and prayed to Jesus for guidance, "leaving it up to the Lord," she explained. Moments later Duda and McDonald showed up, minus the physician. Presumably, Olivares had been scared off by Britton; it would be a few more days before they could line up someone to commence with the treatment.

"That," says Canady, "was sign enough for me to go home."

It was also the end of the serum treatment in Panama.

"When they came to me with this cockeyed idea, I didn't pay too much attention to them," Dr. Britton told me last winter. But when she realized that they intended to treat people there, she blew a gasket.

"I am not one to squelch good research, but this is a bunch

of horseshit, as they say in the United States. Come on, we've been killing mice for years and they have a magic formula? . . . They can go back to Atlanta or wherever they came from and practice their voodoo there."

Alex Marinaccio's response was not to question the science of the treatment he had been promoting for wide human use. His response was to accuse Britton of running a competing cancer clinic in Costa Rica, a charge she dismisses as preposterous. Fellner's explanation of her tirade was similar, that "the gal in Panama had her own research breakthrough and feared the serum cure would overshadow it." (She says, "I wish.") McDonald observed simply, "She's full of bull hunkey."

Duda and McDonald were bewildered and discouraged, but Marinaccio and Fellner were undaunted. By early December they were taking parallel steps to see that the serum cure would survive the Panama snafu. First, Fellner was helping an Annapolis, Maryland, man secure the serum for his forty-year-old wife, who was in the late stages of cancer of the breast, bone, and brain. At length the serum found its way north and, with the help of a friendly physician, the treatment began.

"It's almost absurd to think something like this could come of something so simple," said the husband, a lawyer for the state of Maryland, who spoke to me in the midst of the treatments. "We talked about this and decided she didn't want [to continue with] the chemotherapy. All the chemotherapy would do is buy time and [considering the diminished] quality of life—she didn't tolerate chemotherapy well—she said, 'No more.' We've got some hope this way."

Four days into the treatment, Fellner was reporting some good news. It's hard to say he was gleeful—he speaks in a relentless monotone—but he clearly was buoyed by events: "She had this tumor on the side of the abdomen. It was the size of a grapefruit. As of yesterday, it had gone down to where he stomach looked normal."

That wasn't the half of the good fortune. Marinaccio had run across two prospective patients, one of whom knew a Tijuana physician willing to administer the serum. The patients were a Windsor, Connecticut, woman named Norma and a Georgia man I'll call John. Both were in Tijuana taking the treatment by mid-December—thanks to John's friend, Dr. Jorge Estrella.

Estrella, a doctor with a 90 percent American clientele, for twenty-four years has devoted his practice chiefly to "cellular therapy," the controversial injection of live animal cells into the blood. His friend and former patient John had learned of the serum through a friend of Marinaccio, and had been frustrated by the Panama situation in his efforts to procure it. Estrella was interested in assisting and spoke with Duda by phone.

"I was told [by Duda] 'many patients,' and they were obtaining benefit from this," Estrella recalls.

Furthermore, the argon-nitrogen replacement sounded like an ozone treatment he'd read about, and the use of polyclonal antibodies rang similar to the use of monoclonal antibodies—"magic bullets"—in targeting malignant tissue with radioisotopes and drugs, a promising avenue of conventional research. But mainly he pursued it with "the idea of helping a friend. It was a matter of life and death."

The results were amazing. John, a colon-cancer patient, arrived in Tijuana weak, gaunt, pale, and in constant pain. The injections caused him headache, nausea, dizziness, quickened pulse, and what he describes as a burning sensation "in my hot spots of cancer." Yet within days he looked and felt better. Steve Brenson, an Atlanta business associate of John's, says the transformation was remarkable.

When John left for Tijuana, Brenson said, "we [in the office] had some conversation to the effect of this was the last time we'd see him. When he came back to our facility, a number of people didn't recognize him. He had gained some weight, his color was back, his eyes were bright, and he was in incredibly good spirits. The difference was startling enough that the secretary said, '[John], is that you?' "

For Norma, the effects were similar, including a nearly immediate sense of well-being.

"I feel terrific," the thirty-four-year-old mother said upon returning to Connecticut. "I never felt better. Those people down there are incredible. I think they *have* it. I'm going to go down in history as a pioneer woman."

Suddenly, all the optimism seemed validated, all of the misgivings erased. The stuff actually seemed to work. Marinaccio was exuberant. "We're on the threshold of something so big and so great," he said. Likewise Fellner, who regaled other prospects with accounts of these great successes. "There's absolutely fantastic stories," he was saying shortly after the new year. "They have come through absolutely terrific."

All but one. The Annapolis woman being treated at home died January 12 of kidney failure, presumably the result of the excessive calcium from her deteriorating bones, five days after finishing with the serum.

"I think it [the serum] had a bad effect," said Dr. Simon Tchekmedyian, her oncologist, who was unhappy it was administered. Dr. Tchekmedyian thinks his patient died of the cancer, but it seemed to him that her condition got worse during the serum treatment.

The husband disagrees. "It really never got a chance to work," he said. "The thing I remember most was the impact on the mass in her lower abdomen. She got a direct injection there and within two days it was flat and normal looking, instead of swelled up like a grapefruit. I'm glad we did this thing with the serum. Apart from the substantive effect it had, it did one precious thing for us, and that was give us hope."

Still in all, Art Fellner was disappointed.

"We lost a potential good one there, as far as being able to talk to someone about it."

But with the Annapolis widower's testimony and the glowing

reports on John and Norman in Tijuana, the promoters still had plenty to talk about. Within two days of the death, Estrella would begin treating three more patients. Fellner now was so confident that he hired and dispatched a crew from Compro Communications Projects Inc., an Atlanta film production house, to record a documentary of the fabulous results. One of the patients they filmed was Michael Tartar, a sixty-year-old Ohio man in the final stages of cancer in the liver, colon, and lung.

"I really had no idea what I was getting into, no belief in it," said Tartar's daughter, Diane Heskett of Lancaster, Ohio. "Of course I'd heard all of the horror stories about what could happen [with alternative treatments], but I figured he didn't have anything to lose."

At the time, Tartar was dehydrated and weak, heavily medicated on ten Dilaudid painkillers a day and bound to a wheelchair. His doctor, Heskett said, questioned whether he'd survive the trip to Mexico. But when the treatments began, Heskett was floored by what she witnessed. Each day her father felt better and better.

"He really began to regain his strength. He was able to eat more. . . . He could pull himself out of bed rather than me pulling him out of bed. He was using the walker some instead of the wheelchair all the time. My father started making plans for the future, which he hadn't done in months. I'm sure he was getting better."

When Mike Tartar got back north, however, he was still dehydrated and was hospitalized for replenishment of fluids. Then on February 25, Heskett says, Tartar died as a result of diabetic shock and liver failure unrelated to the serum cure. In the meantime, though, he had been given a CEA test—a crude chemical indicator of the advancement of malignant tissue. His count was 340. Though he'd had no such tests done previously, Heskett says, doctors were amazed the value was so low for a man in such an advanced stage of the disease. They'd have expected a number in the thousands.

"I don't know if the treatment cures people—time will only tell that," she says. "I do know that it improved my father and I do know that he was without pain."

Allan and Jackie Manny sit in Jorge Estrella's outer office waiting for the day's argon treatment, and if you didn't have Tijuana on your mind you wouldn't see a thing unusual about it.

The offices are ordinary-looking—if sparsely furnished—appearing not entirely different from an American practice of similar size. If anything is strange it's what's missing: the familiar array of medical equipment and supplies. The other mild surprise is the selection of books. The shelves have their share of titles on the order of *Clinical Gastroenterology, Clinical Diagnostics, Internal Medicine,* and *Urology,* but they are outnumbered by such works of popular nonfiction as *Gods from Outer Space, Psychic Discoveries Behind the Iron Curtain, The Edgar Cayce Handbook for Health,* and *The Save-Your-Life Diet.* But, all in all, this could be Decatur.

Jorge Estrella sits behind his oversized teak desk and leans back in his tall-back leather chair with his fingertips pressing together. Right now he's looking for all the world like a fifty-three-year-old Tony Bennett. The drapes behind him are white, the carpet beneath him plush, and the air around him heavy with disinfectant.

He has spent a lot of time with Allan Manny the past few days, and is provisionally pleased with his progress. Other patients, he says, had violent reactions during the injections—dizziness, nausea, headache—but Allan's only side effect has been cramping. "He's doing pretty good," Estrella says. "He has been able to eat. He's not thrown up. He's rested."

Estrella is encouraged, but hardly sanguine. He is a doctor who by United States standards operates on the outer fringes of conventional medicine, yet he's no grandstander and he isn't given to sensational claims.

"There is no such thing as a cancer cure," he says. "What we are doing here is research with biological substances. I have been trying to keep that in a low profile. I am not advertising or calling attention to this or trying to give false hope."

Estrella graduated from Universidad Nacional Autonoma de Mexico in 1962 and shortly thereafter joined the practice of Dr. Roman Schenk, an early practitioner of cellular therapy—the injection of live-animal cells said to fortify and rejuvenate human tissue. Schenk has since died, but Estrella has carried on the practice, chiefly for Americans who cross the border five miles away at San Ysidro. They gravitate here because they know this doctor takes a dim view of medical conservatism, which the American Medical Association regards as the prudent and deliberate application of proven science, and which Estrella regards as overly rigid, close-minded, and, occasionally, inhumane.

"Medicine is an art. Medicine is unknown things. Medicine is not a precise science like mathematics." As such, Estrella over the years has administered cellular therapy, laetrile, chodroitin sulfate A, GH3 (a procaine derivative widely advertised in the supermarket tabloids), and other drugs not approved in the United States. "If you incorporate all these little things—cellular here, GH3 over here—you will find some good results. As long as you're using something that gives you results, you don't care if it's legally approved or not legally approved."

Thus he approaches Duda's theory. He saw a remarkable improvement in many of his first few patients, and he'll continue to experiment.

"I think we're on the right track," he says.

Estrella pulls out a medical record describing the case of a thirty-six-year-old Arkansas woman who came to him several weeks earlier 2,000 miles by ambulance. The woman, he said, had twenty-two inches of intestine removed in August, had undergone radiation and chemotherapy, and was near death with cancer in the liver, hip, and brain. Her abdomen was grossly distended. She was on 4 to 6 milligrams of Dilaudid every two hours and still in excruciating pain. She also was on Flexeril, a muscle relaxer; prednisone, for inflammation; Dilantin, for seizures; Xanax, a tranquilizer; and Tagamet, the ulcer medicine.

"In this case we were facing not only a cancer problem with metastasis, we were treating drug addiction. Well, would you believe that she arrived on a Monday evening, Tuesday I started the treatment, and Thursday she was walking around and the abdomen was down flat?"

What's more, he claims, she was off the painkillers and muscle relaxer, on reduced doses of Tagamet and prednisone, "and she was not in pain." The brain lesions continued to prompt seizures, he says, "but the treatment has a virtue.

"Then again, I do not believe it performs miracles."

"EXPECT A MIRACLE," says the little wooden sign above the receptionist, but Allan Manny is oblivious to it as he makes his way to the examining room. He is totally fixed on a tank of argon and an unusually personable physician.

"I'll tell you one thing," Allan says. "When I came down here, I got the most positive feeling from any doctor I've seen. The other doctors are positive—they're positive I'm gonna die."

"I looked at the science and there is no science," says Gregory A. Curt, deputy director of cancer treatment at the National Cancer Institute.

He has reviewed Duda and McDonald's literature—such that it is—a four-and-a-half-page report called "Process for the Eradication of Cancer." Curt is confounded not only by the theory itself, but by the secondary-research citations, which include three outdated textbooks and a journal-article excerpt without reference to the names of the journal or the author. One university medical research director whose research was cited in his report was flabbergasted and enraged that his work appeared in the report. The physician, who pleaded for anonymity for fear of being professionally humiliated, said he merely encouraged the Panama crew to pursue the theory with some conventional science—such as animal experimentation and the collection of data.

Curt is no stranger to purported cancer cures, but to him this whole thing is baffling.

"That's not how you reference stuff scientifically. If there was any evidence that blood types change within tumors, there would have been an article written about it." As for the antigen treatment, "If you destroyed every blood cell that goes through the tumor over three days, the person would have no blood left. It sounds, frankly, very strange."

Dr. Ronald A. Sacher is director of the Blood Bank and Transfusion Service at Georgetown University Hospital, where he is also attending hematologist. In the Duda theory he discerns at least a germ of science. Their description of a blood-type change corresponds vaguely to a phenomenon called "acquired adsorption."

"There is some scientific evidence that tumors can modify the expression of red blood cell blood-group antigens," as observed in certain bowel cancers and hydatid disease, an inflammatory bowel disorder caused by dog tapeworms. "But their approach and interpretation—the expansion of their application—is at best alchemy. . . . They may have been trying to add one and one and get two, but it's incomprehensible to do what they're suggesting. I think it is crackpot nonsense."

Professor Sen-itiroh Hakomori of the Fred Hutchinson Cancer Research Center in Seattle is prominent among biochemists doing research in the chemical identification of antigens. He says Duda and McDonald are very much confused. First, he says, viruses do not cause the vast majority of cancers. He suspects they are reading about viral oncogenes and getting the wrong message. Secondly, says Hakomori, the amateur cancer sleuths mistake the presence of Type A antigens on tumor cells for changes in red-cell blood types—and even that, he says, occurs only in about 10 percent of malignancies among people with Type O or Type B blood.

Hakomori sees a grain of plausibility in the theory, to the degree that the right antibodies conceivably could attack Type A antigens within the tumor. But they would have to be highly specific antibodies—not the variety-pack found in blood-typing reagent—and even then they would be ineffective unless the Type A antigens were present in 100 percent of the tumor, and still that effect would be superficial at best.

In short, he says, "It has nothing to do with science."

Not to put too fine a point on it, the conventional medical world thinks the serum cure is so much quackery. Physicians and researchers require data. They have no use for the subjective anecdotal evidence such as the stories filtering back from Tijuana. (One wonders how they'd react to the random recollections provided by Duda and McDonald by way of documentation. When I asked them, for example, about their first patient, a man they say they treated in Framingham, Massachusetts, in 1980, they couldn't remember if his name was Vince or Vic. Nor did they have a clue as to how I might find him.) Even doctors I spoke to who claimed ignorance in cancer hematology dismissed the treatment out of hand. As Dr. Dennis Bertram put it—he's chairman of the unproven-methods committee of the American Cancer Society—"There's always someone out there with something that appears to cure." Of course, he felt no need to add, the cure never really is.

That sort of institutional skepticism may be justified by the scientific method, but if doctors think it dissuades people from chasing cancer-cure rainbows, they are very much mistaken. The categorical rejection of "unproven methods" may, in its own way, contribute to the proliferation of quack cures around the globe. What is conventional wisdom to an oncologist may be precisely what you don't want to hear if you happen to be dying of cancer. When you are terminal, what you might see is some inattentive physician or some smug bureaucrat turning up his nose at the treatment that—who knows?—could save your life.

"If anything looks promising, if it's going out and eating dandelion weeds, I'd do it," says Bob Holt, a Georgia man and Estrella's third patient. "Wouldn't you? A man forty-two years old with five daughters, hey, man, you'd better do *something*."

Holt resents and mistrusts the medical establishment. He discerns nothing less than a conspiracy to quash unconventional treatments and to perpetuate the chemotherapy-radiation-surgery trinity that does so much harm to patients' bodies while therapeutically, to his way of thinking, doing so little good.

"The reason that I have been *forced* to go to Mexico is because of the unbelievable effect—the monopolistic grip—the AMA, the National Cancer Institute, and the American Cancer Society have on the poor cancer patient. . . . My father died of colon cancer twenty years ago. He got it twenty-five years ago and died five years later. When I found out that I had the same problem—here is the appalling thing—do you know what they wanted to treat me with? The *same chemotherapy drugs they treated my father with twenty-five years ago!* Tell me that's not appalling.

"I met twenty-five or thirty people in Mexico who actually were fleeing the U.S.A., because they would be ridiculed by their own physicians for seeking alternate therapies."

Like the conspiracy buffs who believe General Electric is sitting on patents for an everlasting lightbulb, or that Exxon has acquired and buried the rights to manufacture a 200 mpg carburetor, some cancer patients believe the medical orthodoxy seeks to bury nonconventional treatments—not because the treatments are scientifically suspect, but because they might cut into the cancer-treatment industry. And because the National Cancer Institute sets aside virtually nothing to explore potential merit in alternate therapies, the desperate terminal patient is left with two choices. He can separate the wheat from the chaff on his own, or throw up his hands and die.

"So I have to traipse off to Mexico," Holt says, heatedly. "I'll go to the Bahamas. I'll go to Germany. I'll go wherever it takes to beat this thing."

When Marie Steinmeyer, the Atlanta cancer-patient-rights advocate, told Allan and Jackie Manny about the serum treatment, it was like an answer to prayer. There was simply no way they could raise the cash for a stay at the Gerson Clinic, and Steinmeyer was saying this new serum was apparently both nontoxic and promising. It was not as established, perhaps, as the Gerson regime, but far more affordable.

The Mannys certainly had faith in the recommendation. Steinmeyer's personal horror story about her own treatment for breast cancer had propelled her on a high-profile crusade against medical arrogance. The Mannys, themselves in the midst of a none-too-encouraging relationship with the VA hospital doctors, were further convinced that the chemotherapy and radiation were doing Allan more harm than his cancer and were as *simpatico* with Steinmeyer as could be.

As an officer of the International Association of Cancer Victors and Friends, Steinmeyer counsels dozens of cancer patients a week about a multitude of treatment options. It was she who introduced Holt to the serum, and she continues to be bullish on the potential.

"I don't steer anyone, per se," she says, though she did tell "maybe a dozen friends I'd look into it if I were you. . . . I think there's a great deal of merit to it. I think it should be looked into. The fact is that it is far less toxic than anything we use in the United States."

The toxicity issue was what particularly attracted the Mannys last winter when they met Steinmeyer in an Atlanta cafeteria, and Steinmeyer seemed pleased to learn they had followed through. "I wish he would have tried herbs, too," she says. "Herbs are the most effective treatments."

By April 21, a week after returning from Mexico to Decatur, Allan and Jackie are wondering on their own about what else they might have tried. Allan is in agony.

"I'm terrible," he says. "I don't know whether I'm getting healing pains or what. Nobody seems to know. I'm in tremendous pain all the time."

He is also all but collapsed with fatigue. Even after the treatments began to make him feel better, he had difficulty sleeping and tolerating food. Now Jackie is at her wits' end trying to feed him juices of the Gerson diet, which she's trying to administer at home.

"Gerson's works," she says, "but I'm having trouble implementing it. He's just shot."

The odd thing—the encouraging thing—is his lymph nodes. Before the treatments they had been grotesquely swollen. But ever since they've diminished in size. That the shrinking might reveal a reversal of the disease is where they invest all their hope.

"We've stalled it," Jackie says. "I don't know about how the insides are, but I know what I can see with my own eyes."

As early as February 19, Alex Marinaccio was getting impatient. His protégé Duda was effectively closed down in Panama. The doctor in Tijuana was administering the serum outside the Inventors Club auspices. And, financially, everybody was in a hole. The first five patients had been treated for free—Art Fellner having promised to pay Estrella's fees—but none of them had seen fit to donate anything to the cause, an option that had been plainly encouraged from the momentous August 9 announcement.

"We cure people and they melt," Marinaccio groused. "None of them has even called to say thank you. No one has given ten cents as a donation. So now we're starting to charge. It's a whole new ball game. We're charging $2,600 right now.

"Here we have the discovery of a lifetime and we can't make any money off of it."

Marinaccio's complaints were fascinating, encapsulating as they did six months of mixed signals and misinformation. To start with, nobody—by any measure—had been cured of cancer. John, Norma, Bob Holt, and the Arizona woman indeed reported feeling better—and there was a variety of medical evidence to the effect that their tumors had not grown—but there was no evidence whatsoever of a tumor having shrunk or disappeared. Mike Tartar, as Marinaccio spoke, was on the edge of death. The Maryland woman was dead.

Cure is a word that Marinaccio had used loosely from the outset, such as he randomly dished out figures on the number of people treated. In the same February 19 conversation, Marinaccio claimed that twenty people had taken the serum and that "We can document nine of them." Yet Estrella had treated only five. The Maryland woman who received the serum in her home made six. Duda and McDonald claimed treating five in the earliest stages of development. Among them: Vince (or Vic), a woman named Alice, and "John Somebody-or-other." I could track down only one of them, a New England physicist who reported improvement, but who simultaneously had undergone a half-dozen other therapies.

It is of minor consequence what the principals told me. What they told prospective patients is a different matter. One person says promoters referred to thirty previous cases. Another person says he was told "a dozen" had preceded him. Forgetting for a moment what therapeutic value the serum might or might not have, this raises the question of whether patients were lured into the treatment under false pretenses. When a week later in Atlanta I asked Al Marinaccio about this manner of promotion, he blew up.

"I'm not promoting it. I have never promoted it. I thought it was something to investigate."

And the August 9 press release describing the 100 percent cure rate?

"It's not a press release," he said. "It's a confidential cancer report to me."

Brian McDonald remembers things differently. Three months after Marinaccio's mad retreat from puffery, McDonald was feeling contrite about the original claims.

"We want to get rid of the word 'cure,' " he says. "Al is the one who put that in. We had something that was not anywhere near as fantastic as what he wrote [in the August 9 announcement]. He wrote it and put it above our names. We signed it, but that's about it."

Was it a confidential cancer report *to* Alex?

"Understand," says McDonald, "he was handing them out like they were peanut butter and jelly sandwiches."

In any event, at the time Marinaccio decided to begin seeking payment for the treatments, the team was forty-four patients shy of the fifty documented cases Fellner had hoped to assemble before leaping from an experimental phase to a full-fledged treatment program—a program that suddenly was looking less humanitarian and more entrepreneurial in flavor.

This is not to suggest that the heart of the serum treatment was a money scheme; the enterprise always was in its essence a sincere effort to help mankind. If the principals had turned out to be misguided, they were not the sort of parasites who wantonly lead desperate people down paths of futile hope for the cynical purpose of separating them from their money. In this case, if some patients were misinformed, the road was nevertheless paved with good intentions.

No doubt Art Fellner was very well-intentioned when he said, February 14, "I'm paying for the treatment of these people." No doubt he was sincere when he told—according to their accounts—Bob Holt, John, Manny, Diane Heskett, Estrella, and who-knows-who else that he'd partially or fully subsidize treatment and travel expenses. No doubt he believed what he said from February 1986 to mid-May when he assured me—as well as Compro Communications, the film production house which claims he owes $130,000—that the money was on its way.

"I expect it tomorrow or Thursday," he said on March 11 and a dozen other times. "It's frustrating sometimes when you get those business deals that take longer than you expect to come through."

At this writing, they have not come through. No Hawaiian shopping-center money. No jumbo-jet money. No low-valence-gold money.

Some of the patients said Fellner promised to subsidize their travel expenses as well, but Fellner denies this. "Fellner promised to send me a check to get out of Mexico," Heskett says. "He left me high and dry. All I got from him was a phone call and a lot of lies."

Fellner's reply: "I didn't make no commitment there. I don't know what she's talking about. But you can bet your bottom dollar, the moment this [series of deals] comes through, I'll take care of this because they went through hell."

By the end of May, Allan Manny is in and out of the VA hospital twice a week for hydration and morphine. The weakness is now crippling, the pain constant. He can barely walk even with assistance, and his speech is slurred.

"I've been sleeping more than I want to," he says. "I really don't know what it is. Dr. Estrella can't tell me a whole lot. Hopefully, I can get my strength back."

But he hasn't eaten in weeks. "If he fails it'll be because he starved himself," Jackie says, and Allan agrees: "This is the problem with the juice stuff. The stomach turns sour. I throw up. I dehydrate even more."

In Tijuana, Estrella is at a loss to explain Manny's problems. He thinks perhaps the serum has only a temporary effect, that it should be re-administered every four-to-five months. When I ask him if all the improvements might be the result of the placebo effect, or if the introduction of foreign proteins might be temporarily tricking the patients' immune systems into working overtime, he says no.

"The treatment," he insists, "has a virtue."

Jackie Manny is not quite ready to surrender. The receded lymph nodes give her something to focus on, to cling to.

"If we can just get past this and get some sleep we can turn it around. Something has happened that is not explained. Something has happened. We just don't know what."

Jackie does all of the positive thinking. Allan homes in on the unbearable present. "I'm sitting here thinking, 'If you've got to die, why go through all this suffering?'"

Three weeks later, he was dead.

Well, Well, Well . . .

ABERDEEN, MISS. —There's an expression in these parts: "Well . . ."

It can mean any number of things, one of which is contemptuous resignation, as in, "Just because I'm not hollering doesn't mean I'm pleased," and one of which is a weary sort of surprise, as in, "Well, don't that beat it all, but I suppose I might have guessed."

The first time Joel Harris was arrested for rape, folks around here said, "Well . . ."

Yeah, he was a churchgoing young man who never had so much as a traffic ticket, who worked maintenance at Mueller Brass Co., and hunted and fished and raised a small family. But, you know, Joel was chubby and real quiet, and I reckon you never do know what's going on in the head of a poor ol' fat boy.

The rape victim, a Tishomingo County waitress, had spotted him eating a hamburger in her restaurant two months after the attack. The next day he was in a line-up, scared breathless, as the woman fingered him without hesitation.

"I was uncool," Harris says. "I don't remember, I might have cried."

It happened, though, that Harris came up with an alibi; people at Mueller swore he was at work when the rape took place. But then, three months later, he was arrested again, this time for the attempted rape of a Lee County woman. Then he was charged with trying to rape a Tippah County woman. Three line-ups, three positive IDs. Well . . .

Harris got out of both of the new ones, however. For Lee County charges, he had the at-work alibi. The Tippah County lady just didn't want to go through with a trial. As the *Tupelo Daily Journal* reported in a lead story, "Joel Harris has been charged with attempted rape twice and rape once in recent months. But as of Friday, Harris, 22, of Golden, is not facing any charges."

This is a land of "innocent until proven guilty," but nobody likes to see a criminal slipping through the fingers of justice. By the time the fourth and fifth rape cases came down, Harris had long since been shunned by the people around him. People he thought were friends avoided him. He had to move closer to Mueller because nobody would give him a ride to work. His fledgling fishing-tackle business died aborning.

"I couldn't go buy anything. I couldn't go sell anything," he says. "Nobody knows what I gave up. My truck, my bass boat, my home. My way of life."

All the while, his lawyers were telling law enforcement it was all a terrible mistake. Grady Tollison and Mike Mills, who is also a state legislator and Harris's wife's first cousin, kept saying there must be another man out there who just looks like Joel. Jerry Butler, a state Highway Patrol investigator, cared enough to pursue the possibilities, but the sheriffs weren't buying.

When victim number five picked Harris out of a line-up, Tippah County Sheriff Leroy Meeks said, "With her testimony . . . I think we can get this rapist convicted." He said that on August 12, six weeks before police arrested Sammy Ross—a man who allegedly raped a Union County woman, and a man who is the spitting image of Joel Harris. A dead ringer. A twin.

So the nightmare was over, 17 months of suspicion and paranoia and fear.

"We didn't go out to eat. We didn't go to a movie. We didn't go nowhere. I went to work and church on Sunday. That's all I done. I quit fishing. I nearly quit hunting. I only went deer hunting five times last year."

So fearful was he of another arrest, he refused to be alone for one second he couldn't account for. His diary of his every move included entries such as this one from the morning of June 15, 1986: "Lisa woke me up at 5:48 to get ready to go to brotherhood breakfast. I called over to Ken's, told Theresa, get Ken up and get him ready. Ken come by and got me we left the house at 6:33 and we got to Antioch (Baptist Church) at 6:56 . . . . ."

Joel had considered suicide during his ordeal, rejecting it as betrayal of God and family. Since then he's been tempted to be bitter, but he doesn't have that in him, either. As Mills says, "He rises above all and holds malice toward none." Joel's just happy to have his freedom back, the sweet luxury of going into the woods without needing a witness to vouch for him.

"We didn't know if it would ever end," he says. "My wife— you know what she said when I told her someone got arrested? She said, 'Well . . .' "

The Numbers Man

Norman Bloom was a sixty-seven-year-old homeless man who believed in a unified explanation of the universe built around arithmetic. I had done a story on him in 1988, based on his calculations on the Baltimore Orioles' infamous twenty-one-game losing streak, which he attributed to Divine will, and which he maintained could have been predicted based on certain other numerological expressions, including the Dow-Jones Industrial Average and the date of Larry King's birth. The assertions were, of course, preposterous—but the arithmetical coincidences Bloom painstakingly uncovered were so amazing that I broke my "no psychotics" rule and did the story. Shortly thereafter, I got a call from his daughter informing me of her father's death, and with the call came a suggestion. Her father hadn't always been pathetic and crazy; why not try to revisit the life and numbers of Norman Bloom to try to get some insight into how a bright, loving, ordinary middle-class man can wind up on the streets for twenty-six years, raving about baseball scores and rejected by the world? For the next year, I traveled the East Coast documenting the life and death of the Numbers Man.

[Background noise inside safe-deposit vault, man speaking to someone, saying "195, this must be 207."]

62J, 195, 207. At long last, three numbers that really count for Norman Bloom. The man's affinity for arithmetic isn't apt to be equaled, yet never have a few homely digits meant so much to his life. In fact, they mark the end of it. The numbers belong to safe-deposit boxes in a Paterson, New Jersey, bank. Here Bloom's children sit with a state examiner to inventory the numerological

ephemera he deemed worthy of a Mosler vault. Now they consti-
tute his meager legacy. [Background noise of someone shuffling
papers.]

STATE EXAMINER: Ten-dollar accounts, these are probably
closed . . .

BLOOM'S SON: No, they're not.

EXAMINER: They're not. March '83; I don't know if this is still
active or not. It might be . . .

BLOOM'S DAUGHTER: It's possible . . .

EXAMINER: Yeah . . .

BLOOM'S DAUGHTER: He wasn't your basic normal person.

No, Norman Bloom was not your basic normal person. He was an
eccentric mathematician, composer, and part-time ice-cream truck
driver whose last twenty-six years were a tortured Messianic
odyssey. It was a search, as he once explained, for the relationship
between numbers and God.

NORMAN BLOOM: [As recorded in the earlier program] He
delights in correlating the number of the occurrence with
the number of the date. This is done in all areas; it's done in
the stock market. The Dow Jones averages on 5/3 is plus 15.
Five times three equals 15. On the third day of the third
month of the third year—that's March 3, 1983—the Dow
Jones changes 3 point zero zero. How can blind accident cor-
relate this occurrence which results from the buying and
selling of millions of shares of stock on the idea of a date? You
have to have a thinking, knowing Creator having the power
and the wish to do this.

That's just a taste of the Bloom Proof, which in its fullest form
encompasses biblical text, the Apollo space program, and the par-
tition of Palestine, to say nothing of the Earth's orbit, the date of
his circumcision, and the run-scoring punch of the Baltimore Ori-

oles. For nearly three decades he devoted all of his resources to publishing and proselytizing his theory of divine numbers play, forsaking the comforts of home and hearth for life on the street. Bloom was sour-smelling and disheveled. He slept in his car. He was, in short, a vagrant. But an anonymous vagrant he was not. Carl Sagan, the astronomer, wrote about the "Bloom Proof" ["Larry King Show" theme music begins to play in background], *and millions of late-night radio listeners knew Bloom affectionately as the Numbers Man.*

ANNOUNCER: [Music still playing.] You're listening to the *Larry King Show,* live from the nation's capital. Here again, Larry King.

LARRY KING: Paramus, New Jersey. Hello. [louder] Hello?

CALLER, NORMAN BLOOM: Hello, Mr. King. Do you hear me?

KING: Yeah.

BLOOM: Fine. I issued this challenge to Dr. Sagan, Dr. Teller, Dr. Jeremy Bernstein . . .

KING: What's the challenge?

BLOOM: The challenge is, I issued the challenge that they either prove me in error and win a prize . . .

KING: Why do they have to prove you in error?

BLOOM: Pardon?

KING: Why should they bother to prove you in error?

BLOOM: I'm giving you . . .

KING: You deal with numbers. Why should they bother with that?

BLOOM: Pardon, sir?

KING: Why should they bother with numbers?

BLOOM: Because, sir, if they didn't bother with numbers, you would have no nuclear energy. The very discovery of the . . .

KING: But if you told . . .

[Talk-radio conversation goes on in background.] *For King's listeners, the Numbers Man was irrational and pathetic, but just entertaining enough to put up with. If they wondered how he came to be that way, they got no clues. If they envisioned him as some-*

how always having been a ranting monomaniac, they couldn't have been more wrong . . .

WOMAN: He was a very charming, gift of gab, and good-looking and talented and fun, bright, and . . . very interesting man.

Terry Hulley, now a publishing executive, married twenty-three-year-old Norm Bloom in 1944 *and lived with him for fourteen years.*

TERRY HULLEY: He could whistle whole pieces of classical music through, from one end to the other. We would go to concerts all the time and he would be ecstatic and into the music and very involved in the music, a very talented man.

Or, as his cousin Iris Kaplan puts it . . .

IRIS KAPLAN: He was just a beautiful, beautiful human being. There was something about him that was almost spiritual, and how he reverted to this kind of a *mishegoss*—and I don't know what else to call it—I will never know.

How and why did it all unravel? Terry and Norman were a happy couple with a baby daughter, a piece of the family floor coverings business, and a bright fifties suburban future. But there were pressures, too. Norman's upbringing had been rigid, verging on cruel, by a father who wished to live the cultured academic life vicariously through his children. Sam Bloom was a volatile tyrant. Norman's younger brother Jack, a practicing clinical psychologist, recalls.

JACK BLOOM: My father was a very, very driven, in some ways rigid . . . rigid, but in some ways wanting his sons to have all the culture that was denied him. Norman would have to be up at six-thirty in the morning to practice piano. We'd go to public school, and three times a week we'd go to Hebrew school. The other three he would go to a Yiddish atheist school. Our father used to brag about the fact that he would take Norman and Sol when they were very little kids, six years old, to the organ concerts at City College and how quietly, uh, they would sit. He was very proud of that. They were probably scared out of their gourds.

Even as an adult, Norman was overwhelmed with his father's looming presence. When he and Terry broke away to start their own linoleum business and Bloom rented their first store, Sam Bloom interceded with the landlord to un-rent it. But in the mid-fifties ordinary marriage strains gave way to erratic behavior. One night Bloom awoke screaming, "Leave me alone, go away!" He would seize on strange money-making schemes, such as one to implant plastic-encased girly images into pencils. Norman invested heavily, and unsuccessfully, sending the floor business spiraling into bankruptcy and Bloom into further distress.

TERRY HULLEY: He would disappear, he wouldn't come home at night. He had episodes of, I guess, paranoia, schizophrenia. And finally there was one episode where he got involved with a woman, and the police called me, or somebody called me, and it got just too bad, and I said no, that's enough, you gotta go . . .

They separated in 1958, by which time their second child, Roger, was two. Bloom had been a worrisome husband, but he was one terrific weekend father. [piano music in the background] *For Marcia and Roger, every Sunday was an adventure, frequently a musical one. The piano training Bloom had forced on him he shared lovingly with his children in the form of songs of his own composition.*

CHILDREN SINGING WITH BLOOM: "Sunday morning, Sunday evening, Sunday afternoon . . . Oh how I love to be with you. Weekday mornings, weekday evenings, weekday after-

noon . . . All I do is dream of Sunday, Sunday I share with
you . . ."

WOMAN: [Song in background continues, muted] My father was
embarrassing to both my brother and I because he was loud
and noisy and generous, and he would talk to strangers in
the street, and he would ignore "no trespassing" signs . . .

Marcia Hulley.

MARCIA HULLEY, BLOOM'S DAUGHTER: There was also this incredible love. I mean, he . . . I mean, we grew up singing Walt
Whitman. I . . . [Sings] "Me imperturbed, standing at ease in
nature, master of all or mistress of all . . ."

MAN'S DEEP VOICE: [Singing] "Me imperturbed, standing at ease
in nature, master of all or mistress of all, aplomb in the midst
of irrational things . . ."

[Man continues to sing in background] *This recording, sung by a
baritone Bloom engaged to make a record, documents a turning
point in his state of mind. In* 1962 *he hired Carnegie Recital Hall
to give a concert, one which he said would vindicate and validate
what had become his preoccupation with the Bible.*

MAN'S DEEP VOICE: [singing] "Finding my occupation . . ."

[With baritone in background] *The music was impressive, but
almost nobody showed up and Bloom was shattered. The anguish
and humiliation, his brother thinks, marked the final blow, as if in
one stroke he forever lost his grip on reality. Jack Bloom reads
from a note his brother scribbled on a program after the ill-fated
concert had ended.*

JACK BLOOM: "My dear brother: I guess you are right, and I am
the fool. No critics, no audience except friends and relatives,
even though I distributed 1,600 tickets. This will probably

change many things for me, but one thing will not change: He is my rock, my shield, and my strength. In Him do I place my trust. Your loving brother, Norm."

The odyssey had begun. The passion for music entwined with a fixation for the Bible gradually gave way to a singular fascination with numbers. In early 1962, sister-in-law Helen Bloom recalls him scribbling license plate numbers for future reference. He squirreled away dollar bills with significant serial numbers. He got arrested in New York City in an incident involving a number on a subway turnstile. The disintegration continued until, in 1965, she and Bloom's brothers contrived to get him help . . .

HELEN BLOOM: I couldn't believe that Norman was just going to . . . be mad all his life. That was it, I just couldn't accept it. And somehow I convinced them to have him committed, actually by hiding in the bushes or something near their home with someone from the state institution.

But he was out soon enough. Like many a schizophrenic, totally persuaded of his sanity, he refused all treatment. And because he was articulate and gentle and no physical threat to anybody, he was released, as he was from several other hospitalizations through the next twenty years. However, as my chat with him in mid-1988 revealed, nonviolent is one thing, and mentally healthy is quite another. He had been going on about the Book of Isaiah, chapter 53, when I realized what he was getting at.

BOB: [Talking with Bloom] Are you the Messiah?
BLOOM: Yes, this is who I am, sir. This is definitely who I am. This was made known to me in 1962. There was an anointing without human hands of sacramental wine. I am *Moshiach ben David ha melach*. I am the one who fulfills this. I am the one who reveals the power of God and teaches mankind and brings a new world for mankind. This is my purpose.

Yes, Norman Bloom, rotten teeth and all, thought he was God. This placed him in a category with a fair number of street people, but whatever stereotypes that conjures you may as well discard. For one thing, he wasn't a panhandler. Nor was he, strictly speaking, down and out. In the summertime he worked for the Pied Piper Ice Cream Company in Hawthorne, New Jersey, delivering Good Humor—and sometimes numerical good news—to children just across the state line in New York. This was the job that paid for his real work, the tens of thousands of numbers tracts he would bestow on anybody who cared and many who didn't. Nathan Chernichaw, Pied Piper owner, remembers:

NATHAN CHERNICHAW. He was my one real act of Christian charity. I said, what the devil can this guy do besides something of this nature? He had a job that was quite lucrative. I think he was earning five, six, seven, eight hundred dollars a week. And this job also afforded him the opportunity to do his quote-unquote "work."

In the winter he worked occasionally as a messenger, but mainly he concentrated on his numbers. The morning would find him in the Triangle Diner down the road from Pied Piper, hunkered down over a bowl of hot oatmeal or, in the evenings, a plate of veal parmigiana. Nadya Kubovcik waited on him for years.

NADYA KUBOVCIK: He used to always, you know, read, like take a literature or from the paper first thing in the morning, then start writing things, scribbling things, but I didn't . . . and mostly he used to figure things with numbers, you know. But I have no idea, you know, what kind of theology or whatever he had . . . I have no idea. [Fade up to background sounds of a library.]

LIBRARIAN: Boys and girls, first thing off we're gonna start with a story today.

LITTLE GIRL: I know that one!

LIBRARIAN: You know this one . . .

Bloom didn't have a home, but he did have an office: the Fair Lawn, New Jersey, Public Library. He was a fixture in the reading room there, working feverishly on his computations and serving up reference information when the employees themselves were stumped. There he made a friend of the children's librarian, Evelyn Schoenberg.

EVELYN SCHOENBERG: There were librarians here who were truly offended by him. Some of them who said, uh, he's imposing himself upon us, and I don't see why he's here, because he would occa- . . . you know, he would come over and give you the sheet of paper, I mean, if you evinced any interest in what he was doing at all, and they would become annoyed if he did this more than once.

Mrs. Schoenberg indulged him because there was something about him underneath all that dishevelment that touched her.

SCHOENBERG: He was a courtly man, and the thing that really, uh, made me feel very extremely warmly for Mr. Bloom was his ability to quote poetry. And he did it so beautifully. And very softly one day he began to quote William Blake's "Songs of Innocence" to me, and I was so deeply touched and so impressed that I forever was connected in a way to Mr. Bloom [starts laughing as she speaks], in a very subtle way, I was so impressed with him.

Even in the ascetic, spiritual life, of course, there are moments of earthly intrusion, such as the time Bloom's daughter, Marcia, had some important news. At a loss for a way to reach him, she phoned the library.

SCHOENBERG: She called to . . . called from Boston, to tell him that he had a grandson. This was a very poignant thing to have happen, we were all quite excited about it, actually. Even those who were not exactly, shall I say, friends with Mr. Bloom in the library were pleased that this happened, and even though they probably wanted to eject him and certainly to reject him, he was nevertheless a member of the family of the library.

Yes, Norman Bloom, self-described Son of Man, was also Norman Bloom, grandfather of Willie. It was just another tragic paradox in his life, for he was a man who so loved the world he sacrificed everything to serve it. But as the years went by, when it came to his own family, he became increasingly detached. [Kids singing "Sunday Song" in background.] The model of post-divorce visitation from the early sixties, whose regular weekend adventures inspired the "Sunday Song," referred in his prodigious writings to his own children not at all. He saw his grandchild Willie all of three times. Marcia Hulley recalls her father's first visit to her Boston home after Willie was born:

MARCIA HULLEY: He came up to see Willie, and, uh, they had a little teddy bear. And I was so pleased, y' know? I was so pleased that he, that he thought of that, but y' know what? It was Dotty from the ice-cream truck who made it for Willie. [Softly, barely audible.] It hurt. I don't know why it hurt, but it did. [Deep sigh.]

It's not easy being a child of divorce, especially when Dad is a ridiculous vagabond whose quixotic ramblings mean continual embarrassment, aggravation, and fear—fear for him, and for the psychological future of you and your children. In some ways Norman Bloom's journey for truth was paralleled by his daughter, Marcia's. Was his sickness environmental, all Papa Bloom's fault, or genetic? Was his life, please, somehow romantic, or was it just pain? And did he, after he became ill, really and truly love her?

[Loud bells rings, and a bang in the background]

With a flick of the wire cutters at a rented north Jersey storage locker amid the musty clutter of soiled clothing and carton upon carton of arithmetical tracts, she searches for answers. Here in a 6 X 9-foot cage is the repository of Bloom's life's work.

MARCIA HULLEY: What's this? [Laughs.] One Shark, one Three-Stage bomb, one Fat Frog. [*Still laughing.*] It's an ice cream order! What the hell? One Fruity Patoo!

Marcia and her brother discard crates full of flyers and undelivered correspondence, one to John F. Kennedy, one to Yitzak Shamir, one to Lawrence Taylor of the New York Giants. Presently Marcia uncovers one of her father's journals, his last one, it seems.

MARCIA HULLEY: [Reading.] This is something he said a lot: "My bitterness is beyond any other bitterness. My agony is so profound, so [sound of page turning] limitless, completely rejected by the whole world." [More pages turning, and then she sighs heavily.] I made him some good meals. Oh, y' know, I wish there were something . . . I wish there were something to us in all this . . . [more papers shuffling]

Wish unfulfilled. She can find no letters from her, no photos of her, no references to her, a fact which, months later in Boston, she struggles to reconcile.

MARCIA HULLEY: I know in my heart of hearts that my dad loved me very, very deeply, and I believe that I represented his link to normal life, in a way. Because when he would come up here I would give him dinner and we would listen to music and it would be almost a day of normal life with love and compassion, and, uh . . .

And an emotional farewell.

MARCIA HULLEY: [Fighting tears.] He'd say good-bye, "Pooh," he'd say, "how much do I love you? I love you zillions and zillions of big bunches of zilches." Always. And, uh, "Do great things."

On the other hand, the visits were few, and he'd always veer into mathematical polemics. Even the tender departures were weighted with their mutual knowledge of his return to the street. In that final journal Marcia found heart-rending documentation of his misery. "Cold. Upset stomach. No place to sleep. Leg. Take Pepto-Bismol. Sleep in car. Very ill."

MAN: Uh, Norman neglected his health . . .

John Houston, a refrigeration mechanic at the Pied Piper Company.

JOHN HOUSTON: I remember a day, the weather was below, uh, what was normal, it was a cold spell, and, uh, it was raining outside, and he, uh, instead of going to a hotel he just lay there in the front seat of his car. I told him I think he'd be better off going to a hotel, but he didn't listen.

Nathan Chernichaw.

CHERNICHAW: There's nothing we could tell him. You can't tell God anything, you know. And, uh, he left the depot, not complaining of any illness or anything, went on his route— I think it may have been, uh, somewhere around eight o'clock that we had gotten a call from the local police. The children had come to his truck, and saw him lying on the inside of his truck. They summoned the police and they in turn I believe took an ambulance.

[Ice-cream truck bells ring, fading under as a radio announcer's voice is heard.]

ANNOUNCER: Here again, Larry King.

KING: He did, did he not, get on our nerves, and annoy us? And I almost felt like he was my shadow for some reason. He . . . he became over the years a kind of integral part of this program. Norman Bloom passed away last night at Nyack Hospital in Nyack, New York. You know him, or knew him, as the Numbers Man.

In a life of manifold tragedy, maybe the most heartbreaking fact was the utter futility of Bloom's 26-year quest. His tireless accumulation of mathematical coincidences, according to astronomer Carl Sagan, was classically flawed. In a universe where there are trillions of simultaneous events that can be expressed with numbers, a few thousand such coincidences amount to a drop in the bucket. The genius behind such painstaking enumeration is undeniable. But, in the end, it all amounted to . . . nothing.

MARCIA HULLEY: Oh, Daddy. [Background noise, shuffling of papers, moving things.] "Bide your time for success is near. 88863." [laughs.] A fortune cookie number. Oh, God. He always did love Chinese food. [More shuffling of papers, moving of things.] OK. Empty.

EXAMINER'S VOICE: This is your copy, thank you very much. I can handle the rest.

MARCIA HULLEY: Thank you. I appreciate your waiting for us.

EXAMINER: Thank you, and I'm sorry about your dad. Thank you.

[Music: Instrumental from Bloom's concert.]

Slam

We are at 15 Min, a club on Fifteenth Street in downtown Washington. It's a funky joint, dark and smoky, with dollar Rolling Rocks, beer-sticky painted furniture, and gilt-framed cherubim mounted on bare brick walls. By the time I arrive, Miles Moore, the Washington correspondent for *Rubber & Plastics News,* is already wedged behind a cocktail table, surrounded by friends. Miles, for Miles, is looking reasonably put together. His long-since-amortized dress shirt is neatly tucked into his trousers, for example, and his wispy, wavy chestnut hair is not yet lurching out in five competing directions. As usual, however, his eyeglasses have skied to the tip of his bunny-slope nose and his head is cocked quizzically toward his left shoulder, in the fashion of Nipper, the RCA dog, fixing on his master's voice.

"Hi, Miles."

Although I've told him I'd be here, Miles seems surprised to see me, and he nearly topples a table as he half stands to introduce me to his cronies. He may be the last man who does so strictly according to Amy Vanderbilt. ("Bob, I'd like you to meet Celia Brown . . .") It's an exercise I've been through before—once in a bookstore in Mount Rainier, once in a multipurpose room at the Martin Luther King Jr. Library, once in a lecture hall at the Sumner School Museum, once at the Joaquin Miller Cabin in Rock Creek Park, and once at the Writer's Center in Bethesda. Intimate venues one and all.

Besides being the capital's preeminent rubber journalist, Miles is an accomplished poet. His work has appeared in such publications as *New York Quarterly, Poet Lore, Bogg, Plains Poetry Journal, Pivot, Poetry Motel, Minimus, Lip Service, Black Buzzard Review,* and, believe it or not, *National Review,* yet he has never read anyplace where there was a question of crowd control. This has something to do with our literarily insensate culture, and very much to do with the nature of poetry readings, which have a lot in common with oral surgery, by virtue of combining pain and anesthesia.

At any given forum, half of the poetry is guaranteed to be dreadfully pretentious, or thick with embarrassing clichés about love, nature, and, especially, the art of writing. The other half is insufficient compensation for sacrificing a more enjoyable activity, such as stripping wallpaper. Readings are therefore so thinly attended that the polite listener is obliged to feign attentiveness at all times, including extravagant facial expressions of sympathy and delight during even the most banal passages. None of this, as we shall see, applies to Miles's poems. But, in any event, tonight is no ordinary poetry reading, no routine wine-and-cheese-and-throwing-your-head-back-with-fake-laughter-at-a-meager-literary-joke sort of evening. This is a slam. A poetry slam: freestyle verse in the hooting, raucous format of a wet T-shirt contest. It's *mano a mano*, with the spoils going to the last of twelve poets standing.

"I'm soooo nervous," Miles says to me, in the squeaky pitch his voice achieves when he's especially anxious, splitting the difference between Billy De Wolfe and Big Bird. There are people in our twelve-publication news bureau who have no idea of his wit and astonishing erudition, but who are alternately amused and alarmed by his capacity for becoming unhinged. This can include shrill outbursts of frustration at the fax machine, or hand-wringing declarations of worry about an angry letter from a reader, or *sotto voce* muttering in solitary, but animated, walks down the hall. He is, in a word, excitable, and fear of failure is as sharp a stimulus as any. This is Miles's fifth slam—four here and one in Baltimore—and he's gotten past the first round only once.

"I did so with a poem called 'the Televangelist's Last Sermon,' " he says, "which very nearly got a standing ovation. The next week in Baltimore I read the same poem . . . It died. I lost to a teenage poet who read a very bad poem very badly."

Tonight, in Round 1, he faces Denise DeVries, a George Mason University graduate student with a wry take on poetry, the sexes, and cultural imperialism. But their bout awaits the match between Ed Simmons, an elastic-voiced crooner of rhythmic verse, and Will A. Wyler. Presiding over this and every slam here at 15 min is Art Schuhart, construction worker by day, goateed Slam Master by night.

"WHO ARE YOU?" Schuhart bellows as Wyler takes his place under the lights at the rear of the club.

"Will A. Wyler."

"WHAT DO YOU DO?"

"I own Will's Lawn Service, Arlington, Virginia."

"OKAY . . . DO IT!"

What follows is painful to witness. Wyler's first poem is called "Seaside Passion," romantic verse with conspicuously familiar imagery that draws hoots and laughter from the crowd of seventy-five, establishing what seems to be a hostile tone for the evening. (Slams, Miles explains, follow scorched-earth rules of audience etiquette. "You know: 'We will kill your women and children to the fourteenth generation.' ") When both poets have read their three allotted selections of three minutes each, Schuhart goes through the motions of the hand-over-the-head call for applause, but he needn't have bothered. Simmons prevails in a rout.

Now Miles is onstage, his face shining under the spotlight, his ruddy nose all but glowing under the pressure of his eyewear and of the bloodthirsty crowd.

"WHO ARE YOU?'

"I'm Miles."

"WHADDYA DO?"

"I'm a Washington correspondent for *Rubber & Plastics News.*"

In response to the revelation, wild spontaneous applause; what better icebreaker than an obscure and incongruous job title? Miles couldn't be off to a better start. Alternating with DeVries, he reads three poems. One is "Keats and the Anchorman," which ostensibly is a tirade aimed at the ill-fated nineteenth-century poet, in the voice of an anonymous TV news star. His second selection, one of my favorites, is a lament about the timeless tragedy of war, "Dead Boy in the Road at Fredericksburg (Photographed by Mathew Brady, May 1863)":

You're pictured blankly, in all-neutral tones.
Flung like a starfish on the trampled sod,
You lie still as Virginia takes your bones
And yields them up to Brady and to God.
At least your family was spared the horror
Brought to our time at six in living color,

But not the anguish of the empty chair
At supper, or the lash of each cross word,
Or half-dreamed listening to hear your bare
Feet on the stairs. A century has blurred
How you lost both the Christmases and the quarrels
When those Yanks let you have it with both barrels.

It's old as Caesar. You were starry-eyed
Over a star-crossed flag of bonnie blue
Till that rough monster which no flag can hide
Rose on its haunches and devoured you.
God knows that every cause and every hurt
Are ashes in the equalizing dirt,

So that the men who died on Sparta's slopes
Were dung to fertilize the olive's fruit
And now some living mother's brightest hopes
Lie dying on the tarmac in Beirut.
We turn on our TVs, and hear the cry
Of Belfast and Soweto as they die;

Through the millennia the murdered march
To someone else's tune and memory
And through some other guy's triumphal arch.
You and they are no one. You're history.
Repeating rifles always bear repeating.
The silent beast that ate you keeps on eating.

This is followed by "No Pornography or Rhyme," a poke at poetic pretension, which Miles wrote in defiance of the dually proscriptive submission requirements for a Lebanon, Oregon, poetry journal called the *Yellow Butterly:*

As the lights glow red and bleary, on a midnight bleak and
    dreary.
When the rhymer's wares are shamelessly displayed,
Come the puritanic legions—dressed in Izod shirts and
    Weejuns—
Of the Modern Poets' Anti-Rhyme Brigade.
They have heard of Shelley's lewdness and of William
    Shakespeare's rudeness;
But these goodly folk, who to Parnassus climb
Armed with rage and A.R. Ammons, leap like Pentecostal
    salmons
In the fight against pornography and rhyme.

That's just one stanza, but the audience is loving the whole thing. The applause is huge, rollicking, filled with whooping and whistles of approval. This is a crowd that is two-thirds poets, so Miles is preaching to the choir, and the choir is chanting amen. But victory is by no means assured even in this first round, because Miles has been alternating with DeVries, who is not only clever herself but also blonde and fetching.

"WHO ARE YOU?"

"Denise DeVries."

"AND WHAT DO YOU DO?"

"It's not what I do. It's how I do it," she says with a coy grin. Her first poem is a funny vignette that lampoons the testosterone-fueled nature of a poetry slam by characterizing, somewhat hyperbolically, women's approach to public displays of art:

> *And then I'll read a poem and I'll say, "I know, this is really awful, isn't it?" and you'll say, "No, really, it's wonderful!" and I'll say, "No. No. It's terrible." And you'll all squeal at the same time, "You're CRAZY! It's the most FANTASTIC poem I've ever heard in my life! . . ."*

Comes now the Slam Master. One poet shall live. One shall die. Schuhart places his hand above DeVries's head, soliciting applause. She gets a thunderous ovation, and Miles attempts a thin smile. His posture and state of dishevelment seem to have worsened. The shirttails are fighting to escape his put-upon waistband. Sweat is beading on his brow. A long, shallow sigh seems to deflate him before our very eyes as Schuhart directs a masterful left hand toward him. Miles is resigned to losing, and his head is now tilted so far left that it practically rests on his shoulder. DeVries's ovation was indeed thunderous, but wait— Miles's is more thunderous still. He is stunned. The head is suddenly upright, the thin smile has vanished. For the second time, the second round achieved.

I liked Miles from the moment eight years ago when, on my first day in the Washington bureau of our parent company, he walked into my office, hand extended in greeting. "How do you do, sir?" he asked pleasantly, the first of approximately 2,000 "How do you do, sir?" salutations every morning since. So accustomed was I to perfunctory exchanges of greetings, it was some time before I realized Miles was actually listening to my answers and giving them some thought. This dawned on me the

day I got to the Metro fare-card dispenser with only a $20 bill
and couldn't get anybody to change it for me. By the time I got
to work—by taxi—I was a bit aggravated, and when Miles hit
me with "How do you do, sir?" I answered candidly: "Suicidal,
thanks, and you?" Most co-workers would have let it go at that.
Miles, ever the reporter, availed himself of a follow-up. "Oh,
dear," he said, "I hope it isn't anything serious." So I told him
what happened.

Most people would be inched to shrug off my tale of woe as,
hey, one of those things, or to laugh heartily in my face. Miles
was genuinely pained. He felt my frustration. He felt my anger.
He felt my expenditure. He felt my tardiness. I had forgotten
about the whole thing by midmorning, but later—after
lunch—when Miles apologized to me for the callous indifference of the Washington Metropolitan Area Transit Authority
and the commuters of Northern Virginia, I realized he had
brooded about the incident all day. He brooded not because he
cared particularly about the lack of big-bill changers at Metro
stations. He brooded because, in general, he cares.

He cares enough to remember every one of my birthdays, and
the birthdays of many of his friends. He cares enough to send
postcards from all of his travels, and to give an Easter present to
my children and a Christmas gift every year. He cares when the
copier jams on my copies, when I get nasty letters to the editor,
when my car is in the shop. He isn't just an uncommonly loyal
friend. His qualities as a pal and his poetic gift flow from the same
source: He is the single most empathetic person in the world.

How can you not like a guy like that? Plus, he lets me bor-
row his memory whenever I need it.

"Hey, Miles, what was Laurence Harvey's real name?"

"Larushka Skikne."

"Hey, Miles, who wrote 'La Création du Monde' "?

"Darius Milhaud."

"Hey, Miles, who was born on June 2?"

"Sir Edward Elgar and the Marquis de Sade."

"Hey, Miles. Whaddya call that figure of speech where the part stands for the whole?"

"Synecdoche. Oh, and by the way: Mischa."

"Huh? Mischa? Mischa who?"

"It's Larushka Mischa Skikne."

This is not the result of Miles delving into his *World Almanac*. This is the result of Miles delving into his cerebral cortex. While Miles may not be the most bloodthirsty reporter in Washington, he is among the most knowledgeable, in the sense that, essentially, he knows everything. On matters of fact, for all practical purposes, he is never wrong. This is a handy skill for a journalist.

Oh, don't smirk. *Rubber & Plastics News* is too journalism. There are thousands upon thousands of reporters in this town, and almost all of them don't work for *The New York Times*. Most labor for smaller, more specialized publications such as *Advertising Age* (where I work), *American Banker, Automotive News, Aviation Week & Space Technology,* the *Chronicle of Higher Education,* and *Variety.* The readers of these trade papers and magazines have a tremendous stake in what transpires on Capitol Hill and in the agencies—as do the readers of *Metalworking News, Footwear News, Rural Electrification, Tire Business* (the other publication Miles serves), *Traffic World,* and (my favorite title) *Waste Age.*

So why shouldn't there be a *Rubber & Plastics News,* and why shouldn't it have a Washington bureau?

Granted, trade-press reporters don't show up on *The McLaughlin Group* ("On a scale of 1 to 10, what are the prospects for a new proposed rule on labeling latex products? Miles Moore? . . ."), but how many *New York Times* reporters are perfectly at ease penning free verse?

Oh, no.

Miles has exactly the expression of crushing anxiety he wore the day after his bathtub leaked into the apartment beneath his, leaving him with (1) an angry neighbor, (2) a caulking job vastly beyond his levels of skill and confidence, and (3) uncertain liability for the neighbor's soaked carpeting.

"I'm REALLY nervous," he says in a fretful stage whisper when he realizes who he will be squaring off against in Round 2. The poet is Jeffrey McDaniel, a young man who looks to be in his mid-twenties, outfitted in full grunge. "He's more of a slam poet."

I'll buy that. McDaniel is on stage, eyes three-quarters closed as if he were in a trance, reading an erotic poem while tugging, unconsciously, it would appear, at his crotch. The audience is still and attentive. Miles, tight-lipped and flushed, is on the verge of an aneurysm. Hard to believe that this is the same guy who a few minutes ago was reading "Keats and the Anchorman" with such self-possession and authority.

"He's forcing me to do 'The Televangelist's Last Sermon,' " Miles whispers, referring to his broad and strident assault on Swaggartish arrogance and spiritual charlatanism. He would have preferred to save this poem for the final round—assuming he would finally get that far—but McDaniel's theatrics have put Miles's back up against the wall. "If he's doing rap, I have to fight fire with fire," Miles says, without a hint of irony. He says it, in fact, with fire in his eyes.

For his first two poems, he has performed "A Bluesman in Chillicothe, Ohio," which is a good-natured send-up of lounge entertainment in the cheese-crock-and-polyester atmosphere of a midwestern motor inn, and "The Legacy of Andy Warhol," which seems to find in the pop artist's "happenings" the genesis of American cultural decline. These poems are amusing and satirical, but also relatively subtle. In the face of hip-hop poetry, subtle will not do. Miles takes the stage one more time, with "The Televangelist's Last Sermon," and commences to hollering.

I have SINNED against my Lord and Savior!!! he thunders, his fist waving in the air. *O Lord, OPEN to me thy portals of jus-*

tice! *Those portals, by the way, are closed to all of you. I have con-FESSED my sins, while yours stink like rotting sewage through all the paths of Heaven . . .*

This poetry bludgeon is brandished and swung for three concussive minutes. When those three minutes are over, Miles—by dint of an equally concussive ovation—is propelled to the next round.

Fatslug, the True Lover

It is of no importance
when specks of dust
reach for dim shafts of salvation light,
and so it was of no importance when Fatslug,
searching for a beacon, saw yours.

How kindly you smiled for Fatslug—
smiled with, then at, then not at all.
Was it in his thousand and ninety-one
servile compliments—each masking
a separate self-aggrandizement—
that you smelled the telltale scent of a loser?
Or was it his preening before your mirror,
the posturing of an egregious fool?

Your beacon
is out now, your mirror covered over.
The street is newly faceless, comforting.
In that facelessness you'll never see
a plump speck, belting
his trenchcoat, in his imagination
half Bogart, half Camus,
trying not to see his lack of reflection
as he turns by a lamppost and heaves his bulk
away. He has his destiny, you have yours.

Unrequited love may not be the least of Fatslug's problems; it certainly isn't the only one. This hapless character, a recurring figure in Miles's poetry, is put upon, abused, besieged at all times by a hostile universe and the rude dwellers therein. He is assaulted again and again by aggressive street people, offensive bumper stickers, inflexible bureaucracies, haunting nightmares, stupid teachers, cruel children, indifferent love interests, withering stares, and all manner of other irritants, accumulated evidence of a world that refuses to deliver love and justice to all who seek them.

The petulant thoughts and ongoing sorrows of Fatslug are immutably linked to Miles's own experiences—experiences engendering alternating expressions of self-loathing and moral superiority. Rule No. 13 in "Fatslug's Secret Rules of Etiquette"—the last poem in Miles's unpublished collection, *The Fatslug Papers*—is as follows: "Do not pray to God; everyone knows Christ died for everyone but you." This is a sentiment that can be read, as Miles perhaps intends, in two ways. But in either interpretation, Fatslug is a victim, a meek heir to the earth whose rightful inheritance has somehow been snatched away by bullies.

"Bullies can almost sense, as if by radar, people whom they can bully," Miles says, and he himself has emitted such signals since he was a child, a tubby, awkward, daydreaming kid whom the other children in Sugar Grove, Ohio, teased relentlessly. In their kinder moments, they called him "Miles and Miles Away."

"My family life was very happy, but at school I was like the archetype of the smart sissy kid. I was picked on constantly on the playground," he says. Adults were kind, "but also very likely to take notice when there is an off-bloom of some sort, a petunia in the onion patch, so to speak. I am quite certain they, by and large, thought I was weird—which, no doubt, I was. My whole world was entirely circumscribed by cartoons. I spent my entire year in kindergarten imagining I was Huckleberry Hound."

His retreat into a world of fantasy foreshadowed adult reveries of a different sort, but in no way did it then—nor does it today—fully salve the sting of being a laughingstock. Thirty years later, his poetry is informed both by the pain of his childhood experience and the dubious consolation of recognizing its universality:

Fatslug in the Fourth Grade

"Hey, FATSLUG," yells Fat
Sandra, surrounded
by her harpy cronies.
"There's a new girl here
who wants to meetcha!"

The harpies seize
Fatslug and, claw
by hideous claw, drag him
over to where the pale
new girl fades into the wall.

"Hello," he says,
holding out his hand.

The pale girl cringes
as from a gargoyle.

Fat Sandra's laughter
resounds through the centuries.

Not only does the laughter resound timelessly, but the Fat Sandras of the world have followed Miles into adulthood. He walks into People's Drug to pick up some snapshots, and the cashier berates him for standing in the wrong line. He passes comedian

Rip Taylor on an escalator and declares, "Hey, Rip Taylor! Hello!" and Rip Taylor rewards him with a blood-curdling glower. He buys a condominium apartment on Tuesday, and the condo market collapses on Wednesday. Naturally, Miles takes it all very personally. For instance, he boycotted People's for two years.

"Life is full of Fatslug moments," Miles says, "at least for me. People who are dreamers have a hard time of it."

In a biography of Chopin he once read, the author spoke of differing views of the composer: one as an effeminate weakling, and another as a virile creator. "The biographer's view," Miles recounts, "was that Chopin was neither—and not that he was something in between, but that he was something else altogether: a man who lived in a world of his own creation."

Without in any way comparing his artistic achievement with Chopin's, Miles says, "I too am a person who lives in a world of his own creation." Where once his refuge was Huckleberry Hound, today he loses himself in the universe of art, his own and others'. With the help of his virtual photographic memory, he is a human CD-ROM of the literary, musical, and visual canons. And with the help of an inhospitable city perpetually poking him in the eye, he is a prolific architect of a poetic personal universe. Pass his office on any given morning and look in. There, poised in his chair, back to his keyboard, surrounded by mounds and mounds of Federal Registers and press releases, sits the bemused artist. His stare is vacant. His head is cocked, Nipperlike. His story about proposed latex regulations is well under control, but for the moment he is in a world of his own creation, Miles and Miles away.

"I dream of people who are gracious and kind and strong. I dream of people who can meet the obstacles life throws them, but who will never be thrown anything desperate, a world without poverty, hunger, where everybody has love in his life and everybody lives to be at least ninety. And how I dream of those things, I consider private."

• • •

It has come to this: twelve poets began this evening. Only two remain. One of them is Kate Blackburn, a tiny, forty-something teacher with owlish glasses and an auburn pageboy. She has achieved the final showdown on the strength of a poetic travelogue through the Greek lands, including one tableau where "in the distance a slender minaret needles the air, the goat bells a metallic insult in the Moslem silence," and another vignette wherein her tour guide tries to molest her.

The other poet is Miles.

Four times the Slam Master has put him to the applause test and four times he has prevailed. Or, at least, three and a half times. His last round was to have been the final, but he and Blackburn drew to a dead heat, despite Miles's boisterous rendition of his hilarious poetry-writing credo, "Thou Art a Poet." ("Thou shalt be either a libertine, gleefully raping everything that movest, or else a celibate, writing haunting nature poetry that lingerest pathologically on birds and bees. Thou art a poet; a normal sex life is not for thee . . .")

So now comes the Slam Off. Blackburn reads one last poem, a sentimental tribute to her late mother. A year in the writing, the poem ends hauntingly with, "No one saw Mother burning as always with a fierce, blue flame." Blackburn has touched this cynical crowd, and Miles knows it. He sits in his chair, chin in hand, vibrating. The man is actually vibrating. His diastolic blood pressure, I estimate, is in the low four digits. He is a living, breathing tuning fork and I fear for the glassware. Yet, when he stands he seems somehow becalmed.

Oh, sure, his hair has lost any semblance of organization. His shirttail is completely dislodged. His necktie, with the help of his abdomen, has fixed itself at precisely 45 degrees to the horizon. But he is the picture of confidence as he reads his final selection. It is titled "Stiff Chairs," a tribute to a friend from back home in rural Ohio who died of AIDS:

. . . and now the Methodist minister
who never met you sums you up:
"Let us not judge this poor sinner.
I've sinned myself I'm not proud of it . . ."
As if you'd been the Prince of Abominations
while he, in weakness, had once said, "Damn."

Enter, finally, the Slam Master. Schuhart has his black base-ball cap twisted backward, a cigarette dangling from his lips. "FOR MILES DAVID MOORE, PLEASE!"

Applause. Whistles. Cheers.

"FOR KATE BLACKBURN, PLEASE!" More of the same—only less so.

Miles wins the slam. Blackburn extends her hand in con-gratulation, and Miles, dazed, accepts it. Could this be right? Something must be terribly awry. People are staring at Miles Moore, and yet it is in no way a Fatslug moment. It is a moment of glory, of satisfaction—my God—of victory. He grins from ear to crimson ear. And the ovation resounds through the cen-turies.

About the Author

Bob Garfield is a roving features correspondent for National Public Radio's *All Things Considered,* a columnist and editor at large for *Advertising Age,* contributing editor to *The Washington Post Magazine* and *Civilization,* and frequently appears on *Good Morning, America.* He graduated from Penn State in 1977 with a plan to become a world-conquering Evil Mastermind, but opted for newspaper work because it had better dental benefits. He lives in Fairfax, Virginia, with his wife, Carla, and two children.